2 04

Front Street

Front Street

Resistance and Rebirth in the
Tent Cities of Techlandia

Brian Barth

Astra House
New York

Some of the material in this book was first published in the below articles:

"Homeless in the Shadow of Apple's $5 Billion Campus" by Brian Barth, copyright © 2021 by Brian Barth, originally published in *OneZero*.

"Revealed: How Companies Made $100m Clearing California Homeless Camps" by Brian Barth, copyright © 2024 by Brian Barth, originally published in *The Guardian*.

"What If Unhoused People Designed Their Own Homes?" by Brian Barth, copyright © 2022 by Brian Barth, originally published in *Mother Jones*.

For information about permission to reproduce selections from this book, please contact permissions@astrahouse.com.

Some names have been changed to protect the privacy of the people involved.

Astra House
A Division of Astra Publishing House
astrahouse.com
Printed in the United States of America
Library in Congress Cataloging-in-Publication Data is available upon request
ISBN: 978-1-6626-0161-3
First edition
10 9 8 7 6 5 4 3 2 1
Design by Alissa Theodor
The text is set in Warnock Pro.
The titles are set in Source Code Pro.

For Mama, Granmarie, Kent, Rudy, Tiny, Monte, and all the others

Contents

Front Street

Prologue

I met Monte on a July morning at his camp in Oakland, which stretched for a mile along Wood Street and bulged a hundred yards back from the curb beneath a tangle of overpasses known as the MacArthur Maze. It was infamous among California's megacamps, a place news reports reference *Mad Max* to describe—mountains of junk, hard-looking dudes ambling about, and an incredible number of burnt-out cars. A Hollywood rendering of the apocalypse is an apt, if uncreative, means to explain Wood Street's outer appearance. But the news reports miss the seeds of Eden hiding in the dystopia and the tender hearts residing in the hard-looking dudes. The roughly three hundred residents of the camp referred to the place—their home—as Wood Street Commons.

I walked through the gates of Wood Street Commons to find a small outdoor stage where Monte sat on a canvas director's chair in a loose-fitting leather jacket, pink shirt, blue tie, and cowboy boots. Gathered around him was an assortment of fellow residents, housed friends of the camp, and a handful of city officials who looked rather uncomfortable. Several members of the media were present; a PA sat near the edge of the stage. Soft drinks and snacks were spread on a table as folks lounged about on couches waiting for the event to begin. The stage was backed with walls made from pallets, an Ikea bed frame, and other scavenged material; shade came courtesy of white fabric strung loosely between crooked wooden poles, along with a forest-green café umbrella with STARBUCKS printed on it in white letters. I spotted several hypodermic needles on the ground, along with a dead rat. Propped on a table was a board displaying architectural plans that illustrated how the dystopia might be reorganized a bit to reveal the jewels within.

The plans showed the locations of individual "homesteads," as well as community facilities, including a flea market, bike repair shop, office space, and the Moose Pit Café, located next to a shed belonging to a resident named Moose. All of this and more already existed, though very informally and largely obscured by the cluttered aesthetics of the place. Meals for fifty-plus were prepared daily over a large firepit; an adjacent pantry stocked dried goods and fresh fruits and vegetables, free for whoever needed them. Donated supplies, such as clothes and toiletries, were generally available. Solar panels had begun to replace the power cords that pirated energy from nearby streetlights. Communal water tanks, filled by a volunteer with a water truck, had relieved the need to tap illicitly into city supplies. A pair of steel shipping containers provided lockable storage, a critical step to stability in a place where people were afraid to leave their possessions unattended, for fear they would be pilfered. Security cameras and lighting had been installed in some corners of the camp; if a female resident needed an escort back to her place at night, a call went out on the camp's walkie-talkie network. To accommodate their many Zoom calls with the media, NGOs, and government officials, they'd built an outdoor conference room that included an orange-and-blue wall of padded fabric that made for a professional-looking video backdrop.

The purpose of the event was to convince the city officials, who wanted to tear the camp down, to support the residents in developing the Wood Street Commons vision instead. The city had plans for 170 units of so-called affordable housing on the portion of the camp where we'd gathered, just a few steps away from Monte's handcrafted home, which had a small putting green in the yard and a mailbox that said "1707 Wood Street" out front. Seven units of the city's proposed development were designated for homeless veterans and six for young adults exiting foster care. The majority were designated for households making 60 to 120 percent of Oakland's median income, which translates to an annual salary of roughly $75,000 to $150,000. The city's plan for the camp's residents was to move them into cubicle-like tiny homes inside a fenced lot down the street, where they would be lorded over by security guards and subject to a litany of rules governing their lives.

The meeting was facilitated by Leah, a massage therapist who volunteered at the camp and could sometimes be found kneading her elbows into residents' backs. After she laid out the ground rules and time limits for each speaker, Brian Warwick, a housing coordinator with the city, explained that the $100 million development had been held up for eighteen months "because of the current situation with the site." LaTonda Simmons, the assistant city administrator, struck a more conciliatory tone. "I want to recognize that everybody is frustrated with the city," she said, "and it's one of the reasons that we are here."

The residents felt that this and all the shelter options promoted by the city had the same underlying problem: They were based on a way of thinking that did not reflect the values and needs—or even the basic dignity—of the people they were designed to shelter. The residents weren't interested in submitting to the city's shelters and their wardens—they viewed this as a downgrade from their current living situation.

"We're people. Right? I mean we really are," said Monte to the officials. The city's plans for the community felt like being forced into "a category that does not fit for us," he continued. "This," he said, gesturing at the makeshift village that sprawled out from the stage, "is our category." Monte, a veteran, explained to the crowd that he once tried a housing program for unhoused veterans and it nearly killed him. He said the freedom and autonomy of his current living situation were essential to his mental health. "I'm claustrophobic," he said. "Don't put me in a box—I might hang myself." He was not exaggerating.

The formal portion of the presentation began. Monte's friend Theo, who was wearing stylish glasses and a black blazer, took the mic and read from his prepared remarks. "We the people," he began, "are inviting you all to participate in creating a new model for the unhoused and dispossessed." He implored the officials to "be partners with us in co-creating an historic transformation of Oakland," adding that it was "a chance to be a world leader in solving urban homelessness."

Theo said the residents wanted the city to install basic infrastructure for water, power, and waste management, just like any other neighborhood, but that they intended to develop and manage their "ecovillage" together with their housed allies. He said they planned to raise funds to lease the land and pay the required permitting fees, just like any other developer. "We would like the opportunity to formalize what we have developed in an organic, spontaneous manner," Theo proclaimed. "Great advancements in human life can have a humble appearance in their early stages. We ask you to look past the appearance of trash, visual blight, and the stereotypes of homelessness, and see what people with the least resources can do with sufficient time and space."

A resident named Juanita explained that for her, living in the camp was a choice: the choice between paying rent or paying for college for her boys, who attend San José State University and Cal Poly. "Their dad died and I had to decide, what can I pay for?" she said. "We can't afford to do both." Juanita, who lived in an RV, said she'd looked into one of the nearby "safe lots"—city-controlled places where homeless people can park a home on wheels without the threat of a ticket—but worried she would not, in fact, feel safe there, despite the barbed wire fence and security guard. The closeness she felt with her neighbors in the camp seemed like a more reliable security system. "I'm a single lady by myself and I've never had a problem," she said. "We are the community you should be developing for."

John, Monte's close friend and neighbor, who was hosting the meeting in his backyard, told the officials that the community was developing their own housing, thank you very much, and thus would not be needing theirs. A group of artists cohabitating in one of Oakland's warehouse spaces had befriended the camp and were building tiny homes—ten-by-twelve-foot insulated, lockable structures with windows and porches—that were slowly replacing Wood Street's array of leaking, drafty, tarped-over shelters. John pointed out that the existing housing program on-site was faster and cheaper than the city's approach to housing the homeless, which involves waiting lists tens of thousands of names long for the hundreds of units constructed annually. It can cost more than a million dollars per unit to build affordable housing in California, compared to $3,000 for the camp's tiny homes, which can be built in about five days with volunteer labor. The camp-built housing "can be up and running sooner than you guys can break ground," said John.

Theo, a musician who earns money giving music lessons via Zoom from the camp, continued the pitch, adding that Wood Street Commons already functioned as an "informal social services agency," which ran 24–7, with nary a penny of taxpayer support. Serving as a safe, welcoming space for people who might exhibit difficult behaviors in other spaces was an invaluable service, said Theo, reducing, for instance, "open drug use and sales on the streets of the housed communities of West Oakland. We help to heal and re-socialize people suffering from abuse, PTSD, drug addiction, and over-institutionalization," he said, noting the steady stream of people exiting incarceration directly into the arms of the camp.

Monte, who had just returned from a stint in prison, explained to the officials that the fellowship he encountered on Wood Street—being clothed, fed, and loved through his brokenness—had not made him whole again, but it had kept him from causing harm to himself and others, or at least less harm than in the past. "Let us take care of us, because it doesn't seem like you guys can," he said. "I understand that we're being bad. I mean, we're out here, so . . . you know . . . we're messed up. However, our plan to get better is better than your plan."

Lara Tannenbaum, the city's homelessness services manager, said that the city was setting up co-governed camps—jointly managed by the campers and a nonprofit contracted with the city—and would be open to exploring something similar for the group on a site nearby. "I really hear what people are saying about this being your home and your community," she said.

But Monte was not buying the vague co-governance promise. In his observation, the city's game was to make hollow promises and then bring in the bulldozers. "We're telling you what we need and no one's listening," said Monte, beginning to shout. "You're just putting us out—we're not going!" The crowd, city officials excluded, cheered.

I'd felt the same tender threads of hope in other camps I'd visited, but they'd grown much more robust on Wood Street. They were starting to weave together and form what felt like a viable solution to homelessness—a solution initiated and led by homeless folks. It helped, however, that they'd attracted enthusiastic support from the world of the housed.

The architectural plans, for instance, were drafted by Emma Fraser, a lecturer in UC Berkeley's media studies department who's published scholarly papers on "urban ruin," and Clancy Wilmott, an assistant professor who studies "critical cartography, geovisualisation and design." They'd been contacted by a student volunteering at the camp, who said residents wanted to know who, exactly, had legal jurisdiction over the land where they lived. They compiled a map showing the patchwork parcels of roughly a dozen owners, including the City of Oakland, the State of California, and railroad companies. The pair eventually led a "participatory design" workshop at the site, which yielded ideas such as a series of public fountains and a "rolling garden fort."

"They were very canny and aware that if they had something that looks like a real map, that looks authoritative, it would help convince the council that these are not people to be fucked with," Fraser told me.

"I think the city of Oakland has no idea what kind of force they're dealing with," said Wilmott.

"Wood Street is kind of weird," Monte told me after the meeting. "Because on one side of the coin you have all this negativity going on. But in the center, the nucleus of it, it's a positive thing that's growing outwardly and encapsulating all the negativity that has happened and is happening here. It's slow because change is slow. But there is a jewel here."

Another huge factor in Wood Street's success was that it had remained intact for many years, making it a rare window into what happens organically when a camp is allowed to develop, unimpeded and on its own terms. When I arrived on the scene, those tender threads of hope were crashing into the hard wall of local politics. Allowing the camp to remain risked normalizing what might seem like inhumane living conditions. Helping it develop as a self-governed community risked ceding authority to what might seem like unstable anarchy. The residents' case to the city was that behind outward appearances lay the foundation of a sensible, modest, egalitarian lifestyle—one based on resource sharing, rather than resource accumulation. A fragile social order, based on bonds forged by the daily slog of survival, held the place together; it might not appeal to outsiders, but it was deeply meaningful to the campers. They didn't see Wood Street Commons as a utopic vision, so much as a feasible solution to their situation.

This was not the thesis I had in mind when I set out to write this book. In the beginning, I just wanted to understand the lives of the poorest people in the wealthiest region of America. My journey started in the mask-covered depths of an infamous era in American history, a few weeks before a fateful election and nearly a year before I walked through the gate of Wood Street Commons and caught Monte's smile.

1

Wolves

On an autumn day in the worst year of my life, Kent, the leader of Wolfe Camp, walks his bike across the parking lot of my apartment complex. He wears a dress shirt, as he does every day, completely unbuttoned, as it always is. His hairless chest, tanned and muscular, glints in the light. Lost in the music pumping from the earmuff-style headphones that wrap around his graying head, this slight sprite-of-a-man glides into my field of vision like a character entering a play from stage left: a dystopic drama of greed, heartbreak, Big Data, Little Men, sex, drugs, and the quest for the perfect Instagram image, a tragic farce in which I, too, am a character. It is, of course, set in Silicon Valley, where Kent grew up in a well-to-do family, and where he now pitches his tent. He has been homeless—the politically correct "unhoused" does not yet roll off my tongue—for the past nine of his fifty-eight years.

It is on the basis of Kent's unbuttoned shirt that I recognize him, as his face is covered in a mask, and not of the pandemic kind. He's wearing a black-and-white harlequinesque piece, a ghoulish guise with sad, sinuous streaks falling from the eyes, like a monster who is not a monster but a sensitive, tortured soul trapped behind an ugly image formed by the prejudices of its beholders. It's a variation of a Guy Fawkes mask, which has roots in a seventeenth-century plot to blow up London's House of Lords and has more recently become a symbol of antiestablishment movements in places like Zuccotti Park and Tahrir Square. On the traditional Guy Fawkes mask, the corners of the mouth twist up into a devious smile; Kent's mask just looks bleak. He is not plotting to overthrow anything—it is he who has been overthrown. His current occupation: rebuilding his sense of self-worth from scratch. Perhaps the mask is appropriate attire for the job.

However, when you see a guy walking twenty feet from you in such a mask as you're about to get in your car in a suburban parking lot on a weekday afternoon, your first thought is *What the fuck?* A shriek forms in my throat but does not come out. I look around to see if there are any children about who should be ushered away from this person. When I realize it's Kent, I relax, but only a little. Homeless people—I mean unhoused individuals—have always made me nervous, but I'd felt at ease with Kent. Now I'm not so sure. *He's making a statement about income inequality*, I tell myself. Then, finally, I remember that it's Halloween, and relax a lot more.

"Kent!" I yell.

He pulls the headphones down around his neck and turns. It's an awkward moment. I've been getting to know him in the camp, but now he's suddenly privy to my world—the well-landscaped apartment complex a couple miles from his tent, with its elegantly gnarled olive trees and headily scented gardenia bushes. I've rented a furnished apartment here in Cupertino—the "Heart of Silicon Valley," according to its boosters—so that I can, to put it bluntly and uncomfortably so, study people like him. I have keypad access to a pool ensconced behind a grove of bamboo and a clubhouse with a theater room and an outdoor kitchen cabana. He eats his dinner sitting on a milk crate a few feet from the cars whizzing by at the intersection of Wolfe Road and Interstate 280. I feel like it will make him feel bad to see me getting into my rental car, a cherry-red, way-too-big SUV. But it's really just me who will feel bad.

"Hey," says Kent, waving nonchalantly. He leaves his mask in place.

"What are you up to?" I ask, trying to act as casual as he is.

Turns out he is on a dumpster expedition. Many of the folks in Wolfe Camp make their living, if you want to call it that, by fishing clothes, shoes, handbags, sports equipment, and electronics out of the trash at the low-slung condos and office parks that sprawl across the fifty miles of suburbia between San José and San Francisco—America's infamous, but outwardly bland, techlandia. Its inhabitants often throw out heaps of perfectly good stuff, Kent explains, sometimes in its original wrapping, which he and his buddies collect and post on sites like Craigslist, eBay, Letgo, and OfferUp. One time they unearthed a stash of Gucci.

"This place is a treasure chest for a lot of homeless people," he says, nodding his masked head toward my building. Who said the tech industry doesn't share its wealth?

As I pull out of the parking lot, I catch Kent's image in the rearview. He's put his headphones back on and appears to be dancing his way toward the dumpsters. Steadying his bike with one arm, he snakes his other arm through the air and bounces from foot to foot in a little treasure-hunting jig. *A masked trash bandit*, I muse—*a Silicon Valley phantasm*. Then I scold myself for dramatizing his poverty. His situation *is* dramatic, however. And he is one of the most interesting people I have ever met.

How can homelessness be fixed? Silicon Valley is an obvious place to ponder this beast of a question, given the high concentration of both billionaires and tent cities. California is home to 12 percent of Americans, but hosts a third of the nation's homeless population. The government throws billions at the problem each year, yet the tent cities continue to expand. Not even the infamous innovators of Silicon Valley—the most expensive real estate market in the country—have cracked this code.

Surely something more can be done. Does the problem need to be reframed? Are we looking for The Fix in the right places? Asking the right questions? I had a feeling we were not.

For instance: Why do huge numbers of homeless folks not take advantage of the social services on offer? These so-called "service-resistant" individuals often decline offers of temporary shelter, a fact that local authorities hate to admit. I've discovered that even among those who win the housing lottery and are given keys to an apartment, it's not uncommon to spend their days, and even nights, in their camp, where they feel more at home. Resistance to services is an embarrassing thorn in the side of service providers and policymakers, yet this glaring contradiction is rarely interrogated in the media. Why aren't the solutions to homelessness working? How can they be rejiggered to better meet folks on the street where they're at?

The more unhoused folks I got to know, the more I understood why many would rather live in their camps than be pushed into what they view as a quasi-carceral system to hide them away and control their lives—the goal of the "homeless-industrial complex," as some call it. Remaining in their camps is not an option in the current policy climate, however. All camps are eventually "swept"—a euphemism for the forced removal of unhoused people from their homes on the street—further traumatizing and destabilizing an already traumatized and unstable group of people who have nowhere else to go.

Matt Mahan, the mayor of San José, a former tech executive who once lived in the same Harvard dorm as Mark Zuckerberg, told me that pushing the problem around in this way is "the definition of insanity." Mahan said that "our goal is not to just shuffle people around the city. I think it is a terrible use of taxpayer dollars and it is horribly disruptive for our most vulnerable neighbors." It was an interesting statement, given that he oversees a government that spends exorbitant sums doing exactly that—when I arrived in town, San José was sweeping 1.6 camps per business day.

There's a universe of government programs and nonprofits designed to get unhoused folks off the street. Their employees regularly descend on camps, lanyards around their necks and clipboards in hand, to inform residents about their "options." Names are put on various waiting lists, where they customarily remain for a great many years. I immediately detected a strong distaste for the lanyard-and-clipboard crowd. The campers often talk about "getting housing," but they tend to sigh as they do, before giving various reasons for why that's unlikely, such as not being a senior citizen, a mother with children, a veteran, or some other demographic prioritized for shelter. But many also say that they're not really cut out for housing, at least not in the form offered.

"People think there's all these resources and stuff, but the way it's set up is a fucking joke—it does not work for a lot of people," said Dave, one of Kent's neighbors at Wolfe Camp. "Affordable housing sucks," he continued, "because now not only are you squished in this little box, you have to do all these things on time and in a certain order. I don't see that as attractive. For some of us, coming out of homelessness is worse than being in it."

How can that be? Surely the unhoused desire what the housed have. John, whom I'd met on Wood Street across the Bay in Oakland, was one of many who pushed back on that. "It doesn't interest me to be one of those people who work so hard to go on a vacation and then the whole time they're supposed to be having fun, they're stressed about all the stuff they're putting on their credit card that they can't afford," he said. I was ashamed to tell him how familiar that scenario sounds.

I don't think The Fix is going to spring from the dissected bowels of failed policy. These gruesome dissections exist in abundance, and most arrive at the same obvious conclusion: Real estate prices are out of sync with wages, and we do not build enough subsidized housing at sufficiently affordable price points. Local governments constantly issue new "plans to end homelessness," a sort of absurdist genre of mythmaking disguised as policy. I've read many such plans and found they rest on the same underlying assumption: Fixing homelessness is a matter of preventing people from falling through the cracks of the economy, and returning those who do to the status quo. They do not reflect what I've heard from people on the street, who certainly want access to the resources they need to live comfortably, but do not necessarily see the status quo as a desirable path to obtain them.

The folks on Wolfe Road are very much interested in running water, warmth, and safety, but when I ask about their dreams and goals for the future, no one mentions working a job they hate, or any scenario in which they spend their waking hours engaged in unfulfilling tasks, only to remain in constant stress about whether they can sustain their miserable lifestyle.

Kent says he earns about $3,000 per month through his dumpster-diving and bottle-and-can recycling businesses. It's an ample income for his lifestyle, given that his living expenses are so low. I once suggested that he could move to a less expensive real estate market, where he could afford housing on $3,000 per month, if only in an RV park. Surely that would be better than living on the side of Wolfe Road. I realized how ridiculous this was as soon as the words left my mouth. He makes that much from the garbage *because* he lives in a place where the office parks of billion- and trillion-dollar companies, and the homes of their affluent workers, stretch for miles in every direction. Also: This is his home.

He pointed out a different fallacy in my thinking, however. "The truth," said Kent, solemnly, "is that I would be all alone if I did that. Here, I'm with people. It doesn't excite me to be alone. There's great depression in that." Tent cities function as communities for folks who, for a million different reasons, do not fit in with the communities they come from. They serve as families for folks who may not have much connection with their birth families. And that is priceless.

Monte, John, Dave, and Kent's perspectives are small windows into a larger narrative that I've found is common to all the camps I've visited, a narrative scarcely represented in the media and largely at odds with public policy—which likely has something to do with its failure. Clearly, a paradigmatic shift is in order. What would that new paradigm look like? There's no easy answer, but as a starting point I think it makes sense to address a glaring contradiction: Those designing the solutions generally do not ask unhoused folks for their opinion, at least not in a meaningful way. What do they actually need? How do they really feel? What are their dreams and goals? What do they think The Fix is?

BAD APPLES

My circuitous quest began two blocks from Kent's childhood home, at the intersection of Homestead Road and Wolfe Road, where once upon a time a large oak tree was planted by a large company, called Apple, whose $5 billion campus spreads out behind it. The building, one mile in circumference, forms a perfect circle set in a rectangular green space the size of a city block—Apple Park, the design of which is reminiscent of the home button in the rectangle of an early-model iPhone, but at the scale of an interstellar airport. Locals refer to the building as the Spaceship. You can barely glimpse it through the vegetation behind the towering oak on the corner, which likely cost the company six figures to pluck from its native home and move to the site by truck and crane. It is one of nine thousand trees planted in this 175-acre Garden of Eden—an $85 million landscaping job—including thirty-seven varieties of fruit: plums, apricots, persimmons, cherries, and of course, apples.

Strip away the decadent landscaping and the 2.8-million-square-foot steel building—a gleaming edifice with four stories aboveground and three subterranean ones—gives the impression of a circular Pentagon. Outsiders are not allowed inside Apple Park—employees only!—which a peculiar barrier ensures: The tightly spaced vertical beams closely resemble another fortification being built along the US–Mexico border. The office furniture, according to an employee who leaked some photos from the Spaceship's interior on Instagram, includes "custom-made high-grade leather seats from Louis Vuitton."

Proceeding south on Wolfe Road, past the hummocky meadows of sedge and yarrow—the "ecologically rich oak savanna" that the company's financially rich founder envisioned before his death—another face of the Valley was soon apparent. The tents and tarp homes began a half block from the campus, where several Cupertinians lived on the sidewalk in front of the Hamptons apartment complex. A row of arrow-straight redwoods stands at full attention along the property line, the shiny metal badges affixed to them at chest height affirming that they are official street trees, given the utmost care by the city's horticultural staff. A half block farther, a few more tarps peeked from the bushes along the 280 off-ramp. These scattered abodes were the suburbs of the main Wolfe Camp, which lay another block south in front of a Hyatt hotel, where Kent's tent was found.

Kent grew up on a suburban street a few blocks from his future residence on the sidewalk. When the family's house was built in the sixties it would have been worth around $20,000. In 2012, the Zillow Zestimate of its value was about $1 million. By the time the pandemic hit, the Zestimate was at $2 million. A year into the pandemic it was $3 million. Kent was in prison when his dad died and says his family cut him out of the will. He'd owned multiple homes himself over the years, but various divorces, drug habits, and other instabilities had pried these from his hands. His $3,000-per-month income was about 50 percent more than California's minimum wage, and roughly the average rent in Cupertino, but nowhere near enough to pay both rent *and* other expenses.

"This used to be a blue-collar town," Kent told me during one of our first encounters. "If you had a job, you could afford a home. Now I could work three jobs and still not afford the rent." Actually, if they were minimum wage jobs—$13 per hour in California at the time—he'd need 4.1 of them to earn the $111,680 annually needed to afford a two-bedroom apartment here. "It seems like when things change, there's acceptable loss," he said. "That's what we are here. We're acceptable loss."

The offshoring of unionized manufacturing to less-developed countries, and the stagnation of middle-class wages that resulted, is a well-known chapter in American history, one that played out on steroids in the Valley, where the blue-collar jobs were found in the clean rooms of silicon-chip plants, rather than in greasy, smog-belching factories. The upshot, if you want to call it that, is that Kent's lack of rent or mortgage payments affords him time for the heavy labor of cultivating his self-worth. He's also hard at work on his serenity: "The serenity to accept the things I cannot change, the courage to change the things I can, and the wisdom to know the difference," as they say in his twelve-step program. When I met Kent he was in a monk-like mode, relentlessly practicing inner peace. A lifetime of lacking it had, in a certain sense, made him an expert on the subject. He had cultivated the ability to summon it where it did not seem possible to exist—such as in a tent on the side of Wolfe Road.

As a child, Kent played beneath the willow trees along Calabazas Creek, just a hundred yards or so from his tent. The creek was the safe place that his family home was not—his dad was an alcoholic widower with abusive tendencies—but it is now a concrete-lined channel. The jackrabbits he used to chase after are gone ("There's nowhere for them to run—they need to be able to run," says Kent), but there are still a few trees along the banks. Its proximity is convenient for his recovery. "I still go there regularly for serenity," he told me the first time I met him. I told him he seemed happy. "I am," he said, in a timid tone that suggested a happiness both newfound and tenuous.

One Saturday afternoon I tiptoed into Wolfe Camp, stepping around a green deodorant stick and a plastic bowl of pasta that looked as though it'd been there awhile. Piles of wet clothing and busted furniture alternated with elaborate tent-and-tarp structures. The nest-esque architecture rose from a narrow strip of earth along the curb, forming a modest privacy screen for the sidewalk, which served as a communal living room. Here I found Dave, who worked as a researcher in a biotech lab before moving into a tent six years ago, sitting on the ground, barefoot and smiling, with a few of his friends.

"What's up," said Dave, coolly.

I felt naked in my lack of street cred as this tall, stout man with alert eyes and a devilish smile looked me up and down. He explained how he'd once worked in a research lab at UC Davis, pursuing a career in biotech, and how bipolar disorder, a bitter divorce, and other compounding factors had resulted in his current living arrangement. Later I searched his name online and found it on academic papers with titles like "Proteomic Analysis Highlights the Role of Detoxification Pathways in Increased Tolerance to Huanglongbing Disease." Soon we got to talking about Kent. "Kent is amazing," said Dave. "I'd like to build a statue of him and hide it inside a tent," he joked, "so one day when they tear this all down, he'll still be here." It's easy to imagine a statue of Steve Jobs going up in the neighborhood—it's a company town—but Dave worships at the feet of a different guru. "I never liked Apple," said Dave.

Jen, a camper with pink hair and red toenails, told me how she once enjoyed weekends in Napa with her colleagues—one of the perks at Infineon, a semiconductor manufacturer where she was a sales rep. A layoff was the watershed moment for her journey into homelessness. Jen told me that the Wolfe crew used to camp at other, more discreet locations in the neighborhood, but they kept getting kicked out. So in February 2020, just weeks before the pandemic hit, they moved onto Wolfe Road, knowing that such a conspicuous location would politicize their plight. Under the watch of all the high-minded Apple employees commuting to work, perhaps the sheriff would think twice before evicting them again. Kent pioneered the move, said Jen, and the rest of the campers followed. "We weren't going to let him go it alone," she said.

A few tents down, I found Bobby sitting at a picnic table someone had scored the other day, tinkering with a pile of bike parts. As we shot the breeze, he poked the same piece of wire into the same sprocket for half an hour, with no apparent progress on the repair. Andre fielded my questions and told me, "Don't judge us—no matter what." Roger paced the sidewalk, frowning in a white tank top and fisherman's hat, and muttered at me incomprehensibly. He seemed angry, and I felt afraid to talk to him. His Facebook page, I later discovered, is full of selfie videos in which he parades around the city ranting incoherently about the government. *Already judging*, I thought to myself.

Walter, a mulleted hip-hop artist of Korean descent, told me about that time Snoop Dogg showed up unannounced at his recording studio with a mutual friend. Snoop rolled a spliff, put down a track, and split. Walter was not impressed; he can't even remember the name of the song. "Something about booty," he said. A heart-shaped mail pouch, handmade from gray felt, hung from Walter's tent: "Not home today. Leave msg on other side of heart," it read. No one had ever left a message in it, he said, but on the back side of the heart he'd scrawled his phone number and email address so visitors could get in touch. When we got to talking, I learned that a few years back Walter had lived in the apartment complex I'd just moved into with his girlfriend, the daughter of a local tech founder—not a household-name founder, but prominent enough to have been inducted into the Silicon Valley Engineering Hall of Fame. They had a baby together, but a restraining order prevents Walter from seeing his ex or the child.

Yesenia, Walter's current girlfriend, had a successful career in construction management that fell apart in tandem with her family life a couple years back. Her teenage daughter was suicidal; her son hit her; her husband left. After a brief stint driving for DoorDash, she got a job as a Google shuttle driver but was laid off at the outset of the pandemic. She met Walter on Facebook around the time she became homeless and moved into his tent. Latina, with a dignified bearing, Yesenia could often be found sitting in an office chair, queenlike, at the entrance of the camp, a few feet from the 280 on-ramp. "It's tough on the mind when you're making tons of money and you have your lifestyle that you're used to, and then all of a sudden that just gets reduced to nothing," she said. Her lips quivered.

Steve Jobs grew up in the Cupertino neighborhood where he later built his company. Kent was seven years younger than Jobs but was familiar with the house where he famously fiddled with computer components in his parents' garage. The garage door was often open, and Kent and his posse, a rat pack of prepubescent troublemakers, would ride by on their bikes and harass Jobs and his gang of nerds. "They were always in there tweaking on their little computers," Kent told me one day. "We were always yelling at them—fuck those guys!" he shouted, flashing the corresponding hand gesture to demonstrate. "He was a dork!" said Kent, in an apparent attempt to excuse his bullying. "It was kids being kids," he said with a shrug.

Kent is skilled in the art of allegorical storytelling. One of his best tales involves the neighborhood baseball league, an institution in his all-male family. According to Kent, Jobs also played in the league. He was a laughingstock, in Kent's telling, who played right field—"*when* they allowed him to play." Kent remembered one particularly consequential game, in which first place in the league was at stake. It was a tie game, ninth inning, bases loaded, two outs. The opposing batter launched one into right field—Steve's chance to prove himself at a make-or-break moment. Kent mimed young Steve as he stumbled around trying to align his outstretched glove with the trajectory of the ball. "It went right down his glove and bounced off his head," said Kent. "They lost the game."

I have been unable to corroborate the account, but embellished or not, it's a worthwhile window into the mythology of Wolfe Camp. As Kent and his fellow punks fell into a life of crime, drugs, and chaos, Apple bought up neighborhood real estate for a series of increasingly extravagant corporate campuses—of which the Spaceship is the fifth, if you count the original garage—and made dated bungalows the price of mansions. When Jobs sought city council approval to build the Spaceship, he was pressed about what sort of contributions Apple would make to the community, such as the funding of affordable housing. "See, I'm a simpleton, and I've always had this view that we pay taxes, and the city should do those things," he replied. "As you know, we're the largest taxpayer in Cupertino, so we'd like to continue to stay here and pay taxes."

"They're arrogant!" said Kent.

Kent's childhood bullying morphed into volcanic resentment by the time he found himself inhabiting the bushes next to the Spaceship. He lived for a while on the slopes of 280, across from the Apple parking deck. Later, he and his crew had various camps along Calabazas Creek on the outskirts of Apple Park. Wherever they settled, it was only a matter of time before the police were called in to evict them. As salt in the wound, Apple security cracked down on the campers' dumpster-diving and recycling. "I couldn't even go to the garbage can to make money," said Kent. "Security was all over us."

Dave, who once snuck onto the site during construction, with a hard hat and safety vest as his disguise, said that "they protect their trash like it's fucking gold."

"It became a standoff," said Kent. "But I wasn't going anywhere."

Part of Kent's therapy has been to cycle the Apple Park perimeter, shirt open to the breeze, music blasting from his bike's Bluetooth speaker. "During rush hour I would drink a beer and ride around the place and attack their integrity," he said. "Fuck you!" he yelled again to demonstrate. "Fuuuck yoooou!!!"

Kent works hard to not let anger overtake him. Certain topics, like Apple, get him riled up; but then he returns to serenity. Sometimes it takes him weeks of alone time—in his tent, by the creek, on his bike—to regain it. Other times he's able to correct course on the spot, which is what happened during our conversation about Jobs. His tone and posture softened as he tamed his ranting into a self-reflective soliloquy, which was unintentionally comic in the way that unfiltered earnestness often is. "We were hard on him and he hated his own people because of it," he speculated, matter-of-factly. "Life is hard for everybody, and I don't want to make it harder. Even rich people are living in hell, because that's not an easy life either. I try to break the cycle by dealing with my own problems and keeping positive. I'm not doing hatred—I have to let that shit go."

Kent's homelessness started out with rage—toward his family, his community, and the world at large. But when he finally surrendered to the pain, he found he had a superpower. He said his family not only deprived him of his inheritance but also refused to let him stay with them when he most needed it. "I wanted to hurt my son and brother. I could smell their blood," he said. "But that's a battle you can't win, even if you win. It's lose-lose." Being abandoned by his family felt like unforgiveable treason, until . . . poof: "One day I let it go— they can have it, I'll be alright," he thought. "It turned out to be a blessing," said Kent. "It brought me to a place of happiness where I'd never been before. I was homeless, but I was enjoying life. Which was kind of crazy."

The tremendous labor of moving from us-against-them angst to sober self-reflection is central to Kent's process of recovery. "If I'm happy with myself, no one can take that away," he said one day as he swept up around the camp, wearing black track pants and a white button-down dress shirt, unbuttoned as usual. "It's come with a price, though. To get to this state I had to go through a lot of hurt—becoming homeless is the hardest lesson of all."

It is from Kent's ethos—building something beautiful from the love found beneath the rubble of injustice—that the contours of this book have emerged.

Before coming to Cupertino, I'd spent several years writing stories about how the Valley was ruining the world, riding the techlash until it landed me a book deal. The plan was to come here and write about how tech companies were also ruining Silicon Valley—not the global, metaphorical Silicon Valley, but the actual place. A place where good, hardworking people once made a good, honest living that allowed them to support wholesome families—families now deposed to cleaning toilets on tech campuses at wages that afforded them a cardboard home on the side of the road. The obvious, expected book would depict the horrors of late-stage technocapitalism in excruciating, jargon-drenched detail. It would be a didactic polemic masquerading as equanimous ethnography. It would illustrate how tech-fueled income inequality had gone from awful to unspeakable in a pandemic economy that saw Silicon Valley profits skyrocket while gig workers moved into their cars. The headlines, and the chapters, practically write themselves. My soapbox lay ready, glistening with the sweat of resentment.

To an extent, this is that book—it cannot help but be written. There's ample truth in the narrative. But something happened that bent my trajectory in a different direction—I got to know some homeless folks and discovered that they had a very different tale to tell. The story that took shape through those relationships quickly moved away from simply critiquing capitalism and evaluating policy proposals, and toward an examination of my own humanity and what keeps me—and most housed folks—from connecting across the poverty veil. I came to believe that any realistic, durable fixes for homelessness must emerge one by one through human relationships, and be guided by unhoused communities them-selves. We have the top-down approach churning on steroids; bridging it with a bottom-up movement is, I've come to believe, the missing part of the equation.

This book is my journey from journalist to friend of the unhoused, a transformation that revealed an activist that I didn't know was hiding inside me—at one point I found myself beneath a highway underpass with a guy in a ski mask making "nail bombs," intended to puncture the tires of the police who'd come to evict him and his campmates. Hardly anyone sticks their neck out for homeless folks—like *really* sticks it out—and they desperately need defenders. It's a transformation that dragged me through the swamps of all the attempted fixes, from old-school shelters and Section 8 housing to more fashionable forays, like tiny-home villages, universal basic income, and sanc-tioned encampments. I faced many a beast, from tech executives and politicians to the tired bureaucrats that safeguard the homeless-industrial complex and neighborhood warriors wringing their hands about the tents down the street and the people eating, sleeping, fornicating, and getting high inside them.

Like Kent, I was tired of finger-pointing, and writing a book based on it seemed unlikely to be of any help to my new friends on the street, who clearly valued friendship more than the social services on offer. I didn't want to "get stuck in dwelling," as Kent put it—on whether or not Steve Jobs was a bad dude, the granular details of tech evil, or some sort of hand-waving policy analysis pertaining to wealth redistribution. "My anger is not anger," he told me. "It's my pain."

By going beyond their misery, to create a meaningful life on the other side of it, Kent and many others I eventually met have found a path to empowerment. That transformation is central to the culture of California's unhoused communities. It is the source of power, I believe, from which a camp-based social movement—virtually unknown outside those communities, even among the most hardened social justice warriors—has emerged. "It's deeper than grassroots," one guy told me. This book is my attempt to bring their movement to light.

What I saw in the shadow of the tech campuses, in other words, was not merely another sob story about what's wrong with America. I saw light in that shadow. I saw rebirth. Tent cities are places of extreme suffering and dysfunction, but that's only half the story. Back there behind the veils of our assumptions is a story about colorful communities where people involve themselves intimately in each other's lives—desirable neighborhoods, of a sort—and fight for redemption, both personal and political. The camps feel untenable, yet in making the most from the least, they embody sustainability, which is to say they possess a form of stability lacking in unsustainable affluence.

"This ship is sinking," said Dave, Kent's neighbor in the camp, one day. He was referring to the world we live in. "Everyone's lives have become so unbearable. But guess where the answers are?" He put his hand on his chest. "Homelessness is a recycling thing," he said. "It's like the Prodigal Son." Dave is from one town over in the wealthy enclave of Los Altos, where "everyone I grew up with was filthy rich," so he's familiar with both sides of the coin. He sees his time on the streets as "a spiritual journey" and thinks unhoused folks have something to teach the rest of us: "You learn an immense amount of humility out here," he said.

I wasn't expecting my interviews for the book to sound like self-help sermons, but that's largely the nature of my conversations in camps. People talk more about healing their soul, and that of their country, than they do about getting a job and an apartment. "I've made bad mistakes, but we all have," said Kent. "The question is whether you're trying to fix your mistakes? That's what I'm trying to do."

To the extent that Kent and company are on the leading edge of the apocalypse awaiting the rest of us, I believe they are also early adopters of a new world order. Let me tell you—it ain't utopia. It's a messy experiment in interdependence—a transmogrification of our nation's cult of independence, birthed from the skeletons in the cultists' closets. I came to see homelessness as not just the failure of the American Dream but the opportunity to reimagine it.

OFF WITH THE MASK

I'd walked into Wolfe Camp as a journalist seeking a solution, but I was also walking backward into my own history. In 1952, my grandfather left my grandmother and my mom, then two, with nothing but a goodbye note tacked onto a pincushion. My grandfather had been my grandmother's boss at the *New York Post*, but having recently transitioned to a new career in homemaking, she could not afford the rent on her own. I grew up understanding that being abandoned by my grandfather was a wound at the core of my mom's life story, but all I knew about the period that followed was that she and my grandmother stayed with friends and family for a while. One day I called my mom from California to learn more. "We were homeless," she said. "Not in the sense of living on the street, but we didn't have our own home."

They spent two years couch surfing—what we now call "hidden homelessness." For most unhoused folks I've met, some combo of couch surfing, motel stays, and car sleeping preceded, and often continues to be commingled with, more visible versions of homelessness. Some versions may be more traumatic than others, but I think they all do something similar to the soul and psyche: crush one's sense of stability. "Mommy, where's our home?" my mom often asked her mom during their period of couch surfing, as my grandmother later told her.

My grandmother became a rabid housing activist as a result of these experiences. My mom became a rabid labor activist. I was raised with those values but grew up allergic to the activism aspect, perhaps because of the ideological rigidity I felt bearing down on me from my maternal line. Yet I was primed to befriend the unhoused for altogether different reasons in the fall of 2020—my own suffering.

The worst year of my life was not *just* a product of COVID times George Floyd being murdered times the Orange-Faced One campaigning for reelection. The worst year of my life started in the middle of winter, a month before the World Health Organization made its declaration, when my wife and I agreed to a divorce at the kitchen table in our home in Toronto. I planned to start my new life, fashionably, in New York. But by the time the move date arrived, New York was in the midst of a COVID hurricane, so I moved instead to rural North Carolina, where the houses had been built in a socially distanced manner. My new address was on Solitude Lane, apt nomenclature for the deep tunnel of depression I entered. I had never felt so alone, so ashamed, so shattered as I did during the first months of the pandemic. I honestly didn't know if I would survive.

Six months after moving to North Carolina, I got on a plane to San Francisco—the healthiest form of escapism I could muster. My first in-depth interaction with the residents of Wolfe Camp was with Yesenia, the laid-off Google driver, and Walter, her hip-hopper boyfriend. I offered to take them out to lunch at a sushi bar around the corner from the camp. We sat outdoors—this was pre-vaccine—and shared a lovely meal. We talked about homelessness, and we talked about our rock bottoms. But it wasn't a heavy conversation. They were in love with each other, and they were loving having a meal out. They were rebounding from their rock bottoms, and we dwelled more on other topics—politics, food, travel, music. I felt like I was making new friends, not researching a book on homelessness. I forgot I was there as a journalist. It was the first meal I'd had with anyone other than my mom, who lived down the road from me in North Carolina, in six months; I felt deeply sated. Afterward, we walked a half block to where Yesenia and Walter were parked—their Subaru served as the closet and pantry of their tent—and they gave me a package of shiitake crisps they'd picked up at Walmart.

"Nooooo," I said, sheepishly.

"Yesssss!" they insisted.

Homelessness takes place at an address called rock bottom—if you want to connect with the unhoused, that's the meeting place. Passing through the darkest nights of the soul, for those who survive, instills a unique source of strength, which has much to do with why I'm drawn to unhoused communities, and with the very practical wisdom that I've found my unhoused friends possess in spades. With Kent and his colleagues as my guides, I've tried to swim upstream from us-against-them, to the headwaters of injustice and trauma and suffering, to the busted-ass relationships at the source of it all. Their traumas may be orders of magnitude greater than mine or yours, the intersections of their oppression altogether different, their social status and privilege virtually nonexistent. Those differences are consequential in life-or-death ways. But rather than compare the depth of our suffering to theirs—a slippery slope toward pity and othering—I prefer to see it as the place that we can all connect.

I have some beef with poverty media. As I began spending time in camps, I devoured every article, book, and film on homelessness that I could find, in which I noticed several trends. Their almost universally serious and melancholy tone has the unfortunate effect of rendering characters in a one-dimensional way—we're made to feel sorry for them, perhaps vaguely guilty about their plight, but not much else. Homeless folks drag boatloads of suffering and hardship through their lives, but they also drop their burdens from time to time to be boisterous, make crude jokes, create art, and throw crazy parties. Some of the people I meet on the street have the personalities of rock stars; others have a refined literary sensibility; many are folks you'd want to kick back and have a beer with. Between the hallucinatory swings of shifting mental states and the surrealism of living in a tent village in a twenty-first-century American city, the world of homelessness can feel like an absurdist satire mixed with a magical-realist fable. Can't a book about homelessness be all these things?

Another trend: studying homeless individuals and families in isolation from their communities. A couple and their kids living in a government-regulated shelter is one thing; the tribal thrum of life in an autonomous homeless village of three hundred people is another. To report in these places, you don't call up a social services agency and ask if they can help arrange an hourlong interview in a carpeted room at their office with one of their clients. It's more like entering a war zone, a place where guerrilla rebels make the rules and the only way in is to show a bit of your own humanity; they see right through the stale façade of journalistic neutrality. I knew I needed to write about homelessness through the lens of homeless communities, not just individuals and nuclear families. When you're homeless, the tent village is your family. You are part of a culture that is virtually unknown to the outer world, a culture with its own norms, values, and yes, style. It's impossible to understand that culture by getting to know a single homeless person or family, or even by getting to know a single community. I cast a wide net in the first months of my quest for The Fix, because I felt that I couldn't draw reliable conclusions from only a few fish. I wanted to get the fullest possible sense of the unhoused sea.

I eventually became intimately involved in three camps and got to know dozens of unhoused residents across the Bay Area, some of them quite well. In the following chapters, you'll get to know Wolfe Camp, the community of two dozen or so where Kent lived, along with folks at two of the Bay Area's largest unhoused communities: the Crash Zone in San José, where I connected with a man named Rudy, and Wood Street Commons in Oakland, where I became close with Monte. All three communities have been wiped off the face of the earth— Wolfe Camp within a month of my arrival in 2020; the Crash Zone a year later; Wood Street Commons, an outlier in its longevity, within two years. You'll also take a journey to a commune of sorts where formerly homeless folks live in shiny new townhomes, managing their own affairs without support from government or charities—a vision brought to fruition by a woman named Tiny, whose radical approach to The Fix centers on self-determination for the unhoused. Tiny's community is a rare example of what can happen when the unhoused have the opportunity to stick together and do things their way. They call it Homefulness.

It is not easy to gain the trust of people who are profoundly marginalized, disenfranchised, and often straight-up abused by the people and political system around them. It doesn't help that the media narrative about homelessness is so deeply out of touch with the narratives homeless folks have about themselves. The first thing I learned in the camps is that in order to "report" this book, I had to enter into meaningful relationships with my "sources." This was complicated and uncomfortable. Not only did it require that I set aside the idea of journalistic detachment, it turned out to involve a whole lot of looking in the mirror. Beyond the real estate developers and apathetic politicos, there's a deeper, more personal villain in this tale: fear.

I try to project an easygoing aura when walking into camps, but even now, after having regularly visited several over a period of years, I constantly look over my shoulder and jump at the sight of my own shadow. I've become accustomed to seeing mentally unstable men wandering around with knives, machetes, and baseball bats. Arson is another tool for mediating disputes. "I get mad at you, I burn your shit—that's what we do," a man named Buchi, who resided at the Crash Zone community in San José, told me. Tent and vehicle fires are a weekly experience at some camps. Bullets are occasionally employed as well. "There's a shooting-in-the-leg thing," said Theo from Wood Street Commons. The fear comes in many forms. "The worst thing is the rats," said Bobby, who I befriended at Wolfe Camp. "Some are the size of puppies. They crawl over you when you're asleep. If you have any scabs, they'll gnaw through and try to suck your blood."

Long before I'd been exposed to the rawest sides of homelessness, I was aware that beneath the fears about personal safety lurked a larger fear of the unknown, of darkness, of extreme suffering, like a slippery-sided pit of snakes we would do anything to avoid falling into. Jaz, an unhoused trans woman I got to know, put it this way: "I think people are afraid of us because deep down they think, *It could be me.*"

Whatever the reason, fear had a chokehold on me when I returned to Wolfe Road a few days after meeting Kent in the parking lot of my apartment complex. I was hoping to chat him up about the mask, which I discovered hanging on a post in his postage stamp of a front yard. The post supported a white door that looked as though it may have been hinged, until recently, to someone's condo closet. The door had not been positioned as an entrance to the tent; rather, it faced passersby as they approached on the sidewalk. It was, in other words, a door to nowhere, except the barren soil on the other side of it. *Or perhaps it's a metaphorical door*, I imagined saying to Kent in an embarrassingly serious voice—*a portal to an alternate reality that you hope people walking down Wolfe Road will perceive.*

In front of Kent's multiroom tarp-plex, a samurai sword had been plunged half its length into the earth. The tarp flap was partially open, and I could see a man's hairy arm splayed out on the edge of the couch just inside. *He's sleeping,* I thought, a warm sensation blossoming in my chest. I try to avoid invading the privacy of the campers, who have virtually none, yet my eyes were drawn up the length of the arm, which was clothed in the rolled-up sleeve of a blue dress shirt, and into the dark interior of the structure. My eyes didn't get very far, however, before they froze in a moment of terror. Realizing I'd come across a grisly murder scene, I lurched involuntarily backward—the arm was not connected to a body.

Oh yeah, Halloween was last week, I reminded myself. Condo dumpsters. Faux appendages. The scream in my throat turned into a long exhale as I scuttled out of the camp.

But I later learned that Kent has a collection of masks, which he sometimes wears in public on days that are not Halloween. Kent's job, if you want to call it that, is a timeless one: trickster.

2

Hobo Sapiens

Lost in the contemporary debate about homelessness is the long, highly relevant history of humans lacking a permanent home. There are entire cultures of wanderers, such as the Roma, Maasai, and Persian dervishes. There are those displaced by war, drought, plagues, economic fissures, and other pressures, such as the Okies, who lived in tent cities across California nearly a century ago, and the Central Americans more recently camping on the streets of New York while seeking asylum. Hobos, tramps, train hoppers, gutter punks, vagrants, vagabonds, addicts, winos, ramblers, wandering minstrels, mystic mendicants, migrants, refugees, outlaws, squatters, sociopaths, psychopaths, the neurodiverse and mentally maladjusted: Outcasts and dispossessed peoples of every stripe collectively represent an important archetype in the evolution of culture and consciousness, one that both captures the imagination of the status quo and scares the bejesus out of it.

It can be hard to draw clean lines between the intentionally and unintentionally homeless throughout history; it's more of a spectrum. Certain ancient tribes in arid regions roamed in search of the lush vegetation that fed the animals that fed them, their nomadism a response to Mother Nature—clearly on one end of the spectrum. Perhaps a bit closer to the middle are the homeless ascetics found in the world's religions, from the robed Carmelites of the Middle Ages to the sadhus that still beg for food in the streets of India. Some sadhu groups are known for their body-length dreadlocks and copious cannabis use; others do not bathe or brush their teeth and renounce all worldly possessions, even their clothes, wandering naked in search of God. It can be a murky line between religious devotees on the streets and mentally ill folks exclaiming divine prophecies, at least based on outward appearances.

Other itinerants, such as train-hopping hobos and Rainbow hippies pilot-ing converted school buses, have roamed in search of freedom from the rat race and the soul-crushing norms that come with it, their homelessness a response, in many ways, to capitalism and conformity. To what extent did they consciously reject society, versus being in possession of traits that caused them to be rejected by it? Poverty and idealism are often intertwined.

The unhoused tend to evoke a mixture of disgust, curiosity, and romanti-cism among the housed. Take the Roma, for instance, who are thought to have originated as low-caste traveling performers in India. What is more certain is that they've been looked down on wherever they've roamed throughout the world, and that their persecuted lifestyle has crystallized over the ages into a celebrated cultural identity—many Roma consider *gypsy* a derogatory term, but in pop culture it's synonymous with being a free spirit.

The criminalization of homeless folks has a long and varied past. One early attempt in Europe emerged after the bubonic plague killed a large swath of the population. There were fewer people available to toil for the gentry, creating significant leverage among laborers, who were demanding higher pay and better conditions. Meanwhile, crops were rotting in the fields because there weren't enough peasants to pick them. As a result, people who didn't work, but were perceived as capable of working, were not viewed kindly by the ruling class. In 1349, King Edward III, England's monarch at the time, issued a decree that made it a crime for able-bodied citizens under the age of sixty to withhold their labor. It specifically addressed the nation's "many valiant beggars," who "as long as they may live of begging, do refuse to labor, giving themselves to idleness and vice, and sometime to theft and other abominations."

Vagrancy laws spread as Europe began to urbanize and industrialize. Various "vagabond acts" that criminalized "masterless men" were instituted in England, such as Henry VIII's in 1535, which applied to children as young as six. Upon the first offense of "vagabondage"—the technical term found in his-tory books—one would be whipped and sent back to their hometown to work. "And if he continue his roguish Life, he shall have the upper Part of the Gristle of his Right Ear cut off; and if after that he be taken wandering in Idleness, or doth not apply to his Labour, or is not in Service with any Master, he shall be adjudged and executed as a Felon."

For a time, punishments for British vagrants included slavery: two years for the first offense and a life sentence for the second. You would be branded on the chest with a *V* (for vagrant) for the former, an *S* (for slave) on the forehead for the latter. Historians say this particular provision was not likely enforced, but it is in this context that forced labor for those living in England's streets emerged—the "workhouses" later romanticized by Charles Dickens in *Oliver Twist*—where one would toil breaking stones into gravel, or bones into fertilizer, and hope for a decent portion of gruel at the end of the day.

Homelessness in the earliest days of the United States has not been well documented, but just like on the other side of the pond it is thought to have emerged alongside urbanization and industrialization, its prevalence correlated with downturns in the economy and periods of social upheaval. Historians believe that prior to the Civil War, the unhoused population was composed largely of escaped slaves and former indentured servants. What is known more certainly is that it exploded during the "Long Depression" of the 1870s, when huge numbers of unemployed men took to the rails, hopping freight trains and attempting to have a jolly time while they were down on their luck. They became known as tramps and hobos, and for seventy years they occupied a central place in American culture. The term *homelessness* began to slide from our tongues around this time.

There is limited data on the number of homeless people in the country back then, though the per capita rate was likely higher than it is today. One source estimated a homeless population of about ninety thousand in 1893—a time when the US population was around sixty-three million, making this figure roughly on par with modern-day rates—but it is generally agreed that the population grew significantly over the following decades. Records from New York and Philadelphia in the early twentieth century show tens of thousands of people taking refuge each year at individual shelters—a scale similar to today, but at a time when the general population was a fraction of what it is now. Another early-twentieth-century source cited a conservative estimate of five hundred thousand homeless people, with up to seventy-five thousand in Chicago alone, rates far higher than today. It is clear that homelessness exploded during the Great Depression, when tent cities called Hoovervilles spread across the country. An oft-cited estimate for the American homeless population in the thirties is two million, or about eight times the per capita rate determined by official counts in recent years.

"The homeless were far more visible, and far more assertive, during the industrial era than at any other time in American history," writes Kenneth Kusmer, a rare expert on homelessness in American history, in his book *Down and Out, on the Road.* "Prior to World War II, tramps and beggars could scarcely be avoided. Most Americans regularly encountered people begging for a handout, either at their back doors or on street corners."

The unhoused of this era, as they are today, were generally reviled. An 1873 piece in *The New York Times* declared that "these tramps are always pretending to look for work, but it is very rare that they will accept it if offered, unless to get a chance to steal something." Kusmer cites an 1875 *Times* editorial rendering the tramp as one who "is at war in a lazy kind of way with society and rejoices at being able to prey upon it." There was much talk in those days of an emergent "tramp menace."

But *unlike* unhoused people today, turn-of-the-century tramps were also pop culture icons. They were a staple in vaudeville and an obsession in the first half-century of American film, a period in which hundreds of movies featured tramps as primary characters, if not stars. Charlie Chaplin's recurring tramp character, the most famous of these, remains one of the most recognizable figures in cinema history. Tramp movies were often comical, with the vagrant characters treated as buffoons. But many also contained a jester's satire within the buffoonery, a critical subtext that questioned evolving notions of work in the Gilded Age and the Roaring Twenties, when income inequality rose to levels not seen again in this country until recently. Chaplin—a descendant of the Roma who spent a portion of his childhood in London workhouses due to his father's alcoholism and his mother's mental health struggles—was well known for imbuing his work with leftist sympathies for the lower class. While privileged filmgoers may have found comic relief in tramp films, the poor found a sliver of cultural redemption.

"They show a tension in the American imaginary between viewing homelessness as, on the one hand, deviance, or threat, and, on the other, as freedom and independence," writes film scholar Pamela Robertson Wojcik, whose book *Unhomed* dissects what she calls the "films of the precariat" throughout American history. "But while the tramp can be seen as someone who has failed to achieve the American dream of success and home ownership, he ... is more often shown as resisting, opting out, offering a critique of the necessity for home."

Writers, academics, and public intellectuals were fascinated by unhoused Americans at this time. "What miles of smooth road, or crisp, half-trod grass-paths, are covered," wrote one chronicler of tramps in the late nineteenth century, his adoration evoking the rugged individualist vein of Muir, Twain, Thoreau, and, later, Kerouac. He goes on and on about "dallyings by moss-grown bridges" and "drinking of deep, pure draughts from sparkling springs," rendering an ultra-romanticized image of homelessness as an expression of a timeless masculine quest to experience nature and freedom, one with a grand historical context. "Jesus Christ was himself a tramp," he writes, noting how this transient carpenter from Nazareth valorized poverty and simplicity. "Exalt the inquisitive, vagabond tramp through all ages and in all countries," the author opines. It makes one want to cast off the shackles of rent and march right down to the nearest encampment.

In this account of the glories of Western nomadism, American tramps emerged from the lineage of medieval traveling musicians, indigent peddlers, and itinerant craftsmen of the Old World. Some of these were serious workers. "Journeymen" were the tradesmen of the day, such as carpenters, masons, and tinkers—an old-school word for tinsmiths, which became a pejorative term for the unhoused in the British Isles—who roamed in search of the next gig. Others read palms and offered an array of esoteric services. Each region of Europe had its nomadic groups, broadly known as Travellers, but each with distinct customs and dialects—Woonwagenbewoners in the Netherlands, Skøyere in Scandinavia, Camminanti in Sicily, Pavee in Ireland. The author, who grew up in Scotland, claims to have crossed paths with many a wanderer in Europe. He says that the vagabonds of the day, despite being heavily persecuted, held such a mystic allure that citizens of means regularly emulated them. "Their wandering and seemingly happy mode of life induced many of the romantic to copy their manners and become themselves wanderers or tramps," he writes. "Suddenly the highways and hamlets were filled with them."

You might be surprised to know that the author of these accounts was Allan Pinkerton, founder of a sprawling private-security enterprise known for ruthless tactics to break up strikes and labor unions. The name of the book was *Strikers, Communists, Tramps and Detectives.* "Pinkertons," the precursor of the Secret Service, were the sort of law-enforcement authority figures despised by tramps and hobos. After several chapters waxing about tramp life, Pinkerton finally gets around to his real point, which is that this pure archetype of the wandering man who he so reveres had become polluted by the political and economic forces of his time. The Long Depression had "manufactured tramps with an alarming rapidity. Where they previously existed as single wandering vagabonds, they now have increased until they travel in herds." He says that this more destitute, more communal homeless person was also more dangerous, referring to them as a "highway pirate." Of this new wave of homelessness, said Pinkerton, "there is no doubt that the majority of those now upon the road are there from necessity, and not from choice."

The biggest danger, in Pinkerton's estimation, was their politicization. The bulk of the book is about how, in his view, a coalition of tramps, communists, and railroad workers were responsible for the Great Railroad Strike of 1877—the first nationwide strike in American history, it evolved into a multi-industry work stoppage that became known as the Great Upheaval—which shut down the country for fifty-two days before it was violently squashed. In Pinkerton's telling, communists imbued the workers with the necessary ideology, while tramps brought a criminal mindset and a general desire to see the ruling class dead in a ditch. Having transformed homeless folks from heroes to savages, Pinkerton indulges the same linguistic excesses to describe their role in the rioting of 1877, describing them like rats and roaches. They "seemed to suddenly spring from every conceivable spot like some magical yet dangerous growth of the night," he writes. "The slums and alleys turned out their miserable inhabitants. . . . Every fresh accession of communistic laborers and communistic loafers was welcomed with an intelligence only begot of murderous hate in one common purpose."

It's hard to separate fact from fancy in Pinkerton's writing. Like the Orange-Faced One, there is a certain form of cultural truth-telling in his hyperbole—saying publicly what some think privately in order to plow an agenda forward. There is definitely truth in Pinkerton's assertion that tramps leaned hard to the left. Many less sensationalist commentators have noted that as radical leftist ideology spread through the lower classes in turn-of-the-century America, homeless folks were very much in the mix.

A CERTAIN KIND OF PARADISE

By the twenties, many large American cities contained a neighborhood where the unhoused congregated, which became known as *hobohemias*. This was in part because the hobos were known for having a bohemian outlook, and in part because housed bohemians—leftist intellectuals, drug users, labor union activists, and other radicals—often congregated in the same neighborhoods. Radical bookstores were a primary gathering spot, serving not only to disseminate subversive ideas, but as clubhouses of a sort, where a homeless person could have a drink, store their belongings, collect mail, and even spend the night. In addition to the downtown hobohemias, hobos lived in camps on the outskirts of towns called *jungles*. Here was a different type of bohemianism, one with communal meals over campfires and skinny-dipping (or bathing, as it were).

Operating under their own norms and customs, and largely beyond the tentacles of polite society, the homeless communities of the era fell within what Kusmer describes as "the anarchist streak in the American character." In their autonomy, they possessed both the grassroots power of striking workers and the build-your-own-destiny mentality of the pioneers who were at the time still colonizing the last pockets of North America. "By adopting extralegal forms of government," writes Kusmer, "these groups carried forward a tradition long associated with the American frontier, where communities often preceded formal government. The hobo jungles, with their unwritten rules of conduct, reflected a similar mentality."

In hobohemias, one could pick up a hobo newspaper and read the latest developments of the class struggle, while also gleaning tips about the best train-hopping routes and the towns with the meanest, or most lenient, sheriffs. *Hobo News*, the biggest of these, with a circulation of twenty thousand at its peak, was filled with sharp-witted editorials, lyrics to popular campfire ballads, and poetry inspired by life on the road. The homeless-centric publications of the day evidenced a rich subculture, with its own music, vernacular language, and even secret symbols that were posted, graffiti-like, to communicate with fellow travelers. According to one source I unearthed, a *U* with a dot in it meant "town generally leaves hobos alone." A triangle with stick-man arms meant "man with gun lives here." A crude drawing of a cat meant "kind lady lives here." A Christian cross meant "religious talk will get you a free meal."

This was the soapbox era, and the sidewalks and parks of hobohemias were prime locations to spew one's beliefs. The hot topic among hobohemia soapboxers was the battle between labor and capital. Many of the soapboxers were proponents of the Industrial Workers of the World, a massive union at the time with a mission to "abolish the wage system" and "do away with capitalism," according to its constitution, which declared that "we are forming the structure of the new society within the shell of the old." Unlike most unions, the IWW was agnostic to one's trade—anyone who was not an employer could be a member, including an out-of-work hobo. However, many in the hobohemia universe did work, primarily in seasonal and short-term positions that were critical to some industries, including agriculture, logging, and construction.

There was a range of lifestyles in regard to employment in hobohemias. A saying attributed to Ben Reitman, a hobo who became a doctor and ministered to his colleagues across the nation's hobohemias, distilled three classes of homelessness: "The hobo works and wanders, the tramp dreams and wanders, and the bum drinks and wanders." The lines between them were fluid. A housed person might lose their job and become a hobo traveling in search of work. But as the years went by and the lifestyle became more entrenched, they might find themselves a tramp. If their woes got deep enough, they ended up a bum. The migrant workers of the day were the higher-functioning denizens of hobohemias, and they had a personal stake in the labor movement, one that resonated among the less-functioning denizens as well.

In the early days of the IWW, the union was not just welcoming to hobohemians—its political identity was centered on them. Todd DePastino, another rare historian of homelessness, wrote that the IWW "delivered a floating subculture to the very center of American labor activism." The IWW's position, according to DePastino, was that hobos, "by virtue of their footloose detachment from the bonds of settled community, were by nature the 'real proletarians' and more revolutionary than other groups of stationary workers."

This homeless renaissance a century ago did not remove the stigma or the criminalization inherent in homelessness, but it had a significant impact on political discourse. Besides the fictionalized accounts of tramp and hobo life, a number of firsthand accounts appeared, including those of Jack London, who credited his time tramping as a major influence informing his socialist leanings. Many lesser-known homeless folks also published memoirs. In Chicago, a young sociologist named Nels Anderson, who had been a hobo in his youth, published a treatise on the city's hobohemians, which mixed journalistic reportage with academic rigor, analyzing everything from the mental and physical health traits of the population to their politics and sex lives (he noted a high incidence of homosexuality). Anderson immersed himself in the emerging institutions of hobo life, which he found to be very disorganized. "Hobo colleges" emerged in cities across the country in the early twentieth century—which were not formal colleges, but more like hobo-run community centers that offered programs on topics of interest to their constituents, such as vagrancy laws and labor history— but most quickly fell into disarray, Anderson explained, and closed their doors. He attended a convention of the International Brotherhood Welfare Association, a large homeless-helping-the-homeless group at the time, reporting that it "continued in session for three days and did not get any farther than to argue about the power of the convention to act in the name of the IBWA."

Most shoestring nonprofits suffer from petty jealousies and toxic personalities, but those run by homeless folks carry the burdens of a traumatized population known more for its distaste for bureaucracy than its organizational talents. Rather than trivialize these shortcomings, Anderson plumbed them for meaning. "In pointing out the repeated and seemingly inevitable failures of hobo organizations, the fact must not be lost sight of that they are absolutely necessary to his social existence," he writes, adding that "they satisfy this fundamental need of the social outcast for status. . . . were these organizations destroyed, the anti-social grudge of the individual would undoubtedly be reflected in criminality."

These tensions are no less present in the modern homeless empowerment movement, which shares an ethos of anarchy mixed with the politics of wealth redistribution. Whether one is running from society or feeling spit from it, there's an inherent apathy toward the institutions at play. This muddles the work of building new institutions, which is ultimately how new norms become, well, *normal*. Yet, in this mess, love remains. "With no status in organized society, he longs for a classless society where all inequalities shall be abolished," writes Anderson.

Hobohemias, along with their institutions and culture, faded away after the 1920s. The Great Depression hit, making tramps out of large numbers of Americans, which undoubtedly shifted the dynamic on the streets. New Deal investments in the social safety net made a huge impact on how poverty was experienced, and the federal government, for the first time in American history, took responsibility for addressing homelessness on a large scale. At the same time, unions grew in power and World War II boosted the economy. By the 1950s, the working class, which had grown ever closer to the edge of destitution as industrialization advanced, was moving steadily into the middle class, at least among white folks. As extreme poverty became less common, homelessness receded from the American imagination.

What historians refer to as "modern homelessness" emerged in the eighties as a result of several factors. One was Reaganomics: Huge cuts to the social safety net were made alongside fiscal policy that benefited corporations and the wealthy, steering income inequality back to Gilded Age levels; union jobs dwindled, and good-paying factory work shifted to cheaper overseas labor markets. The second factor was the loss of single-room occupancy hotels, or SROs, which transformed homelessness from something largely hidden behind the walls of dirt-cheap rooming houses to more of a street-based phenomenon—gentrification, coupled with changes in zoning laws, led to the loss of an estimated one million SRO units by the turn of the millennium. The third reason drastically changed the image of homelessness: a movement to "deinstitutionalize" severely mentally ill people, removing them from inhumane asylums and setting them loose on the no-less-inhumane streets. In 1980, the number of people committed in state-run hospitals was one-fourth that of 1960.

Homelessness became a story of Vietnam veterans, HIV-positive men, crack addicts, and people of exceedingly poor hygiene wandering the streets while speaking with invisible companions. There was nothing romantic about it. Then came the opioid epidemic and the Great Recession. The era of the Orange-Faced One melded a pandemic with earth-shattering gentrification and corporate power. And . . . *badda-bing, badda-boom* . . . the tent city age of homelessness took hold. It has much in common with hobohemia, though the average American does not understand it as such—yet.

Anarchy is a common thread of unhoused cultures, past and present, and in both a positive and negative sense. Anarchy, in essence, is how humans live in the absence of state power and entrenched, large-scale institutions that control the distribution of capital and privilege. They may live very well, or they may devolve into depravity; it depends on the situation.

It's likely that if you group a bunch of highly traumatized and dispossessed individuals in an environment where there are no institutions governing or supporting them, things will get messy. There's a lot of trash in homeless camps, a lot of screaming, a lot of intoxication, a lot of dysfunction. Pinkerton writes of a camp where he found some residents busy "making rude toilets with almost toothless combs, and old rags for towels." But he also describes redeeming qualities. They cooked collectively, for instance, and obtained the food and other goods they needed in the simplest ways possible, thus maximizing time available for recreation. He observed that "when they get out of provisions, they either take to the roads and beg or steal a supply from the farmers, or stroll into the meadows and gather mint and other herbs, or flowers, which they take into the city and sell for whatever they can get, the proceeds of which they usually invest in nine parts whiskey and one part food, and then, returning to camp, inaugurate a regular debauch, when they make the woods ring and ring again with songs and laughter." Their shelters were equally modest: "They have a cabin built of limbs of trees and bark for the more aristocratic of their number, but the majority sleep upon the ground, with any arrangement for protection which their ambition may suggest."

The recurring theme is informality, figuring it out in the moment with whatever people and resources happen to be on hand in an unscripted and anarchic way. For those perpetually planning the next nine moves in the chess game of life, homeless camps provide a harsh culture shock. But their worldview can also be liberating. My observation is that for most homeless folks, there's a solid baseline of satisfaction that comes with a life situation where they can simply be—whatever that happens to look like for them.

Pinkerton found heaps of contentment in the camps he visited. "All that is requisite for admission to this Druidical tribe is the certain evidences which a tramp or outcast wears; the lower you are, the more sure of a welcome you are. While you remain, you may have as good as they have, providing you show yourself willing to assist to the extent of your ability." Some of his descriptions sound like a free love commune, only a deeply impoverished version. "Sequestered in the dark, cool recesses, beneath these heavy clump willows, would be gathered between fifty and a hundred tramps of all ages, conditions, and sex, and all lying about promiscuously, alone or in little knots, near smoldering fires . . . joking and chatting, and possibly making love in their rude fashion." One of Pinkerton's most insightful observations was this: "It matters little how the elections go, whether the banks break, or whether revolutions occur. They are all contented, at least for the time being, and are well satisfied with life from what it has brought for the day."

For an anarchist, the culture of homelessness makes perfect sense. Election drama, bank failures, and the impetus to mount a coup are not likely features of a world built by anarchists. While the word *anarchy* conjures chaos, disorder, and dissent—not to mention the violent overthrow of governments—that's only because of the intense friction between anarchist values and the reality in which we live. An anarchist utopia is really just about getting together and being human. When you don't aspire to accumulate wealth and status and compose enormous bureaucracies to that end, the stakes of conflicts and poor judgment are relatively small. They're closer to household scale—Who's going to take out the trash? Why is so-and-so acting so passive-aggressive lately? What are we going to have for dinner tonight?

The idealized image of an anarchist community is, in a sense, a scaled-up family bound not by blood, but by geography and lifestyle affinities—very much the feeling one has in a homeless camp.

Peter Kropotkin, the grand Russian poo-bah of nineteenth-century anarchism, defined the slippery term with elegance: "The name given to a principle or theory of life and conduct under which society is conceived without government—harmony in such a society being obtained, not by submission to law, or by obedience to any authority, but by free agreements concluded between the various groups, territorial and professional, freely constituted for the sake of production and consumption, as also for the satisfaction of the infinite variety of needs and aspirations of a civilized being."

David Graeber, the late anarchist anthropologist credited as one of the architects of the Occupy movement, has said that "anarchists are simply people who believe human beings are capable of behaving in a reasonable fashion without having to be forced to." In his essay titled "Are You an Anarchist? The Answer May Surprise You!," he wrote that "at their very simplest, anarchist beliefs turn on to two elementary assumptions. The first is that human beings are, under ordinary circumstances, about as reasonable and decent as they are allowed to be, and can organize themselves and their communities without needing to be told how. The second is that power corrupts."

Graeber arrived at his anarchist views in part from studying Indigenous groups and other so-called primitive societies who lacked formal governance structures. He found that while there may have been plenty of violence and turmoil in such societies, it was often dealt with using self-organized, cooperative, participatory democracy. When government does not exist, those are pretty much the options. Which is very much the basis of unhoused communities. They are free-for-alls in a sense, but within the chaos there's still the inescapable order and logic of a species with a large frontal lobe, and the unspoken rules of the emotional bonds that we form.

"Most of all, anarchism is just a matter of having the courage to take the simple principles of common decency that we all live by, and to follow them through to their logical conclusions," wrote Graeber. "Every time you work out your differences with others by coming to reasonable compromise, listening to what everyone has to say rather than letting one person decide for everyone else, you are being an anarchist." In Graeber's view, it's human nature to be an anarchist, and much of the time we behave that way—"even if you don't realize it."

The fact that anarchism has gotten so mixed up with leftist ideology has less to do with mohawks and tattoos than it does with the anarchist perspective on labor. In this view, the world would not come to an end if formal employment disappeared—work does not equal job, it's just a thing that happens in the form and timing needed. This purportedly radical perspective is also a very familiar feeling to billions of human beings. In his book *Bullshit Jobs*, Graeber, who was a proud member of the IWW (which still exists today, though in a greatly shriveled form), wrote that "hell is a collection of individuals who spend their time working on a task they don't like and are not especially good at." In the era of digital nomadism, the Great Resignation, quiet quitting, and the anti-work movement, it seems that the working masses have caught the whiff of freedom as well.

Being housed is deeply tied up with mass-scale economic and political systems, in large part because of the nature of the jobs required to sustain membership in that class. To withdraw from those systems, as painful as it might be, presents an opportunity to reimagine them, to live differently. In this sense, unhoused humans, as horrible as their circumstances may be, live in intimate proximity to the ideals of anarchy, a state of possibility limited only by human nature.

ANTI-ERASURE

There's a common tension coursing through the history of homelessness and its modern expressions: They are beautiful experiments in anarchic self-determination, yet they are intensely oppressed by the political economies in which they are enveloped. Perhaps there were ancient humans who found themselves in utopic anarchies, but the nature of anarchy situated within a social system that hotly contests its existence is one of extreme friction. There's easy evidence supporting the argument that the absence of state power leads to antisocial behavior and reduced quality of life: Often when states fail in the modern world, organized crime syndicates or authoritarian groups take over. The anarchy of homeless camps has some of that flavor. They also have plenty of peace, love, and harmony—the lesser-known side of anarchy. There's ample evidence indicating that the uglier side of unhoused anarchies has much to do with the fact that their existence is persecuted, both culturally speaking and in the juridical sense.

One thing that binds the unhoused communities of past and present together is the policeman's boot. The unhoused are constantly told that they cannot be wherever they are. Nels Anderson's book includes an account of a Chicago jungle being swept, as told to him by one of its residents: Someone was mugged the night before and an angry mob, fronted by local police officers, has descended on the camp to drive them out of town. The campers resisted with impassioned speeches and "a fiery song of the class struggle," but were eventually "ordered to hold up their hands with 'You damn bums' added to the command," said Anderson's source. "Some comply, others refuse. One even has the courage to shout, 'Go ahead and shoot, you damn cowards.' This starts a general shooting into every pot, pan and can in sight. The men scatter."

It sounds like a script from a poorly written Western. But police violence is no joke. Being evicted from one's house is trauma enough, but being evicted again and again from one's home on the street—the plight of virtually every homeless person not residing in a shelter—is an unimaginable trauma. Maybe you're in a wheelchair. Maybe you have kids. You've scrapped together a shack and made it as much a home as you can, and then one day you're forced under threat of violence and imprisonment to abandon it and start over. In modern times, the sweeping is done with heavy equipment. The sound of plywood shacks being crushed in the jaws of bulldozers is burned into one's neurons.

All three unhoused communities I befriended were eventually swept, but the most intense carnage I witnessed was on Wood Street in Oakland. This was in part because the community had lasted much longer than most and had built extensive infrastructure. The place was so big and so entrenched and so hostile toward its evictors that it took a small army of workers a couple months to do the physical crushing. What made it feel even more soul-crushing, however, was the historical context of the place. There's a maze of train lines that meet in and around the Wood Street camp, part of an enormous industrial area surrounding the Oakland port, which historically employed large numbers of Black Americans, including Monte's father. It was a place where wages were low, discrimination high, and resistance baked into the culture. In the thirties, the Brotherhood of Sleeping Car Porters, the first African American union in the country, was established at the now-defunct Sixteenth Street Station, a Beaux Arts edifice at the south end of the camp. In the forties and fifties, a strip of jazz clubs, known as the Harlem of the West, emerged nearby. In the sixties, the Black Panther Party was born in the neighborhood. The area is known generally as West Oakland, which has always been poor, Black, and radical. But Wood Street is in a sub-district known as the Lower Bottoms. This alludes to the flat land around the port, barely above sea level, but it also alludes to being the place where the poorest of the poor have lived in Oakland for generations.

In Oakland, the median income of white households is nearly three times higher than Black households. It is an intensely gentrified city in which nearly half of residents were Black in 1980, compared to less than 12 percent today. Seventy percent of the homeless population is Black, however. Oakland has been inundated by a gentrification tsunami emanating across the Bay from San Francisco and Silicon Valley, and Wood Street is on the front lines of the destruction. Condo developments ooze down the street, replacing the tents, block by block. Within a year after I started hanging out there, construction began on one kitty-corner from the camp; another broke ground on a lot in the middle of the camp that had been swept before I came along. The Sixteenth Street Station has been out of service for years, but recently has been rented out for Burning Man parties and other events. The station's forecourt is now occupied by Boxcar Flower Farm. After picking up a fifty-dollar organic bouquet, one can sip espresso on the sidewalk out front at the Monster Java coffee cart, which has a view of the camp on one side and shiny new $700,000 condos on the other.

The homeless folks were there first, however. Many of them grew up in the neighborhood, and for many years, the Oakland police, when conducting a sweep, told unhoused residents they'd be left alone if they went to Wood Street. Monte was one of those who was directed here when being evicted from elsewhere. He'd been there about eight years when I met him—significantly longer than I've lived in one place since leaving my parents' home. Monte was very attached to Wood Street. The day I met him, city officials were there to persuade the residents to leave voluntarily, which was of course not going to happen. But they would eventually bring in guys with guns.

"We need to fight," Monte told me. "And we need to make the fight large enough that the world is watching."

New Friends

Who is homeless in America today and why? One night in the dead of winter every other year, thousands of volunteers hit the streets to count the people sleeping in them, while shelter operators tally their occupants. Each person is asked their age, race, ethnicity, gender identity, family situation, history of military service, and length of time being unhoused. The resulting dataset—the Department of Housing and Urban Development's biannual "point-in-time" count—is the federal government's answer to the first part of the question.

In the winter of the worst year of my life, COVID disrupted the count, but the following year HUD found that six out of ten unhoused folks were male. Six out of ten stayed in shelters, the official variety, as opposed to the so-called "unsheltered" homeless, HUD's term for those in tents, vehicles, shacks, abandoned buildings, and other forms of unsanctioned shelter. Thirty-seven percent of those counted were Black, though only 12 percent of the general population is. Of those who identified as members of a family with children, half were Black. Five percent were people under twenty-five without a parent or guardian looking after them, and 7 percent were veterans. About a third fit the criteria for chronic homelessness—"an individual with a disability who has been continuously homeless for one year or more or has experienced at least four episodes of homelessness in the last three years where the combined length of time homeless on those occasions is at least 12 months," according to HUD's extraordinarily obtuse definition.

The West Coast has higher-than-average rates of homelessness compared to the rest of the country, especially the chronic, unsheltered variety. Overall, rates have stayed fairly steady in recent years—the national point-in-time count has been hovering around 550,000 to 650,000—but in California, Washington, and Oregon the numbers of unsheltered individuals has gone up between 30 and 50 percent since 2007. Hence the proliferation of tent cities during that time period—and the accompanying exclamations of "crisis" on the left coast. It's not because unhoused people are moving west in droves to take advantage of welfare handouts in liberal states; studies have shown that the vast majority of homeless folks live in the same region where they were previously housed (a California study, for instance, found that 90 percent of homeless residents surveyed were last housed in the state and three out of four had not left the county where they were last housed). The West Coast's disproportionately high housing costs clearly have something to do with the trend, though the region's relatively mild climate also contributes to the tent city phenomenon—in colder climes, one is more apt to submit to a cot in a congregate shelter or ask friends and family if you can couch surf.

California is the undisputed capital of both the crisis and the unhoused empowerment movement. Nowhere are there more homeless people living in tent cities, where they are in our faces, unlike New York, in contrast, which has an enormous unhoused population, but with most of it confined to shelters at night. California has the nation's highest per capita rate of homelessness and half of the nation's total unsheltered population—those living outdoors, that is—which is nine times more than the next-closest state. Los Angeles County has the most unsheltered residents in the country, nearly forty-five thousand, which is enough to fill the Angels stadium in Anaheim. But Silicon Valley wins the prize for the highest overall rate of unsheltered among the total unhoused population of any urban area, at 83 percent.

In 2022, California conducted its first comprehensive census, which drills much more into the "why" than HUD's does. The conclusions are fairly obvious—low income, trauma, addiction, and mental illness predispose one to homelessness. The more of those boxes one checks, the higher the likelihood you lack a permanent address. Eighty-two percent of respondents said they'd experienced "a serious mental health condition" at some point in their lives; 27 percent had been hospitalized as a result. Half considered themselves seriously depressed, and half reported anxiety; an eighth reported hallucinations. Sixty-five percent reported regular drug use, and 62 percent reported heavy drinking. Meth was the most popular illicit substance (31 percent), followed by nonprescription opioids (11 percent). Sixty percent said they suffered from a chronic disease. Nineteen percent became homeless after exiting the carceral system. A quarter said they had experienced sexual violence at some point in life, though among nonbinary and trans respondents, three-quarters had.

Median income prior to becoming unhoused was $960 per month. Seventy percent said a rental subsidy of $300 to $500 per month, or a lump sum of $5,000 to $10,000, could have prevented their homelessness; even more said the same amount of financial assistance could end it. Eighteen percent received some income from working, and 55 percent of able-bodied individuals under the age of sixty-two said they were looking for work. Only 9 percent said they'd received mental health counseling while homeless, but 30 percent said they'd been to jail. A third identified as Latino, a quarter Black, and an eighth Indigenous. The average age? Forty-seven. The average number of months they'd been unhoused? Twenty-two. The percentage of income they'd spent on housing prior to losing it? Roughly half.

Surveys of the unhoused have limited value for understanding unhoused communities. There's a lot of subjectivity at play when asking questions of folks who are likely to be traumatized, intoxicated, and unwell, physically and mentally speaking. And there's a lot of bias at play in the ways those surveys, invariably designed and conducted by housed people, are carried out. They are deeply suspect even as a one-dimensional census of warm bodies. We know the population numbers are a vast undercount—unhoused people can be hard to find, especially if you only spend a single night each year looking for them. Experts believe the actual number is around two or three million, or about four to six times higher than the annual HUD counts. Also, HUD doesn't consider people living with friends and family due to hardship, like my mom and grandmother were, to be homeless. The Department of Education does, however, and they've found that there are several million children and parents experiencing this form of hidden homelessness on an annual basis. With this more expansive view, a realistic estimate for the country's unhoused population is in the neighborhood of six million, or nearly one in fifty Americans.

The story of who is homeless and why is much more interesting, much more meaningful, than any figures that can be plucked by parachuting into someone's life for a few minutes. The people I meet in camps are a rainbow. Some come from generations of poverty. Others have wealthy parents. Some are so possessed by drugs, demons, or faulty brain chemistry that you can't have a coherent conversation with them. Others come across like a churchgoing grandma, all done up in curls and pearls. Stepping into a camp is like stepping into an alternate dimension—the rules and norms that govern that world are not the same as those that govern the housed world. There's a distinct subculture in camps that extends to language, dress, and codes of conduct, which I slowly came to understand. And there are subcultures within the subculture—Black, Latino, hippie, punk; lifestyles based around particular drugs or illegal activities; and so on.

One thing they have in common, however, is their shared reality on the other side of the poverty veil. The unhoused I've come to know are unified by a pervasive sense that they do not belong, that there is nowhere they can freely exist, and that they are in fact hated by housed communities. They are, in many respects, a persecuted minority—not having a home is aggressively criminalized in this country. Yet even in this era of extreme debate about what it means to be a persecuted minority—for people of color, of certain ancestries, of various gender identities and sexual orientations—the unhoused are scarcely mentioned.

There are some serious homeless haters out there, such as the San Francisco shop owner who sprayed a woman sleeping in front of his store with a garden hose. A former San Francisco fire commissioner was accused of assaulting people who were asleep on the street with bear spray, on multiple occasions. He'd pressed criminal charges against a homeless man he said had attacked him out of the blue, but during the trial it became clear that the guy had simply fought back after being sprayed. Another homeless man in San Francisco died when someone set his sleeping bag on fire with him in it. In Southern California, a man who had worked as a "gang interventionist," according to the *Los Angeles Times*, shot and killed three homeless men in a four-day period.

The internet seethes with homeless hate. For a while I collected anti-homeless content posted by tech bros. Justin Keller, founder of Commando.io, said that wealthy people had earned the "right" to not have to see homeless people in their city. "I shouldn't have to worry about being accosted," he wrote. "I shouldn't have to see the pain, struggle, and despair of homeless people to and from my way to work every day." Greg Gopman, founder of AngelHack, referred to homeless folks as "hyenas" that "spit, urinate, taunt you. . . . If they added the smallest iota of value I'd consider thinking different, but the crazy toothless lady who kicks everyone that gets too close to her cardboard box hasn't made anyone's life better in a while."

Of course most folks don't go out of their way to ridicule or assault homeless people. Most of us simply avoid unhoused people like the plague, which in this case is more than a simple idiom—consciously or not, we see them as different and dangerous, a group we should not engage with, even if they lay dying on the curb in front of us, screaming for our help. I remember once in San Francisco passing a figure crying their lungs out under a blanket on the sidewalk. It reminded me of how I cried under the blankets after my divorce, except I was at home in bed. I wanted to stop and talk to the person. I didn't know how, so I shuffled along with all the other guilty passersby.

"I call that the violence of looking away," Tiny, the cofounder of Oakland's Homefulness community, told me. The poverty veil is an illusion that that enables us—encourages us—to look away as we walk past a person who we have the means to help. In most cities these days, especially on the enlightened West Coast, we do exactly that as part of our daily routine. In the perverse innocence of our bliss, we are the villains.

The hate compounds another noxious element common to the air that the unhoused breathe: trauma, and a long history of the dysfunctional relationships that generate it, and are spawned by it. Almost universally, there is trauma wrapped up in the *why* of homelessness, which is then compounded by the trauma of experiencing homelessness. I found myself observing a notable contradiction: There is no greater empathy than that elicited by a child who has been raped, beaten, or otherwise abused—but when the same child is grown, evicted, addicted, and wandering around talking to themselves in public, with God-knows-what living in their eight-year beard? We don't hesitate to let them rot on the sidewalk, sweeping them as expediently as possible toward their grave, where they'll finally be out of sight. This is homelessness.

KENT

Among the unhoused communities I've visited, Wolfe Camp was on the clean-cut end of the spectrum. Substance abuse, mental health maladies, and all the other "risk factors" were present in the camp, but on the whole, the group was relatively clean, cool, and collected—if you were to pass them in a grocery store aisle, your first thought would probably not be, *Yikes, homeless person!* Most folks even have their teeth, with the exception of Kent, who comes off less as a bum than a badass who probably has some crazy story about how his teeth got knocked out.

But he and his campmates get plenty of hate anyways. After the tents went up on Wolfe Road, the Cupertino chat rooms on Nextdoor.com lit up with complaints. Someone spray-painted "leave" on the armchair of a camper's outdoor den. Objects were hurled like grenades from passing cars—one camper barely dodged a container of yogurt—along with rants and obscenities. Kent even gets the cold shoulder at the church across from the Spaceship where he was baptized. "Sometimes I go sit there and the priest will pop out, like, *Who are you? What are you doing here?* And I'm like, *Who are you?* It's kind of weird to be an outcast in the place where you've lived your whole life."

Part of what first drew me to Kent is that he was so damned elusive—he seemed to have better things to do than talk to a journalist. Though I saw him constantly, he tended to keep conversation brief. When I went to Safeway for groceries, there he was, cruising right past me on his bike as I walked across the parking lot, not recognizing me, or maybe just pretending he didn't. One day I crossed paths with him on the 280 overpass, but he excused himself after a few minutes of small talk. I stopped by his tent nearly every day, but usually it was full of people hanging out without him—it was the social hub of the camp, though more often than not he was off on his bike somewhere. One time I called his name from outside the tent, and, after several minutes, a petite middle-aged woman in reading glasses emerged. "Kent is not available right now," she informed me in a polite, but firm, tone. "He's busy with some important matters."

Sometimes I found him in a top hat. Usually he wore his sailor's cap, however. He is definitely the captain of his destiny. Finally, I managed to corner him outside his tent. His sound system was pumping—Kent provided the soundtrack for the camp—as was the generator that powered it. Despite this and the traffic noise, he spoke in a library voice. I could barely hear him, much less record an interview. Kent is the undisputed leader of Wolfe Camp, where he possesses something of a guru vibe. The first time I visited, a guy I chatted up was like, "You've *got* to meet Kent." It took persistence, but I eventually learned how his sparkle came to be.

Let's start with the numbers: Kent has broken relationships in abundance, between his dad, three ex-wives, nine children, and nine brothers, none of which are typos. His mom died young, leaving Kent in a hypermasculine household in which he was the youngest. His dad never remarried, passed out drunk each night, and focused family life on the athletic pursuits of Kent's older brothers. "The routine was violence at night and love in the morning," says Kent, who grew up feeling like he had to prove his worth to the ten other men in the house.

That insecurity led him to a path of increasingly dysfunctional behaviors. They started innocently enough—picking the pocket of his own father, an architect who had a habit of keeping large sums of money in the house. "When I was a kid I started pinching $10 from him when he was passed out drunk," said Kent. "$10 turned into $100; $100 turned into $1,000. I did it for years. He knew about it and accepted it. It was a game that we played." When Kent was twelve, a year after his mom died, he started smoking cigarettes in the house. "Nobody said anything," said Kent, who then quickly progressed to smoking weed, dropping acid, and losing his mind on PCP, which he says was available in his seventh-grade class. "PCP is the hardest drug I've ever done," he told me. "It's like getting hit in the back of the head with a baseball bat—you wake up somewhere else, not knowing how the hell you got there."

Along with drugs came love—both progressed at an absurd rate. Kent and his girlfriend had their first child when he was thirteen. By the time he graduated high school, they had five kids, two of them twins. The relationship fell apart, as did all of Kent's romantic relationships over the following decades. "I think that's why I ended up on the streets," he says. "A little boy shouldn't be having sex and getting involved with someone at that level, because it's hard when they leave you. I've never handled heartbreak well." Alongside all that child-bearing and drug-abusing, Kent spent his teenage years running from the law for petty theft and other misdemeanors, a lifestyle set to a Black Sabbath soundtrack. "I was a punk," says Kent. "The sheriffs in Cupertino have been chasing me on my bike since I was a kid. It's always been us against them: the sheriffs, the companies, society as a whole."

Kent and his buddies spent a lot of time riding their bikes and goofing off along Calabazas Creek. Next to it were the remnant fields of an old orchard—during his childhood, the Valley evolved from a place known for fruit production to one known for the production of silicon chips—which Hewlett-Packard eventually bought for their headquarters, later selling the land to Apple for the Spaceship. Kent says that before those fields became office parks, local dudes raced dirt bikes back there. He was mesmerized and soon joined them, thus launching Kent's first career: motocross, a subgenre of motorcycle racing that involves doing tricks on the bike while speeding up and down hills of dirt. Kent was a fearless rider and had raw talent—suddenly he'd won the love of his father, who became his de facto manager and financier. They traveled all over the West to pro competitions, which Kent often won.

Kent was thriving for a time, living it up on the road with his pops, boozing, womanizing, getting cranked out of his mind on meth. Then he crushed his elbow at a race in Anaheim. His arm nearly required amputation, but a skilled surgeon saved it, installing hardware to replace the crushed parts. "Now my elbow is half fake and half real," he said, flexing it to show me. "I still have a bump where there was a five-eighths-inch bolt that they'd use to tighten it up when it got loose."

It took a decade to recover full use of the arm, a period in which Kent attempted domestic life. He had four other kids from a pair of marriages and worked as a manager of a lumberyard in San José to support his family. He enrolled in rehab and went to night school for a credential that would allow him to counsel drug users who were coming out of prison. For a while he worked seven days a week at the lumberyard, plus several nights as a counselor. The money was great, but the stress was not. "I got assigned to counsel people coming out of prison who were out of my league in terms of hardness. I'd only been in trouble with the law for small stuff. I knew nothing about people who kill other people. It was too much for me. Everybody who knows me knows I'm vulnerable to other people's problems—if they're crying and bitching and moaning, next thing you know I'm doing the same thing. I couldn't handle it." Kent went back to drugs and made a comeback on the motocross circuit, which quickly ended with another injury. "Everything kind of went to hell after that," he said.

One day Kent was driving his Monte Carlo on Foothill Expressway in Los Altos, a suburb a few miles from Cupertino, when the car started to overheat. He pulled over in a library parking lot next to a Mercedes, steam fuming from the hood. Noticing that a window of the Mercedes had been left half open, he peeked inside and saw a purse on the seat with hundred-dollar bills sticking out of it. On the floor was a paper grocery bag; it was heavy with gold jewelry, and the handles tore when he tried to lift it. Later, when he went to court for the crime, he learned that it was Hindu ceremonial jewelry that the owner of the Mercedes, an Indian woman, had inherited from her grandmother. He took it to a pawn shop on Saratoga Avenue on a Saturday night and spent hours haggling with the owner over its value. He finally left in the wee hours of Sunday morning with $62,000 in cash. "I've been paying for that $62,000 ever since," said Kent.

He spent two years at the penitentiary in San Quentin, north of San Francisco. "I lost a lot when I was in prison," he said. "Everyone cut me off—my wife, my kids, my brothers." One day he received an envelope through the prison mail system. Inside was a sticky note from a friend with six words on it: "Hey bro, sorry about your dad." He knew what it meant. "When I got out I went straight to my dad's house," Kent told me. "I went in the door and these Chinese people started yelling at me." His father had died, and his brothers had sold the house.

Kent's self-destruction deepened after his dad died. He kicked in the door of one of his brothers. He screamed and writhed and threw things during a divorce proceeding. "I was in pain, but it came out as anger," he said. "All of a sudden I had multiple restraining orders on me. I lost my house. I had nowhere to go." Kent said he'd paid for the house—"I got it for seventy grand and next thing I knew it was worth six-hundred-some thousand dollars"—but due to his legal issues the deed was in the name of his oldest son and youngest brother.

They initiated eviction proceedings against him, and the sheriff came and threw him out. Kent became homeless two days before Christmas. "It was forty-two degrees out and raining," he told me. "I ended up locked out of my house in a pair of shorts, a tank top, and no shoes on."

At some point—he can't remember exactly when in the sequence of his unraveling—Kent woke up from a coma. Swine flu, according to his doctors. No one came to the hospital to visit. The nail in the spiritual coffin was losing contact with his youngest daughter, still a toddler when he lost his home. "She used to follow me around like a baby duck," he told me. "Losing your family is a wound that never heals. It's a nightmare and it's happened to me three times."

Kent fits squarely into one of the dominant narratives about why people become homeless: He made bad choices. But he still has a right to exist, to redeem the choices of his past. Ruptures in relationships are a theme in every story of homelessness I've heard. It's an obvious thing, but it points to an overlooked facet of The Fix that's too intimate for the coarse hands of the homeless services bureaucracy to touch: healing those ruptures.

Kent spent his first year on the street imagining he would soon be one of those unhoused people you read about in a tiny blurb in the local paper: unidentified man found dead in the gutter. He found a shovel and dug a pit on a slope above 280. It resembled a grave, but it became a home. Working only at night, he expanded the pit into a cave ten feet deep and wide enough to spread out his belongings. He built a roof with logs, over which he unfurled a tarp; he spread a layer of soil on top and transplanted ragged clumps of grass and shrubs from the roadside brush as camouflage. He lived there for about five years, licking his wounds, waiting to be reborn. As a lonely felon rejected by his family, he'd felt homeless in the most profound sense. But as the leader of a community fighting for its survival, he felt a profound sense of purpose.

MONTE

Kent checks the boxes for bad choices and addiction, but he doesn't "hear voices and stuff like that," as he often pointed out to me. Monte, however, checks that other box on the list of what we imagine to be wrong with homeless folks: poor mental health.

After losing his father, a grandmother, and a brother in short succession—the latter a wheelchair-bound man who died at the hands of the Oakland police—Monte quit his job at a property management company, moved out of his apartment, and found his way to the camps of the Lower Bottoms. Plenty of people were camped along the labyrinth of train tracks and highway overpasses that parallel Wood Street, but this was long before the community became known as Wood Street Commons. At first he slept in a crevice between two giant slabs of concrete that form part of an overpass at the back of the camp, the traffic whizzing by day and night overhead, with giant trucks violently thrumming the walls of his cave as they made their way to the nearby port district.

"I came here to kill myself," Monte told me during one of our first conversations. He meant it literally. He jumped in front of a truck, but it hit the brakes just in time. He tried to jump off a nearby overpass, but he had a particular vision for how he wanted to do it and was unable to figure out the logistics for making it happen. Another time he jumped into the Bay from the crumbling Berkeley Pier, a century-old ferry landing that extends 2 miles into the Bay, an iconic landmark pointing toward the Golden Gate Bridge, which on clear days is visible in the distance beyond. Only the half mile closest to shore was still open to the public the night that Monte ventured along its length; ghostly, barnacled pilings were all that remained of the rest. There was a barrier at the end of the intact part, and Monte ran full speed toward it, launching his body over the rails and into the water. But he didn't anticipate how shallow the Bay is there at low tide—the reason the ferry landing had been built so far offshore. He ended up stuck in the mud beneath a few feet of water, still alive.

"A lot of things intervened every time I tried to kill myself," he told me, as we sat one rainy January night by the fireplace inside his shack. The ultimate intervention was the brotherhood he eventually found on Wood Street. After Monte came down from the crevice in the overpass, he began sleeping in a pine tree, a lone sentinel of green in the camp, his body draped gracefully in the fold of the branches. Then he built a shack next to the tree and got to know his neighbors on Wood Street. They cooked together, swapped stories around the fire, and laid plans to improve their plight. But most importantly, there was an unspoken rule of welcoming, or at least tolerating, anyone and everyone, no matter what they were going through, no matter what dysfunctional behaviors they were engaged in. "I found friends and family that gave me a sense of cama-raderie, a sense of purpose—my community saved my life," he said. "Nobody judges you there—that alone is enough to make a person think about bettering themselves. It's infectious." Like Kent, Monte was reborn.

Monte is short for LaMonte, and he pronounces the *e* in his name à la the French—LaMon*tay*. He has Cajun roots but grew up mostly in Oakland and Sacramento, pursuing a degree in psychology and entering the Air Force, like his dad. One version of his origin story paints Monte, a thin, muscular, middle-aged guy, as the progeny of a conservative working-class Black family—straight-as-an-arrow, a bit stuck-up, and intolerant of wastrels on the street. Other parts of his story, such as his parents' crack habit, help to explain how he ended up on Wood Street. In Oakland, as in cities throughout the country, the crack epidemic coin-cided with a period in which unionized manufacturing jobs moved overseas and inner-city neighborhoods underwent massive gentrification, forces that sparked an increase in drugs, crime, and housing insecurity within those communities. At the height of his family's struggles, his parents split up, and his mom moved herself and the kids temporarily into a homeless shelter. He later watched as multiple relatives and family friends descended to life on the streets.

In many respects, Monte's social skills are better than mine, and he cleans up well—I've seen him strut through a room in a three-piece suit, turning the heads of affluent women as he passed. But he is not well. His depression was relatively mild when I met him, though he says that during the suicidal period that coincided with becoming homeless he ended up in a local psychiatric ward more than twenty times. Monte does not walk around talking to people who aren't there, but he does hear voices. "It's not like I hear voices telling me to kill people or anything like that," he says. It's more like unintelligible grumbling, he explained, demonstrating something that sounded like gremlins arguing with each other.

Monte's attention span is about a millimeter in length, and he suffers from a state of disorganization and forgetfulness so severe that it makes basic life func-tions difficult. He jumps restlessly from one unfinished task to another, leaving chaos in his wake, his tools and electronics abandoned in the rain, important papers blowing away in the wind. He describes himself as claustrophobic, which shows up not just as having a fear of confined spaces, but in the form of a severe allergy to the confines of expectations—the more one suggests that he might consider doing this or that to improve his situation, the more apt he is to stand up and walk away. He is almost constitutionally incapable of keeping an appointment. I've attended a number of social events with him, for which he was always late, and from which he usually disappeared, without notice, before it was over.

He constantly breaks or loses his phone, and his shack was so jammed with stuff that there wasn't much room to stand, let alone sit. He bought a car at one point, which quickly became broken in umpteen ways. There was a stretch in which, inexplicably, he was getting a flat tire on nearly a daily basis. He repeatedly lost the key fob, which cost several hundred dollars to replace each time. Monte does not have a license or insurance, so each time he drives, he risks going to jail. You might think this would make him a cautious driver—Monte is the opposite of a cautious driver. He peels loudly out of intersections and weaves through traffic on the highway at absurd speeds. Once when stopped at a red light next to a cop, he suddenly sped through the intersection. The cop pulled him over but, amazingly, let him go.

It was hard to get a straight answer out of Monte about why he decided to run a light knowing a cop was watching. But I sensed a self-destructive vibe in his dysfunctional behaviors, as though something in his brain causes him to act in ways contrary to his best interests and well-being. Sometimes the result is risky behavior; other times it comes out as rage. "When I'm hurt, I get angry," he told me. I could tell there was more to the story. "I have a secret to tell you at some point," he said. He never told me the details but alluded to highly traumatic experiences that were difficult to talk about.

On one visit to Wood Street, I sat by a campfire with John, Monte's neighbor, as we watched from a distance while Monte screamed at someone. It appeared to be a disagreement related to car repairs. At one point I saw Monte's silhouette in the headlights, his arm raised with a hammer in his hands that was aimed in the direction of the guy he was yelling at. He argued frequently with people in the camp, including John, his closest friend, and sometimes the spats came to blows. On another occasion, upon hearing that a friend was being harassed by a security guard down the street, he stormed into his shack and emerged with a rifle. Fortunately, his campmates disarmed him before he got down the street with it. I've learned to see the anger coming. His face changes, and I can feel his brain chemistry beginning to overheat.

Meth appears to be part of the cycle. Monte has been trying to quit as long as I've known him. He says he never touched drugs before becoming homeless, a choice motivated by growing up in a family of users. Becoming homeless coincided with not only suicidal intentions, however, but copious drug use. He was methed out of his mind for years, but when I met him he said he'd managed to reduce his $200-per-week habit to $50 per week—a maintenance approach to drug use that he was forever setting deadlines to end. Sometimes he would simply smash his meth pipe in anger at the addiction, thinking that he would stop if he didn't have the necessary tool. Problem is, it's not hard to obtain a new meth pipe.

One time he invited me into a tent with a couple of his friends, Johnathan and Tamara, because they were in the midst of a conversation about drug use that he wanted me to hear. Tamara, who I once saw huffing Endust through the tiny red straw that comes with the canister, produced a small packet of fentanyl from her bra and explained that she used it to "numb myself." Meth, however, is "for socializing," she said, passing the pipe. Monte hit it and said this was the last time he would be getting high. He held the pipe in his hand and said, solemnly, "This represents my unemployment. This represents medical issues. This represents failed relationships." He went quiet for a moment and then said, angrily, "This represents men trying to fuck me."

"Me too," said Tamara.

Monte then smashed the glass pipe on a metal canister of butane he had in the tent, the sort used for refillable torch-style lighters, which are a popular accessory among drug users. The pipe didn't break, but somehow the butane canister did, making a loud pop and filling the tent with a white gaseous fog. Everyone screamed. Then they collapsed in a fit of giggles. It was not the last of Monte's meth use.

Monte's difficulties do not begin to define him. They are mere aspects of who he is, and much of the time he manages them with grace—perhaps not in the way a housed person would define as successful or functional, but in a way that works for him. The key to his sanity, as for most folks, is to maintain a low-stress lifestyle. If he can wake up when he wants and do what he wants each day, while also having essential survival needs met, he's more or less OK. Living in a shack on Wood Street, as horrible as it seems from the outside, provided this for him much of the time.

When he is in a stable mental space, his other sides come out to play. Monte is a renaissance man. He plays golf in the park across the street at midnight and composes abstract paintings that enchant my eyes. He can fix anything (if he doesn't get distracted), performs headstands of impressive duration, and is the life of the party. He writes haunting blues ballads, improvises classical sounds on the piano, and absolutely owns the dance floor. One of our many adventures together was to crash the Oakland mayor's inaugural ball, where he boogied with his city council representative. In his suit, new shoes, and leather handbag, he looked more than simply "cleaned up." The accoutrements enabled a sort of celebrity aura to ooze from Monte—supreme confidence, preternatural cool-ness, and a feeling that he was tapped into something that everyone else in the room was not, even the mayor.

I was at the event with a documentary film crew, and at one point a member of the mayor's security detail, noticing the cameras trailing Monte, asked me whether I was making a film about him or about the mayor. I could see him trying to figure out *who* this VIP was.

"It's about him," I said.

My feeling is that Monte's magnetism, his unique juju, flows from the depth of his self-knowledge. He looks you squarely in the eye when he talks to you. He is sincere without being pretentious. When Monte's mind is at ease, deep presence and tenderness are his default state. It's comforting to be around him, at least at the times that it's not disturbing to be around him, which in my experience is only a minority of the time. I found Monte's charisma, intellect, and spiritual sensibility—traits not typically noted in government-sponsored surveys of unhoused people—to be far greater than his dysfunction.

As I got to know more folks on the street, I observed another trend never noted in the media or in government reports: Being homeless brings out not only the worst in people but also the best. Becoming homeless is very much the product of being dealt a bad hand in life, and then playing it badly. But while one is homeless, there's an opportunity to reconfigure the pain into something else. Monte feels very strongly about this. "The people out here are damaged—like *really* damaged," he said, pausing and staring at me intensely after he said the words, as if to make sure I understood the degree of that damage. "No one that comes here comes here for no reason," he continued. "And once they get here, that reason tends to change."

Monte says that people on the street often find what he calls "their spark," an inner light more valuable than anything else. Monte says that one reason why he and so many others are reticent to return to the housed world is they fear losing what they've gained—community, purpose, and, perhaps, something deeper. "Why would anyone out here who's found their spark want to give it up for something that's less than that spark?" he asked. His conviction would soon be put to the test in front of a line of police and bulldozers.

RUDY

It can be hard to track exactly how and why a certain individual becomes homeless. At some point in the story there's always a transition from a relatively stable roof over one's head to a not-so-stable one. It might be an abrupt eviction, or a gradual process—deciding to couch surf for a while to save money, moving into an RV parked in a friend's driveway, bunking at your parent's house. At some point, the roof may be as thin as a tent or tarp. Along the spectrum from relatively stable to completely unstable is a series of circumstances and events that precipitate the descent. I like to think of these as red marbles—placed on the scales of life, they tip one toward the abyss, while green ones counteract those forces and move one back toward security. Some marbles we're born with; others we acquire throughout our lives.

What I've seen is that it takes many red marbles to tip one's scale into tent life. Macroeconomic forces, such as astronomical rent, can make for a fat red marble, but that marble alone rarely seems to do it—it just means a higher portion of people carrying lots of other red marbles will spill them onto the street when a rent hike hits. There's virtually always some combination of childhood trauma, adult trauma, addictions, mental illness, poor physical health, bad choices, bad luck, and dysfunctional relationships that primes the scale in the wrong direction.

There's another fat red marble that I've found is highly prevalent among the unhoused: a predisposition to rebel, to question authority, to live from the soul rather than the status quo. It's another trend that the media and policy-makers don't mention. There may not be data to support it, but rebelliousness is practically baked into the reality of being unhoused—when you feel like you don't belong, that the world around you is not designed to support you, it's hard not to develop antiestablishment tendencies. I think it has a lot to do with who becomes homeless and perhaps why some seemingly choose to stay that way—they don't want to go back to the world that spit them out. People lose trust in the system, if they had it in the first place. Anarchist tendencies sprout from the cracks in their lives.

In San José, I met Rudy, a Latino man in his mid-forties who carries a particularly large, juicy red marble of subversiveness. Rudy lived at the Crash Zone, which was located in a series of dusty fields near the end of the San José airport runway. At the time, it was one of the largest camps in the state, and the city was under tremendous pressure to clear it. I met him on a hellishly hot summer day, just as the sweeps had begun. The day before, the police had come to evict a friend of his, and as Rudy walked toward her tent, he saw an officer pull down a wall of the makeshift structure. His friend was in bed, naked beneath the sheets. Rudy filmed parts of the encounter that followed, which he proceeded to show me on his phone.

"Hey lady, you need to wake up," said the officer. "Get up and go."

"No, she doesn't," said Rudy to the officer.

"The mayor sent us here to do this, so you can complain to the mayor if you want," said the officer to Rudy.

"The mayor can't authorize this," Rudy replied, snarkily. "It has to be the city attorney, bro."

"You tell him that," said the officer.

Rudy is well versed in his legal rights. He enjoys reading municipal codes and legal briefs, which he files away as ammunition to deploy in situations such as this. One bit of legal trivia rises above the rest: the case of *Martin v. Boise*.

The case may not be a household name, but among the unhoused it has the cachet of *Roe v. Wade*. It has become lore, a defining and shining emblem of camp culture, its text a bible-slash-manifesto. *Martin v. Boise* changed the game for people living on public land because it enshrined their right to be there. In evicting Robert Martin from his camp in Boise, Idaho, a federal judge found that the city had violated his constitutional rights, specifically the Eighth Amendment: It was cruel and unusual punishment. After an unsuccessful, decade-long appeal process, *Martin v. Boise* entered the canon of case law in 2019, when the Supreme Court declined to hear a final appeal.

"As long as there is no option of sleeping indoors, the government cannot criminalize indigent, homeless people for sleeping outdoors, on public property, on the false premise they had a choice in the matter," the ruling decreed.

The key legal principle asserted in *Martin v. Boise* is that if a city is unable to provide shelter to an unsheltered person, they have the right to remain put. Kent carried a paper copy of the ruling in his pocket in case he needed to bust it out. Rudy had it ready on his phone, and as the altercation escalated at his friend's camp, he suggested that the officers might want to take a look.

"There's a federal court ruling!" he shouted. "Don't you go by the ruling?" He continued to press the case. "Hey! You never provided shelter! Look at your law books," he said, to no effect. "I'll go get the book and read it to you. Because you're acting really amateur."

Rudy instead went to get a cigarette for his naked friend. He didn't record what happened next, but as we stood limply in the sun, he narrated the rest of the story, sans video.

"It gets crazier from this point," he said.

While Rudy was searching for a cigarette, more officers arrived on the scene. They told him he had to leave or he would be arrested. "Whatever," he replied. "I'm just helping my friend out because she's scared right now," said Rudy to the officers. "Next thing you know, the officer grabs me and twists my arm all the way behind my back," Rudy told me. "I heard a pop." Rudy showed me his hand, which was bandaged at the wrist, apparently sprained. His friend's shelter was constructed in part with wooden pallets, and Rudy explained how the officer "slammed me up against them, and then pulled me back and hit me against a vehicle that was right behind me. Then he walked me, like forcefully, about one hundred feet, and I kept tripping. Then he pushed me and said, *Stay there.*"

Rudy's wrist throbbed; he felt lightheaded, and like he couldn't breathe. I could see he was reliving the experience as he told me the story. "Having to go through that—it's trauma, physically and psychologically," he said. "It messes you up."

He sat there in the dirt, reeling, and decided to call 911. The officers laughed at him, he said, and insinuated that he was faking an injury. Rudy said the cops prevented the ambulance from leaving for an hour and a half, questioning him about this and that, such as the nature of his tattoos, which they lifted his shirt to see. "Then he starts taking my jewelry off. When he tried to take my ring off, he contorted my hands, and I started screaming. Then I shit in my pants. Excuse my language—I defecated. Because it was real painful and I had to use the restroom. I was practically in tears. Before he closed the door, he said I was going to be arrested when I got to the hospital."

A plane roared above us, pausing the conversation. Rudy looked increasingly ashen as he continued, reciting the events in a rambling stream of consciousness. "They get me to the hospital, and I'm being a little bit belligerent and I say I'm not getting out of the stretcher. I'm just, I'm going numb. They told me that the force they're going to use is gonna hurt me really bad." Rudy said he was eventually extricated from the stretcher, treated, and transferred to police custody. "I told the nurse and the doctor, please don't give my medical information out. They stretchered me all the way to the police car, and I get into the police car and they hand the paperwork to the police officer—my medical paperwork! It has personal things on it. I'm dying. You know what I mean? I have something that's wrong with me. I'm not *dying* dying right now, but it's eventually gonna happen with what I have. So I didn't want nobody to see that." This is how I learned that Rudy has AIDS. Studies have found that HIV rates among unhoused populations range from two to sixteen times higher than the general population.

Rudy continued the story. "That's a HIPAA violation, you know what I mean? That's a violation. I just, I just..." He trailed off. "I'm sorry, I just..." Eventually he composed himself and continued. "I stay for about fifteen hours in the police station. I fell asleep in there and then I woke up. It was nighttime by then. It was cold. I had to walk back. That's everything."

Rudy's roots at the Crash Zone run deep. The dusty fields of the camp once had houses on them, including one where he was born in 1976. Around this time, the neighborhood was deemed unsafe for habitation by virtue of its proximity to the runway, despite the fact that the airport had been there for decades when the place was built. By the early eighties, 630 homes had been bulldozed from the site through eminent domain. It's the sort of thing that never seems to happen in wealthier neighborhoods.

"I remember my aunt putting me in the bathtub when I was about two years old and hearing gunshots," Rudy told me. "It was a high-crime area. I think that's the reason why they got rid of it."

Rudy grew up hearing that his parents did not get properly compensated by the government for the loss of their home. But for the most part he did not grow up with his parents. Rudy never said much about his biological family, but after they were forced out he ended up in a series of foster homes, which is another marble common to homelessness—studies have found that up to half of the unhoused population has spent time in foster care. Many foster kids exit state-mandated care at the age of eighteen and quickly find themselves homeless, but Rudy held down jobs, and his rent, for two decades.

In his late thirties, Rudy was working as a property manager at an apartment complex occupied mainly by low-income immigrant families, not unlike the one he was born into. He describes the owners as "slumlords" who were skilled in the art of raising the rent—rent control laws allow for modest annual increases based on inflation, but if you can induce someone to move out, you can set the rent for the next tenant at whatever rate the market will bear. Such tactics include stonewalling on maintenance and repairs, bullshitting tenants about renovations that require the unit to be vacated, and concocting a story about a desperate family member who they need to give the apartment to. Rudy was informing the tenants about their rights and coaching them to resist. He was fired, and because he had an apartment at the complex as part of the job, he also lost his home.

Like Kent, Rudy was drawn back to the geography of his childhood when he became homeless. When Rudy arrived after being evicted, about six years before I met him, the camp was small and dispersed. But during the pandemic it mushroomed into one of California's largest unhoused communities, with three-hundred-plus residents spread over the forty acres of fields. Rudy says they used to call it Harmony Fields, but after the masses arrived, the camp became known as the Crash Zone.

Rudy told me about other Crash Zone residents who had returned to the site where their childhood homes had been demolished, including Riverman Dave and Mama Shark, a respected elder in the community. Mama Shark was a rock for Rudy, who I could tell saw it as an obligation to introduce me to her, as a newcomer in the camp—part of the tribal etiquette. "She's one of the first people I met when I came out here and didn't have anywhere to go," said Rudy. "She had open arms."

As we walked over to her spot, Rudy explained that he and Mama Shark were among a core of Crash Zone residents who formed an informal "council" that attempted to maintain order and ensure that folks are cared for. "It's like a family here," said Mama Shark. "We've learned from each other. We've fought each other." Rudy chuckled. "And even after that, we're a family. We just are."

Mama Shark pointed to a spot about two hundred feet away from her camp where her parents' home once stood. "Second house from the corner on Emory Street," she said, in a raspy, slightly garbled voice. The asphalt had long ago been removed, but rows of distressed-looking trees still marked the old grid pattern of the streets. Rudy was too young when he lived there to have many memories, but Mama Shark pointed to where there used to be a laundromat, a beauty salon, and an elementary school. She remembers playing carefree in the river at the edge of the neighborhood, but says that now "there's spirits and stuff out there. It's real dark out there." She was not referring to the lack of nighttime lighting.

Rudy concurred. "There's a lot of supernatural things that happen out here," he said.

"Like what?" I asked.

"Uh ... just ... just ... sounds ... and ... imprintations on things ... and stuff like that," he said. "I'm not crazy. I know it's not part of my imagination."

Mama Shark told me that one of her sons was "brutally murdered" in the camp and her other son "was suffocated." She said she has colon cancer and that her husband has diabetes. "He has holes on the bottom of his feet," she told me. "You can put your thumb in it and touch his bone." At some point when she was still young, Mama Shark "cracked up," she said. "I've got multiples," she explained, as in personalities. "I've lived with them for over forty years." She paused and considered her statement. "They live with me, actually," she concluded.

Rudy's spot was beneath an elderberry tree in the location of his old front yard, what was once Walnut Street. He's not in touch with his parents, but his aunt showed him where they once lived. "Same exact place," he said. "That's why I chose it."

As the pressure grew to shut down the Crash Zone, Rudy became a spokesperson for the community, liaising with the city, social service agencies, and the media to let them know that they weren't going down without a fight. He wasn't going to give up his home yet again. "They're going to have to drag me out of here," he told me. He, too, had found his spark—like Monte's, it would soon be tested by a posse of men armed with guns and bulldozers.

TINY

One morning a couple days after I met Rudy, a busted-ass minivan—its driver calls it her "hooptie"—pulled onto Crash Zone dust, sending up a small plume. A petite woman emerged, her blond pigtails poking out from the red-and-black bandanna that covered her face. She wore bug-eye shades, a camo jacket, and a baseball cap printed with two letters: *Po.*

Po, of course, is short for *poor.* But the colloquial version enables the woman beneath the hat to construct wordplays, such as *po'lice*—lice of the po—which is her name-slash-metaphor for the gold-badged forces ostensibly in charge of keeping our streets safe, but which are a massive annoyance to street folks on a good day, a life-threatening presence on a bad one. The woman beneath the hat is fond of wordplay—*crap*italism, gentri*fuck*ation, *devil*opers. She grew up more houseless than not, and then, after being housed for a few years, she and her young son ended up on the street again after a $700 rent increase. When I met her, in her late forties, her housing situation had stabilized, and she dedicated nearly every waking hour to helping her comrades on the street achieve the same.

Her name is Tiny. She is the preposterously humorous mind behind *POOR Magazine*, which I'd discovered after arriving in California. In some ways, the publication reminds me of *The New Yorker*—sharply intellectual, provocatively nuanced, and adept in the arts of comic satire. In most every other way, it is the antithesis of the highbrow *New Yorker*. *POOR* is a modern incarnation of the street-based publications of the hobo era, which in the Bay Area also include *Street Sheet* and *Street Spirit*. In the quarter century since Tiny and her now-deceased mom, Dee, founded *POOR Magazine*, it has evolved into a media empire—blog, radio shows, podcasts, theater, film, and a literary imprint—though that empire, to be fair, nests within the minuscule genre of poverty-centric content.

That morning in the Crash Zone, Tiny was all business; she had a schedule to keep—lots of unhoused people's stories to tell, starting with those facing eviction at the Crash Zone. She marched over to Rudy's elderberry tree, where a flock of boisterous birds greeted her from the branches, chirping and shitting. She called Rudy's name, and as he emerged groggily from his tent, Tiny flipped on her Instagram video feed. Slightly perplexed, he submitted to the interview.

"You're listening to Poor People's Radio," said Tiny, who has the calm, practiced delivery of a professional DJ (she has an actual radio show called *Poor People's Radio*, but refers to her live social media broadcasts with the same name). "We out in the occupied Muwekma Ohlone territory known as San José, where they are sweeping people like they are trash," Tiny continued. "Tell us what's going on," she said to Rudy, who proceeded to describe his recent arrest, how he was in fact born in the Crash Zone, and how he had nowhere else to go. "This is the only open land that we have here," he said. "I'm losing my home."

"That's real," said Tiny. "I'm so sorry, hon."

Rudy explained to listeners that San José was building tiny homes for people displaced from camps, but so far there were just a smattering ready for occupancy, despite the city initiating a sweep of hundreds at the Crash Zone. Not

that he would move to a tiny-home site—he calls them "concentration camps"—
if it was offered to him. "The rules are too strict, the fences are too high," he
said. "We don't want to go to those. We're human beings."

Tiny pounced on the thought and pivoted it toward the vision that
courses through her veins: self-determination for the unhoused. She posed a
question that reporters on the homeless beat never ask: "If the city of San José
gave you land, what would your dream be?"

Rudy said he'd do what the core family of residents had been planning
before the hordes descended on Harmony Fields—growing crops and selling
the produce. They'd use the proceeds to construct modest hand-built homes
for themselves. "It would be co-op-type living," said Rudy.

"That's called sovereignty!" said Tiny, as she prepared to sign off. "Shout-out to
Rudy for being a warrior. *Ometeotl!*" Tiny uses the word *Ometeotl*—pronounced
ohhhmatayo, with a slight grunt on the *ohhh*—as a sort of rallying cry on the
caboose of many a sentence. It took me a long time to figure out what *ohhhmatayo* meant. Tiny shares information when, and with whom, she deems
it necessary.

Tiny says things like "private property is a settler-colonial lie" and "wealth
hoarding is a disease," for which "radical redistribution is the cure." She's not
waiting around for "politricksters" to enact a wealth tax. Her idea of redistribution
is for wealthy people to hand over large amounts of cash directly to poor people.
She doesn't look to charities for solutions to the homelessness crisis—her
version of The Fix is to empower the unhoused to come up with their own
solutions by paying them "poverty reparations."

Tiny is a cultish figure with a mesmerizing sway over certain segments of
Bay Area intelligentsia, an asset in her quest to persuade people to part with
their dollars. She's built a "solidarity family" of folks with means, more than one
hundred strong, who have redistributed hundreds of thousands of dollars in
the past decade (perhaps more than a million—Tiny doesn't keep track) to her
and her formerly unhoused friends, who then pass it along to others in need.
"We turn blood-stained dollars into love-stained dollars," she told me.

Tiny has channeled a big chunk of those dollars into real estate: She's transformed a foreclosed property in Oakland into a small townhome complex,

where she lives in a commune of formerly unhoused folks, all rent-free. She and her crew conceived the project, hung the drywall, hammered the studs, and now collectively manage the space. "This is a poor-people-led solution to our own problems," said Tiny, who sees the built-by-and-for-poor-people version of The Fix as an antidote to the housing solutions proffered by what she calls "nonprofiteers."

"Change won't come from a savior, a pimp, or an institution. Change will only come from a poor-people-led re-vo-*loooo*-shun," says Tiny, who sometimes speaks in hip-hop-inflected rhyme.

Building multifamily real estate is an uphill slog for seasoned professionals—zoning, permits, design, financing, construction, management—and even projects initiated by folks with money and connections are routinely thwarted. Tiny dropped out of school in the sixth grade when she and her mom became homeless and has scarcely ever held a "real" job. But she possesses a gold mine of doggedness, and with it has managed to coax homes for about two dozen people out of East Bay air. Architects, engineers, and tradesmen donated their services. The solidarity family put up the money for permits and supplies, and to pay unhoused laborers to help build. When I met Tiny, she and her tribe were putting the finishing touches on the place—Homefulness.

Tiny grew up in Los Angeles as the daughter of a mentally ill social worker. She herself is quite stable and has never touched drugs, but she does check the box for intergenerational poverty and trauma. Her grandmother was an Irish orphan who immigrated as a teenager to New York, only to endure an abusive relationship with an older man. When she was eighteen, she left him and their three children behind, fleeing to Philadelphia, where she soon had a fourth child with a Black Puerto Rican man—Tiny's mom, Dee—who she also abandoned.

Tiny grew up hearing how her grandmother did not feed or even touch Dee during her first several days of life. She nearly died. Baby Dee was then repeatedly molested by an acquaintance of her mother. Around eighteen months of age, she was sent to the first of many foster homes, where the trauma continued. Tiny later wrote a memoir, *Criminal of Poverty: Growing up Homeless in America*, which describes the horrific sexual abuse that two-year-old Dee survived at one foster home, and how she survived at another—where she was barely fed—by stealing cat food.

Dee met Tiny's father, the scion of a wealthy Southern California family, while still in high school. "His was a life of extreme privilege and extreme insanity," she writes. "Into this strange American family walked my mother, a sexy mixed-race . . . embodiment of all that was other." The marriage ended when Tiny's father, a newly minted psychiatrist on the verge of a breakdown, broke Dee's arm. Tiny was four. This was the end of a "brief period of very rich times" and the beginning of a "bloody wound of pain, betrayal, and fear," Tiny continues, "one that would never properly heal."

Dee and Tiny moved onto a houseboat in LA, from which they were booted several months later, the first of many evictions they weathered together. Dee's mental health spiraled downward after losing her job as a social worker when Tiny was eleven, at which point Tiny stopped going to school to serve as her mom's caregiver. Procuring housing was one of Tiny's main duties. At the age of twelve, she convinced a landlord that she was twenty-six and gainfully employed, a triumph that led her to cultivate an increasingly sophisticated alter ego: a responsible adult with good credit and money in the bank. Nonetheless, by the time Tiny was a teenager, she and Dee were houseless more often than not.

As her mother's caregiver, Tiny was a child without a childhood. She became a pawn in her mother's dysfunctional and sometimes violent relationships with a series of men. Central to this pattern was financial reliance on her mother's boyfriends: "It was a testimony to our level of desperation," she writes, describing herself as "11 going on 40. . . . I began dreaming of the ways I could kill myself. I imagined the kind of gun I would use, how it would feel in my hands and the relief it would give me."

Tiny is a rarity. But she represents the flower of a common seed in the camps— pain and suffering fertilized with rebelliousness and grown into a movement that remedies the root causes of the pain and suffering. Tiny's answer to the question of who becomes homeless and why reads like a communist manifesto, one that she's hell-bent on reciting in the halls of power.

In 2018, Tiny was invited to give a talk at Talks at Google, the speaker series conducted at the company headquarters in Mountain View and broadcast live to employees worldwide. You've certainly heard of some of the people who have given them, such as Hillary Clinton, Henry Kissinger, and Lady Gaga. Tiny's talk was a little different—it ended explosively, illustrating the fundamental clash between Tiny's brand of radical activism and Silicon Valley's reshaping of California, and the world.

4

The Ecosystem

Fuckers. I couldn't get the word out of my head, because he wouldn't stop saying it. I was sitting in the tiled courtyard of the Mediterranean-style home of an old acquaintance, a venture capitalist and serial tech entrepreneur, who lived a few blocks from Zuckerberg in Palo Alto. Next to us was a massive stone slab over which water dribbled into a reflecting pool. A Buddha sat on the stone, contemplating the flow. Above us sprawled the canopy of a century-old olive tree, which had been raining its fruit onto the courtyard. It would have been an idyllic scene, were it not for the presence of my acquaintance, who kept smacking and berating his dog, a puffy, pure-white Alaskan-looking thing, who wouldn't stop eating the olives.

In my previous career, I was a landscape designer, and this person was my client. I'd lived in Santa Cruz then, a hippie-surfer town about an hour away on the other side of the mountains that separate the Valley from the ocean. I was not alone in commuting over those mountains—many of Santa Cruz's hippies and surfers make the trek to stick their straws where the wealth is. I went to college at the University of California in Santa Cruz—home of the fighting Banana Slugs!—and spent the entirety of my twenties there. When thirty approached, I began to think of things like owning a home, which even an hour from the Valley's gravitational center was out of reach with my income at the time. So a few months after the Great Recession hit, I moved back to Georgia, where I'd grown up. I bought a house on seven acres for $90,000.

I'd been away from California for twelve years. Much had changed. The real estate costs I'd fled had tripled; 2008 prices now seem quaintly affordable. I don't remember ever seeing a tent on the streets of Santa Cruz back then.

It was known as a place with a lot of panhandlers and drug users, but not so many that they made their dwellings in places obvious to the casual observer. When I drove over after arriving in Cupertino, however, a camp lined the main road into town; hundreds of unhoused residents inhabited another area along the river.

My client had also changed. I remembered him as a charming, progressive guy, but he'd grown older, crankier, and more libertarian in the decade since I last saw him. Apparently he'd become fond of calling people *fuckers*, and when I broached the topic of homelessness, he erupted in a lava flow. Employees of NGOs who concoct idealistic plans to address the housing crisis? Fuckers. Activists who valiantly defend the less fortunate among us? Fuckers. He couldn't stand to go to San Francisco anymore because of the hordes sleeping and shitting right there on the sidewalk, in front of businesses run by people who actually contribute to the economy.

"If we can figure out how to get a package from China to your doorstep in two days, we can figure this out," he said. Whether it's houses made of shipping containers or building artificial islands in the Bay to house the homeless, he assured me that "innovators" like himself could come up with a solution—if only the incompetent, naïve, and corrupt fuckers in the public sector would get out of the way. In fact, he would personally love to dig his entrepreneurial hands into the issue. But the poverty space was dominated by inefficient nonprofits and he wouldn't waste his time consorting with them—the profit motive is what drives efficiency, after all, and efficiency paves the way to viable solutions. Nonprofits are in the business of self-congratulation, not getting things done, he said. His evidence: They hadn't fixed the problem yet. "It's like a car or your phone," he said. "Either it works or it doesn't."

The last time I'd seen my client he was plotting his first trip to Burning Man. He'd shown me some of his paintings and we'd chatted about organic farming and his time in a kibbutz. Though he worked sixteen hours a day (he claimed to sleep no more than a few hours a night), he nevertheless found time to feed his omnivorous intellect, which snacked on cybernetics and chewed on transcendentalism after dinner. He was the archetypal boomer tech entrepreneur, kissed by the antiestablishment, but in the business of re-establishing the establishment in his own image.

The Valley overlaps geographically with the hippie homeland of San Francisco, Berkeley, and their environs, and there's long been cross-pollination, if not orgiastic copulation, between the two spheres. As a barefoot college dropout in the early seventies, Steve Jobs's interests included Ram Dass, Hare Krishnas, and fruitarianism; his connection to apples stemmed from a stint at the All One Farm, a commune where he worked in a Gravenstein orchard. The commune fell apart as residents realized they were being conned by the spiritual leader, a close friend of Jobs, into providing free labor for his apple cider business. The apple cider guru later became a billionaire mining magnate notorious for labor and environmental abuses. Jobs, however, sought to bring his spiritual values with him in founding a company to disseminate what he considered the ultimate tool of enlightenment—the personal computer—to the masses.

This trajectory is such a prominent feature among the Valley's founding fathers that it has spawned a minor field of academic study. "To pursue the development of individualized, interactive computing technology was to pursue the New Communalist dream of social change," writes Fred Turner, a Stanford historian, in his book *From Counterculture to Cyberculture: Stewart Brand, the Whole Earth Network, and the Rise of Digital Utopianism.*

Turner's book focuses on Stewart Brand, a Merry Prankster turned evangelist of enlightened capitalism, who once roamed from commune to commune selling back-to-the-land supplies out of his 1963 Dodge truck. The Whole Earth Truck Store, as he called it, morphed into the *Whole Earth Catalog* magazine, which begat the *Whole Earth Software Catalog*, which begat *Wired* magazine. Brand, writes Turner, "brokered a long-running encounter between San Francisco flower power and the emerging technological hub of Silicon Valley," in which "counterculturalists and technologists alike joined together to reimagine computers as tools for personal liberation, the building of virtual and decidedly alternative communities, and the exploration of bold new social frontiers."

One can imagine a young Steve Jobs digging the communalism of today's Bay Area camps, whose countercultural idealism shares many threads with that of the Valley's early hippie-nerds—ironic given the bulldozing of camps in the shadows of contemporary tech campuses and their tightly conformist corporate cultures. The commonalities don't stretch very far: A rather thick thread in the hippie-techie braid is individualism, a whole lot of which hid behind the Me generation's "New Communalist" movement. The marriage of these Bay Area cultures is alive and well, but today has more of a New Age–Burning Man vibe. Brand, now in his eighties, is an ardent Burner. He's gone from libertarian to the even-harder-to-define "post-libertarian" and is building a five-hundred-foot clock inside a Texas mountain owned by Jeff Bezos, which is designed to tick once per year for ten thousand years. A cuckoo will emerge at the end of each millennium.

Brand shares a certain intellectual hubris with my acquaintance, who asked if I would like to read an eighty-two-page white paper he wrote regarding the human brain and why Darwin's survival-of-the-fittest theory applies not just to biological evolution, but to the optimization of social structure. I stared at the Buddha and tried to think of a way to change the subject.

RHIZOMATOUS

Unhoused communities don't randomly burble up from the sidewalk. They are born of the housed communities around them, which in the Valley's case is a particularly curious one. The Valley's valley is wide and smoggy enough that some days you can't see the mountain ranges that form it. The scorching Diablo Range, where cattle roam oceans of desiccated grass, lies to the east. On the other side, the lusher Santa Cruz Mountains, a place of dank redwood forests, organic farming communes, and uppity vineyards, form a verdant curtain between the Valley and the ocean. Here the tech elite build their villas and take to the fog-kissed ravines for athleisure-clad recreation.

The valley started to become the Valley in 1943 when IBM opened a factory to manufacture punch cards in San José. At the time, orchards carpeted much of the region. When the trees blossomed in early spring, the honey-scented flowers intoxicated bees and lovers alike. During the late summer harvest, the air was a punch bowl. Maps referred to it then as the Santa Clara Valley, but romantic minds of the day christened it the Valley of Heart's Delight, after a 1927 poem by a local writer with Wordsworthian sensibilities, named Clara Louise Lawrence.

No brush can paint the picture
No pen describe the sight
That one can find in April
In "The Valley of Heart's Delight."

Cupertino did not exist back then. The Glendenning family farmed the land where the Apple Spaceship now sits. Prunes were their specialty. The farm was on Pruneridge Avenue—the valley was considered the prune capital of the world, supplying 30 percent of the global market—which passed through their orchards near the present location of Steve Jobs Theater, a smaller circular building next to the mothership. But Apple bought the road from the city—$23,814,257 for a half mile—so you can't drive through there anymore. Between the steel bars of the fence you can still catch a glimpse of the Glendennings' old fruit-drying barn, which has been renovated and is now storage for landscaping equipment. The new orchards and the old barn help soften the Pentagon vibe with a little farm-to-table ambience.

The Valley's valley is not a stereotypical one because it lacks a mighty river meandering between the mountain ranges. Instead, there is the southern leg of San Francisco Bay, a shallow, brackish estuary fed by measly creeks that barely run in the dry season. It's a bird and crustacean paradise, but the lack of fresh water and ocean currents make for a putrid aroma that's further intensified by the landfills, wastewater treatment plants, and commercial salt-harvesting operations clustered around the waterfront. The smell is so intense that it's spawned a South Bay Odor Stakeholders Group "dedicated to identifying and resolving odor issues." One finds Reddit threads with titles like South Bay Fucking Smell: "south bay people, you know what i mean. where the fuck is this rancid ass smell coming from. it's pretty common for it to smell like shit here, i've smelled it my whole life, but i just want to know where it's comin from. my guess is the shitty salty shallow south bay water spewing out smelly air, but idk."

"That, or else it's your mom," replied another user, who referred to the odor as "the ass cloud." The poetics of the region have shifted since Lawrence's day.

The ass cloud did not dissuade the early tech settlers, who followed the money flowing from the patron saint of the Valley's venture capitalists: DARPA, the Department of Defense's secretive research agency, which commissioned much of the basic science from which the IT revolution sprang. While farms like the Glendennings' continued to pump out prunes on the arable land between the Bay and the mountains, the military-industrial complex set up along the mud flats. The Navy built an eight-acre dirigible hangar in Mountain View, still one of the largest freestanding structures ever erected. The CIA quietly rooted itself among the reeds and spread rhizomatically. During the Cold War, aerospace companies blossomed between DOD installations. Lockheed was the Valley's biggest employer when Kent and Steve Jobs were growing up in the suburbs that slowly consumed the orchards.

The American tech industry was born in the Bay Area because its defense industry parents came here to ward off the Japanese—during World War II, this was the gateway to the "Pacific Theater," as the Asian front of the war was euphemistically referred to. This first generation of the Valley "seeded companies that repurposed technologies built for war to everyday life," writes Margaret O'Mara, a tech industry historian. "Today's tech giants all contain some defense-industry DNA." Jeff Bezos's grandfather, for instance, was a high-ranking official at the US Atomic Energy Commission and at ARPA, the precursor to DARPA. Jerry Wozniak, father of Apple's other Steve—Steve "The Woz" Wozniak, the company cofounder and part of the gang tweaking on computers in the Jobs' garage—was an engineer at Lockheed. The military forefathers of the Valley must have been horrified at the hippies their children became, though by the eighties the arc of flower power had bent toward the common ground of Wall Street.

The Navy's dirigible hangar still looms over the Bay, but Google now rents the property from the government for the parking of private jets. The company dominates the neighborhood to the west of the hangar, a spread of dull office buildings revolving around the central Googleplex, with its employee swimming pools, volleyball courts, and eighteen cafeterias. There are no houses or apartments in the neighborhood, though there are residential districts—of a sort. These are surprisingly affordable, which means that some of the folks who smear avocado on the techies' toast and stock the kombucha taps have the good fortune to live nearby. It's easy to miss their humble abodes, however. An out-of-towner who gets off at the Google exit to take a leak could be forgiven for thinking they'd stumbled across some sort of RV convention. But those aren't *recreational* vehicles lining the backstreets of the Google-burbs—those are homes on wheels.

RVs parked on the side of the road are the new desirable real estate, and like the old industrial cores of American cities that have evolved from rough-shod hangouts for unemployed artists to haute loft developments for upwardly mobile professionals, their inhabitants aren't immune to class stratification. Most of the rigs are older, ramshackle models, but here and there shiny coaches broadcast the relative wealth of their inhabitants—techies who could afford an apartment but don't want to waste their money on rent. They roll out of bed, hop on a company bike, and are at the office in three minutes, in the meantime saving up for a big house in the outer, outer, outer burbs, where you can still get a McMansion for under $3 million. Some already have the McMansion and use their RV as a workweek crash pad.

The more-rickety RVs belong to the avocado smearers and lawn mower operators. Crisanto Avenue, five minutes from the Googleplex, is the Latin America of Mountain View's homes-on-wheels community. It's like a museum of 1980s RVs—Toyota Escapers, Winnebago Braves, Chevy Lindys, Fleetwood Jamborees—most of them emanating Spanish banter, many with blue tarps over the roof, and some leaking unmentionable juices from onboard septic tanks. Apartments line one side of Crisanto, but the side with the RVs fronts onto train tracks. A shaded strip of earth along the tracks, maybe twelve feet wide, serves as a communal front yard, complete with potted plants and patio furniture, for pets and kids to play.

An older Peruvian woman named Ida invited me into her RV, where a half-eaten pineapple sat serenely on an otherwise empty table. She used to live in a two-bedroom apartment with sixteen other people—"Fue imposible!" she said—until she learned of the RV scene. She couldn't afford to purchase one, but there's a growing industry in the Valley for old-school RV rentals; residents on Crisanto told me they pay between $500 and $1,000 per month, depending on the RV, plus a $75 fee to pump sewage. Since Ida arrived in the US in 2003, she has worked mainly as a nanny, often for around six dollars per hour. Work was sparse during the pandemic, so she accepted whatever pay she was offered. One family gave her twenty dollars for taking care of their two children for twelve hours. She'd held America in high esteem before living here. "La vida en los Estados Unidos es terrible," she said.

My visual experience of the Valley began to shift. My eyes had once flashed at views of the water, clever billboards ("Hey Facebook, our planet doesn't like your climate posts"), and homes with the billowy, buff-colored grasses and scrawny wildflowers that signify the aesthetics of people who can afford expensive landscaping designed to look feral. But the more time I spent with the Valley's have-nots, the more my focus became trained on the visual language of the income inequality ecosystem: the camouflage patterns of desiccated vegetation pocked with blue tarps and plastic bags flapping in the branches; the hulking silhouettes of recreational vehicles parked in non-recreational environments; the bodies splayed out on the sidewalk.

Here and there, artistic aberrations emerge in the motif. I met a thirty-year old man named Ariginal who lived with his family and dogs in a 1983 Chevy camper van that he'd hand-painted marine blue with school-bus-yellow trim. A blue neon light mounted to the undercarriage illuminated the street in a cool glow as they motored around in their Scooby-Doo mobile at night. Ariginal went to school to be a fireman but became an Uber driver. He's also a rapper, fashion model, and inventor—there are a few things he's hoping to patent, and he wanted to show me the drawings, but his daughter was napping in the van. "I have a lot of dreams," he said. Within twelve minutes of meeting Ariginal I learned that he recently "discovered a couple of lumps . . . uh, in my testicles." They were cancerous. He'd just had the tumors removed and would soon be undergoing radiation to make sure they don't come back. "Just another obsta-cle," he sighed.

"Vanlife has become the norm here," a veteran gig worker named Chase, who's driven for Uber, Instacart, and Amazon Flex, told me. He was not talking about hipsters who move into a home on wheels because it sounds like a fun and Instagrammable lifestyle. He was referring to his colleagues who have no other choice. I found there is significant overlap between the gig work commu-nity and the unhoused community. Some full-time gig workers end up living in their vehicles; some camp residents become part-time gig workers because it's a way to make a buck that doesn't require a home address or the scrutiny of a human boss, only a working phone. Rudy, for instance, began delivering for food apps—using Lime scooters he rents by the hour—after he became homeless.

The mobile communities stretch along the Bay up to Meta's headquarters at 1 Hacker Way, on the outskirts of Palo Alto. East Palo Alto, the historically Black community surrounding the Meta campus, is one of the least gentrified, most impoverished places in the Valley—a 2017 study found that 42 percent of students in the local school district were homeless. A sixty-acre nature preserve across the street from the Meta campus is home to endangered species such as the salt marsh harvest mouse and Ridgway's rail, a chicken-sized bird with a long, pointy beak and special glands that allow it to drink salt water. A local variety of *Homo sapiens* lives there too, who are endangered in a different sort of way. The authorities want them out because their "presence is compromising the health of the estuary," according to *Palo Alto Weekly*. Their poop and trash are considered pollution under the federal Clean Water Act—grounds for eviction. "The welfare of wildlife and the health of Baylands ecosystems is pitted against the very real human needs of people," the paper opined. Their camps keep getting razed, but like the marshland reeds, they sprout right back.

RIPARIAN

Different regions of the Valley lend themselves to different expressions of homelessness. In the suburban areas, there are lots of vehicle dwellers because it's (relatively) easy to find a place to park. In densely developed San Francisco, homelessness is largely centered along sidewalks, pushing the lives of unhoused individuals up close and personal, but keeping camps small and dispersed. Golden Gate Park is a would-be homeless haven, but local authorities have managed to keep camps from proliferating. In San José, however, local green spaces have been commandeered by the unhoused, with camps that have developed into villages, especially along the Guadalupe River, where the Crash Zone was located, and its tributaries.

San José's waterways are hideously un-scenic—views are of rubble and trash; the vegetation appears to be in a fight for its life. And although the Guadalupe is called a river, it's more like a creek that bulges into a torrent on the rare occasion of a multiday rainstorm. Its abused hydrology forms the armature of a shadow city—a new form of urban infrastructure that is unplanned and unwelcome—within a city that does not acknowledge its shadow. At a community meeting in 2017 to solicit input on a homeless shelter the city wanted to build, a horde of angry residents expressed their discontent over efforts to accommodate the unhoused: "Build a wall," they chanted.

The Guadalupe River and its camps pierce downtown San José, meandering past the Zoom campus and Adobe's four-tower headquarters to the Children's Discovery Museum on Woz Way (as in Apple's Wozniak, the Apple cofounder), where a community of Latinx campers have chiseled terraced gardens into the riverbank to grow food. People call it the Shelves. Downstream from the Crash Zone, the Guadalupe flows north along the edge of the airport on its way to the Bay, passing dozens of camps and acres of office parks populated by household names—PayPal, Google, Hewlett-Packard, Roku, Cisco, Intel. One of the biggest camps in this part of town emerged on vacant land owned by Apple, just north of the airport, where the company plans to build yet another campus. Located on Component Drive, it was known as Component Camp. As word spread that displaced Crash Zone residents might soon inundate the place, the company announced they would spend "several million dollars" on a high-end sweep—evicted residents were given vouchers for nine months in a hotel—just weeks before the Crash Zone sweep began.

The Guadalupe's tributaries tell further stories. Los Gatos Creek leads to the headquarters of eBay and Netflix, as well as Downtown West, a neighborhood being built from the ground up by Google. The city approved a development proposal that included office space for twenty-five thousand folks, but only four thousand units of housing—the sort of job-supply-to-housing-demand ratio that helps put a $3 million sticker on a bungalow. A report by an economic research firm found that the project's job-to-housing imbalance would translate to a $765-per-month increase for San José renters over a decade—to offset upward pressure on rents, they said more than four times as many units would be needed, a third of them at subsidized rates. The San José Chamber of Commerce declared the report "fundamentally flawed" and dismissed findings like the $765 rent increase. "I don't think that the stark reality presented in the report is realistic," a representative told *San José Spotlight*, "nor something we can expect to happen in the next 8 to 10 years." In the previous decade, however, median rent in the area had gone up by exactly $763.

Coyote Creek is home to a camp called the Jungle—I never deduced whether this was a reference to hobo jungles or the dense vegetation, or both—on which national media descended in 2014 as it was being swept. It was similar to the Crash Zone in scale, and headlines touting it as the "nation's largest homeless camp" became a mantra. It was a feast of poverty porn. "Living in The Jungle means learning to live in fear," said *The Atlantic*, quoting a resident who displayed "a machete that he carries up his sleeve at night." For the UK's *Daily Mail*, it was an opportunity to get Dickensian. "Dilapidated, muddy and squalid though it was, it was all they had to call home—a shantytown in the heart of Silicon Valley," the reporter lamented. "In the last month, one resident tried to strangle another with a cord of wire and another was nearly beaten to death with a hammer." The Jungle, they said, was "a crime syndicate ruled by gangs, where police do not enter." *The New York Times* was more restrained, striking a valiant tone, with a photo of the mayor himself helping a resident to "wheel his belongings up a muddy embankment." The local CBS station reported that displaced residents immediately formed a "New Jungle" a half mile away. Before long, they recolonized the original Jungle.

The Crash Zone had grown to the size of the original Jungle, if not larger, by the time I first visited. The fields outside the airport fence technically belong to a city park, but when driving by they appeared like a cross between a junkyard and a refugee camp, in which explosives were periodically detonated. RVs in various states of disrepair butted up to tarp compounds that overflowed with debris, from bottles and cans to appliances and vehicles. This visual buffet was a mix of freshly prepared, putrefied, and charred—one resident had a tidily landscaped yard with a pair of pink plastic flamingos, while other homesteads were a mix of rotting garbage, blackened grass, melted tarps, and burnt-out vehicles. My eyes flowed over suitcases and furniture and school buses to unexpected items, such as a piano, several boats, and a limousine. The first residents I met cautioned me against wandering into certain sections, where I might be mistaken for an undercover cop—the confetti labyrinth of structures left many a hidden nook where bad things might happen. One guy had cobbled together a two-story wood cabin; around it were huge piles of wood chips and logs. I wanted to knock but was told the owner wielded an axe and did not like visitors. They called him the Woodchucker.

It was midsummer when I first visited the Crash Zone, height of the dry season in California. Large portions of the landscape were barren earth, and the powder-dry soil coated the skin of its residents. Here and there, people sifted through the loose dirt with their hands; occasionally someone held up a small trinket they'd discovered, inspecting it in the harsh light of the sun. A woman walked by with a mixing bowl and a toy unicorn, stooping to extract a scrap of blue tarp from the earth, before she continued on. A minimally dressed man pulled clothes from a dumpster and tried them on, not necessarily in the way they were designed to be worn, and quickly took them off again. He spoke incomprehensively to himself as he did this, tsking and looking annoyed, as though he just couldn't find the outfit he was looking for. He was thin, barefoot; I wondered how he stayed alive.

I saw a man thrashing his body in anger as he crossed the street. A dreadlocked white guy in a hoodie wandered by with a baseball bat in one hand and a small, sweet-looking dog in the other. The wind picked up; a dust devil spun. A car crawled out of one of the fields with a flat tire, its rim scraping the asphalt as it entered the street. Every five minutes or so, a plane roared overhead like an angry avian dinosaur.

The Crash Zone spilled from its gills, extending beyond the end-of-the-runway fields and into the surrounding cityscape. One end spilled into a series of baseball diamonds, the dugout now housing, the clubhouse a drug den, the bathrooms given over to the sex trade—"People pull through in $100,000 cars trolling for people to blow them in the car," a resident told me. On an adjacent street, a man on crutches lived on a bench next to what was once a demonstration garden for drought-tolerant plants, according to a small sign, which had devolved into a garden of rocks and bare earth. The street proceeds across a large bridge where a solitary tent occupied one of the little nooks designed as a place for pedestrians to linger and look out over the Guadalupe. The bike and pedestrian paths that weave through the riparian corridor below provided access to a neighborhood of tents and shacks, a leafy suburb of the Crash Zone known as the Enchanted Forest. Its inhabitants pulled their cars over the curb, using the paths as driveways. Joggers and cyclists and parents pushing strollers paraded through nonetheless.

The tents flowed along the river to the San José Heritage Rose Garden, where thousands of rare and forgotten varieties have been arranged in concentric rings of paths and beds. Some of those varieties disappeared following the Crash Zone's pandemic-era population explosion, when incidents of arson and "rose rustling"—horticultural theft—were reported by garden volunteers on the site's Facebook page, the insinuation of who was responsible clearly legible between the lines of the posts. The tents trickled past the roses and collected in clumps along the edges of the Historic Orchard, whose few remaining trees appear murdered and maimed, where they bumped into the six-foot fence that protects the children at the Rotary PlayGarden, a gift to the city from the local Rotary Club. A gate attendant keeps the you-know-who from wandering in to the $6 million playscape.

As San José's camps have spread, the Guadalupe River parklands have become the frontlines of a local culture war. "The city's homeless problem is becoming a PR problem," a CBS anchor said in a 2019 segment. "From their airplane windows, arriving visitors are greeted by a shantytown of tents, blue tarps, and RVs," they said, describing the trail network that parallels the river as "an eleven-mile stretch of human misery and suffering."

The campers swim in the animosity that drenches the airwaves and cyberspaces around them. I wondered how my new friends on the street felt when they heard these things. How much does the angst directed toward them undermine their prospects of recovery? I found myself reading the Tripadvisor reviews of Guadalupe River Park, which encompasses much of the trail system. They felt like a beating. "The once beautiful walking, running and biking trail has been taken over by homeless, garbage, rats," wrote Robin G. "Really bad," wrote hob0525. "It was basically . . . a tour of homeless camps. We walked for over an hour thinking it would get better. . . . It did not."

In a 2019 survey by the Guadalupe River Park Conservancy, 77 percent of respondents did not feel "welcome and safe" in the park. "It's something that I've never seen before, honestly," Jason Su, the conservancy's director, told *The Mercury News*. "This is just on a scale that's just so, so large."

It's as though the city feels it's been invaded by the unhoused. But turn San José inside out and it's a giant homeless camp being invaded by a city.

Fronting

Life in a homeless camp is extraordinarily stressful, but it is still a life. People fall in love and break up. They adopt pets. They are active on social media. Cliques form and fall apart. Neighbors try to outdo each other. People choose sides. On Wolfe Road, the people at the north end of the camp tended to have more resources than the folks at the south end, who they derided for leaving too much trash piled around their tents. But all of them made it their home in their own way, adorning the camp with dumpster-sourced decorations, including an American flag, a scarecrow, several nonfunctioning clocks, and an autumn-themed wall-hanging that said "Harvest Blessings." Someone fashioned a shower out of PVC pipe and a hand-pumped herbicide spray tank, with a blue tarp for a curtain. A handmade sign on one tent provided the URL for the group's GoFundMe page. "Be happy, life is a gift" had been spray-painted on the wall of another home. They were not, in fact, homeless.

Unhoused communities root themselves in place with a hand-built infrastructure for power, water, waste, cooking, and bathing and cobble together outdoor gathering places for socializing and community events. These were just beginning to coalesce on Wolfe Road, but other camps are like self-contained villages—the longer they are allowed to remain in place without being swept, the more extensive their infrastructure. I found irrigated gardens, both edible and ornamental, chicken coops, and, at Wood Street Commons, a rabbit hutch. One guy in the Jungle had air-conditioning and burglar bars on his four-hundred-square-foot streamside cabin. A guy at the Crash Zone had planted a fig tree next to his dog's grave in the front yard of his compound. Urban campers do most everything people living in houses do. They even go on vacation—once when I bumped into Moose, proprietor of the Moose Pit

Café at Wood Street Commons, he surprised me by telling me about his recent trip to Tahoe.

Political correctness aside, there's not an adequate catch-all term to describe the various living arrangements and degrees of permanence one finds on the street. Most refer to themselves as homeless and their place of residence simply as a camp, but I've also heard inventive terms, such as "marginally housed community" and, my favorite, for its simplicity, clarity, and power: "settlement."

Food is a primary focus. An assortment of grills and camp stoves were scattered among the tents on Wolfe Road, and some campers had generators that powered mini-fridges and microwaves. One day I found Walter clutching a clear plastic bag filled with a brown liquid in which chopped meat, herbs, and vegetables floated—his mom's Korean ribs recipe, marinating in preparation for the grill. Troy, a clean-cut Black man with a soft, round face who loves to cook, whipped out his phone to show me a recent camp-stove feast: bourbon-apple-glazed pork chops stuffed with garlic, onions, jalapeños, potatoes, and four types of cheese.

The Wolves had more money than you might expect, but since it wasn't enough for rent, they tended to invest in other things, like computers, cars, and drugs. Sometimes when I arrived at the camp, Troy was pedaling down the bike lane to where he parked his car, a late-model Acura with leather seats. "Going to work!" he yelled, waving cheerfully. He'd recently started a holiday-season gig at UPS, one in a string of jobs he'd held since losing his apartment several years prior. The previous one, with the Santa Clara County Registrar of Voters, ended with a round of pandemic layoffs that spring. "I spend most of my time in my tent staring at the walls or crying," said Troy, who shared his home with a cat named Butterscotch. "I'm broken inside. I don't know how to get past it."

There was a sense of vitality in the camp, but also morbidity. A visitor was killed on his bike in a hit-and-run by the 280 overpass. A seventy-four-year-old man was run over and killed while sleeping in a strip-mall parking lot up the road. Sometimes a woman from a neighboring camp wandered through with a dead bird in her hands, singing a screeching death wail. "She thinks she's bringing it back to life," said Jen, the former Infineon employee with pink hair. "The first time I heard her, I thought someone was getting murdered. I came out of my tent with a knife in my hand."

Jen explained some of the dynamics of camp communities as a woman. "One of the biggest struggles is being able to shower," she told me over a plate of orange chicken chow mein from the Asian supermarket up the street. At her camp on Calabazas Creek she'd fashioned a patio with a tarped-off area for bathing, employing an electric pump for water pressure. On Wolfe Road, the communal herbicide-sprayer shower offered less privacy. "I wore a bathing suit the first time I used it, just because I didn't feel safe out there, you know, right on the road. When I got out of the shower, two guys were sitting there in front of it."

Jen says she's generally felt safe living in camps, though there's always an undercurrent of fear. Early in her time on the street, she fell asleep in the tent of an older man, a father figure she trusted, and awoke to him tugging on her leg. "I woke up disoriented, not realizing who it was, and kicked the shit out of him," she said. Turned out he was just trying to take her boots off so she could sleep more comfortably. Finding the Wolfe Road clan felt like finding home, she said, one where she felt both connected and protected. "I felt like I completed a puzzle for the group—having a woman around seemed like a positive thing for them."

Jen became the indisputable matriarch of the clan, everyone's mom. She's warm and grounded and speaks in a tone of don't-worry-honey-everything's-gonna-be-OK. But beneath the optimistic aura, she was having a very hard time. Her cat, Littles, had just been run over by a car. They were very close. She used to carry Littles in a frontpack that Kent scavenged for her, but one day she climbed onto Jen's shoulder and claimed it as her perch. She would balance there when Jen rode her bike and fall asleep there when Jen was still. Littles roamed between Jen's tent and Calabazas Creek, which doesn't involve crossing any streets, but she'd recently taken to exploring on the other side of Wolfe Road. And, well . . . that was that.

"Poor Littles," moaned Jen, as we shoveled down the greasy noodles.

Littles was a gift from her boyfriend, Smurf, who Jen parted with around the same time. Smurf and Jen's troubles put the whole camp on edge, so they both left for a while to let things cool off. When she returned to the camp, she started hanging out with Dave, who may or may not have been her new boyfriend. He built her a new living space, bigger than all the others, its shiny new tarps projecting new possibilities. "Dating out here is really hard, but for a woman it's almost necessary to be safe," she told me. It's complicated to be both camp mom and one of the only women in a community of unpartnered men. "It's a bunch of men who don't have women in their lives, but they've got you and they want more," said Jen.

One of Jen's biggest challenges is maintaining her sense of self-worth. As a woman on the street, there's an added layer of shame, she said, telling me about the harassment she'd experienced from workers hired to sweep previous camps she'd lived at. "They harass everybody, but as a woman it's worse—hooting and hollering and saying all sorts of disrespectful things. They seem to think that if you're a woman out here that you do certain things. That's not the case, not everybody has to resort to things like that."

In other camp news, said Jen, huge sums of money had recently fallen from the sky. It felt that way, anyways, when the campers learned that they were eligible for unemployment benefits. The government normally cuts you off six months after becoming unemployed, but the rules changed with the Coronavirus Aid, Relief, and Economic Security Act. By the time the campers caught wind of this and figured out how to apply, some had accrued tens of thousands of dollars in retroactive payments.

Suddenly, a change in lifestyle was possible for the Wolfe Road crew. After lunch, Jen was heading over to the Amazon lockers at 7-11. "I went on a shopping spree and my guilty little pleasures are coming today," she chirped. I imagined things like chocolate-covered goji berries and organic argan-oil face cream, but it turned out she'd ordered a Taser, a flashlight, and a knife. The latter, I was disturbed to learn, was a gift for Roger, the one person at Wolfe Camp that I was truly afraid of.

Upon learning of the campers' newly inflated bank accounts, I assumed that the packing would soon begin. Here was a gift from God; now everyone could find a cheap place to rent (or at least try to), start applying for jobs, and slowly rebuild their lives. They had runway, a cushion.

Some campers bought cars with their unemployment income. Kent spent $10,000 on an electric bike and a new bike trailer to better transport the fruits of his dumpster dives. But mainly he bought it because he loves bikes more than almost anything. He told me that his retirement dream is to hand-build a tiny, ultra-light Airstream-style bike trailer, just big enough for him to sleep in, and cycle around the country with it. In the meantime, he's busy with his caretaking career. "I could get off the streets, but I don't because I'm out here with the people who can't get off the streets"—his friends who are too traumatized, too mentally ill to function in the 9-to-5 world. "Like the old and the infirm, we should be taking care of them," he said. Higher-functioning residents taking care of their lower-functioning neighbors is a hallmark of camp culture.

There is a range of attitudes, and a fair amount of disagreement, among the campers about whether, and under what terms, they would return to society. Yesenia, who'd only been on the streets for a few months, was eager to get off them. Troy would do so in a heartbeat, and he was hoping to use the publicity of camping in front of Apple to leverage himself into an apartment. "Give us six months in a stable environment with a roof over our heads, the opportunity to wake up in a bed, take a shower, and go to work," he said. "I need that foundation."

As Jen and I walked back to the camp after lunch, she mused about her future. She had no interest in going back to the tech industry, but she was open to participating in the mainstream economy again if it was "something that fills me up, gives joy, and makes a difference of some sort." Perhaps she'd become a teacher for autistic children, she said, or open a flower shop. She sees herself building a tiny home one day with volunteer labor and scavenged materials. "I think a lot of us are trying to figure out how we'd like to make our next impression, to change our major, so to speak," said Jen. "To be stuck in the rat race is hard, so it's good to be able to take a time-out and reorganize. How many people get to do that?"

After visiting Wolfe Camp nearly every day for several weeks, I began to feel like a part of the community—still very much an outsider, but a thread of their fabric nonetheless. I sensed that the residents were seeing me less as a journalist and more as a person. I was drawn in as my relationships grew, and also unnerved by how rapidly I was becoming subsumed by the camp's interpersonal intricacies.

One day when cycling by I saw Walter standing with a bouquet of roses clasped in his hands like a prayer, his body arched over Yesenia, who was sitting in her usual office chair next to the 280 on-ramp. The look on his face said, *Please don't leave me.* As soon as their separation was final, they both began confiding in me about their difficulties. Walter blamed them on her alcoholism. Yesenia blamed them on his resignation to life in a tent, which she did not see as her future, and on his violence. After one dispute, Yesenia called the police and said he had raped and beaten her—information I learned from Walter, who said he was arrested for battery.

Things got complicated for me at the camp. I spent an afternoon with Cheryl, a new arrival who said she had been raped and beaten nearly to death and had a brain injury as a result. She trembled and cried as she told me her story. Cheryl had tented up with Roger, the angry, incoherent camper I tried to avoid, who she said was making bombs in the tent and scared her to death and she didn't know what he'd do to her if she tried to leave, and could I please help her?

Cheryl is a lovely person. She has no filters, which inspires an immediate and profound affection. Muscular and freckled, with cropped blond hair, she wore mismatched Converse All Stars, a short sundress, a black choker around her neck, and a pink bow atop her head. We sat on a bench outside Philz Coffee at Main Street Cupertino, a mixed-use development down the street from the camp, where she said she comes when the bars let out at night to find work (I didn't inquire what she meant by that). After a while she got nervous about people recognizing her while she was crying, so I proposed a walk through the neighborhood. Piecing together bits of her story, I gathered that her lifestyle involved rotating from one sketchy guy's tent to another. Most recently, she'd tented with a guy in the parking lot of the gas station that was kitty-corner to Apple's marquee oak at the corner of Wolfe and Homestead. They eventually got the boot, which gave her an opening to escape from that guy and move in with Roger.

She said that she and Roger were not together, but that he wanted to be. She paid him to watch her stuff when she was out, but she brought her most important stuff with her everywhere she went so he didn't meddle with it, which is why she had a very heavy-looking day pack on her back and another bulging bag in her arms. As we strolled past the stucco homes and their topiaries, I offered to carry one of the bags. Then, good fortune arrived: Someone had left a stroller at the end of their driveway with a "free" sign taped to it. Cheryl loaded her bags into it, and we strolled together back toward the camp, her tears and anxiety having subsided a bit in the calm of the leafy streets.

But ten minutes later, as we proceeded down Wolfe Road looking like a couple enjoying the sun with our newborn, the anxiety sprung back: Roger knew she was out with me and might know that she'd been telling me about him and his bombs and it was very important to act chill when we got back to the camp, so as to give the impression that nothing eventful had occurred between us. "I don't know what he's going to do to me when I get back," she whispered, as if he might be listening. I wondered what he was going to do to me as well. A half-block before the tents, I decided to peel off on the little street that runs between Wolfe Road and Main Street Cupertino, where I was parked, telling Cheryl that I had to go and would see her soon. I handed her a ten-dollar bill I'd found on the ground earlier that day. Journalists aren't supposed to pay sources, but it wasn't actually my money, so I figured it was OK.

I wanted to help Cheryl. But I didn't want to meddle in camp affairs. I'd pierced the veil, yet I was terrified to step on the other side of it. I was also unsure of how to interpret everything she'd said. Was he really making bombs? How much of her anxiety was PTSD, versus present circumstances?

I stayed away from the camp for the next few days, suddenly too busy for the daily visits the campers had grown accustomed to. When I finally ventured back, Roger, naturally, was the first person I saw. My usual tactic when I saw Roger coming down the sidewalk was to cheerfully wave hello while maintaining a brisk stride, as though I really must get to an appointment down at the other end of the camp.

"Hey Roger!" I said.

"That bitch is stealing my stuff," he growled, turning to glare at me as I scurried by.

I decided to consult with my most trusted camp confidants about the situation. They were surprisingly nonchalant. "Roger is a different bird," said Jen. "He's been through some things. I can understand why he is the way he is. I've learned to live with him."

Kent told me that just the other day Roger had missed his court date for assaulting someone. But he didn't seem concerned for Cheryl. His take was that Roger is not particularly dangerous, just mentally ill. "He hears voices," Kent explained. "But I like the guy; he's a friend." In Kent's analysis, Roger's anger stemmed from the death of his father, who Roger believes was murdered by the sheriff, though Kent says he actually died in a car accident. Roger's paranoia blends with antiestablishment rage. When the group set up on Wolfe Road, he interpreted it as the beginning of the revolution. "Within an hour he's out in the street with a stick in his hand acting like he's Rambo shooting at people," said Kent. "People would show up to talk to us and he's yelling, *Ahhhhhrrgghhh, I'm going to break out the arms and call in the boys. I'm like, Calm down, Roger, we're here to show everyone that we're just normal people.*"

A week passed without seeing Cheryl again, but knocking at Roger's tent and asking for her didn't seem like a good idea. Then, finally, there she was, standing in front of a different tent—Andre's tent—wearing a short-brimmed hipster's cap and flashing long, bling-y nails with faux rhinestones set in them. I made nervous small talk and wondered when Roger was going to appear with a baseball bat. I hadn't hung out much with Andre, but he seemed much mellower than Roger, and Cheryl seemed better. "I hope you're behaving yourself in there, Andre," she said, sternly, toward the tent.

I got the feeling that she was dancing around things she wanted to tell me, out of concern for who might be overhearing them. Eventually she asked, in a hushed tone, if she could call me that night.

"Uh . . . sure," I said, noncommittally.

Before I left, she asked, "Would it be inappropriate to give you a hug?"

"Maybe not the best idea," I said. "You know, with the virus and all."

Cheryl didn't call, and we didn't cross paths again. A few weeks later I heard she'd moved on, but no one seemed to know where to.

The campers are nothing if not tolerant. Dave has a schizophrenic friend who repeatedly slashed the tires of his Prius, which sat immobile in a parking lot up the street. "It doesn't really bother me," he said with a shrug. The deflated tires greatly reduced the capacity of Dave's dumpster-diving business, but he seemed to feel it was more important that his friend was able to release some rage without hurting anyone. "I've had a friend swing a bat at my head and come this close," said Dave, holding his hands a few inches apart. "I didn't even move—I knew he wouldn't actually hit me. You become fearless out here."

Dave and his friends swam in detritus—the camp looked as though giant celestial hands had picked up a dozen dumpsters and shaken out their contents along the sidewalk—which scarcely seemed to faze them. Refuse was piled several feet deep around each tent and, in some cases, covered the floor inside them. The heaps, which were mined for daily needs as well as eBay material, struck me as a digestive process: the campers metabolizing the Valley's shit. "Homeless people are going to make a mess, but that mess is actually the same garbage you guys threw in your can," said Dave. "It's not more garbage—it's the same garbage."

I found myself in a state of cognitive dissonance on each visit, simultaneously alien invader and brother-in-arms. Camps are like that: both riveting and repulsive, overflowing with antisocial behaviors, yet earnestly egalitarian. The tarps and trash fit the stereotypes; the intellectual sophistication does not. Anarchy reigns, in every sense of the word.

Dave attempted to soothe my distress over the camp's contradictions. "I've had to accept these things," he said. "I've had to accept a lot of people who I know have beautiful hearts, but are also pretty fucking awful." We were sitting on a bench outside Philz Coffee on a weekday morning. Adjacent benches were a buffet of pastries, espresso drinks, and laptops. "I became a thief and a liar and a cheat," said Dave. "But I'm not really those things. Why do people steal? Some people are assholes. But a lot of them probably get started because they're hungry and desperate. Is that really stealing? I don't know."

Dave is an evangelist for the idea that camps are not the problem, but the solution. "A lot of us want to be here," he told me. "We love the compassion of it. We love the fact that we belong. Out here I can cry and be pathetic or loud and angry, whatever I need to be." Dave helped me understand that it's not just a lack of other options that maintains camp communalism, it's because when you pack a bunch of broken souls in a small space, a rare trait blooms: the unspoken sense that your neighbor will tolerate your imperfections because they know what it's like to stare up from rock bottom. In the camp, no matter one's flaws, "they accept you and they love you," said Dave. "Which is a really magical thing. I would never be able to heal anywhere else."

TARP PERIOD

Camps are pressure cookers for human suffering, no doubt about it. But I recognized something of unmistakable value. It was somehow familiar. A quarter century before, in the autumn of 1998, I was merrily sleeping under a tarp in the redwood forest on the UCSC campus, which is situated on a large nature preserve overlooking the Pacific. This was a trend: intentionally homeless students communing with nature while undermining capitalism. I was inspired in part by Satish Kumar, who'd given a lecture on campus about "voluntary simplicity." Kumar had become a mendicant monk at the age of nine—he later traveled the world barefoot, begging for food as he went—and said things like, "How much I can learn from a tree!" Having too little causes suffering, he said, but so does having too much: "Human happiness, true prosperity and joyful living can only emerge from a life of elegant simplicity."

I wanted this elegance. What did I truly need? Not much more than my Nalgene bottle, notebook, and bedroll, I decided. I also needed to feel connected with nature, which would be easier if I lived outdoors.

While stumbling around the forest high on mushrooms my freshman year, I'd encountered various shacks and tents hidden in the underbrush. Friends pointed to a rope hanging from a tree—we tugged on it and down came a rope ladder that led to a wooden platform, barely visible in the branches above, where a fellow stoner made their home. I was invited to a fire circle where the forest dwellers gathered at night, a strange scene where granola activists and liberal arts students, fresh off the bus from high school, mixed with some of the gutter punks and dreadlocked transients I'd become accustomed to seeing downtown, a social scene that treaded the fine line between the intentionally and unintentionally homeless.

In the fall of my sophomore year, I set up a tarp in a thicket just a few minutes' walk from the lecture hall where I attended a Psychology and Religion class twice a week at 8 A.M. I commuted to my tarp each night, feeling my way along the dark forest floor with my feet—I thought of it as a walking meditation, and a flashlight would have muted the vibe. The woods on campus are notorious for the mountain lions that creep through the redwoods at night in search of a deer, or maybe a wayward hippie, to dine on. My nightly meditation focused on facing this fear—and, as I told myself, on facing the darkness within.

My Tarp Period lasted only three months—then I shifted to tents and other non-house dwellings. I spent the winter backpacking across southern Chile while conducting research on an endangered Andean deer, sleeping mostly in a tent. When I returned, I lived for a while in a gussied-up shed in a friend's back-yard. Then I dropped out of school and spent six months tenting it in Hawaii, mostly under a giant mango tree on a remote, off-grid homestead. Later I spent four years living in a yurt at an organic farm on the outskirts of Santa Cruz; the canvas-walled structure, ten feet in diameter, barely held a bed, desk, dresser, and altar. Outside was an open-air kitchen, a fifty-five-gallon drum with a toilet seat on top, and a horse trough for bathing. In my first twelve years after leaving my parents' home, I was unconventionally housed for six.

My period of intentional houselessness was motivated by spiritual reasons, but they were intertwined with worldly considerations. If I saved money on rent, I could avoid having a regular job and follow my passions instead—a path that led me to establish the aforementioned saving-the-planet-through-landscaping business, called Dreaming of Eden, which specialized in transforming con-sumptive lawns into organic food forests—without having to worry much about the financial implications. And if I consumed less, I told myself, there would be more resources for others.

I miss my voluntary simplicity. The more money I've made, the more stressed about money I've become—a pervasive pressure to avoid losing my buying power seeps through me. What if I had to go back to two-star lodging and a car held together by duct tape, like the one I'd bought in my early thirties for $200? Who would I be? Sometimes I think I'd rather go back to living in a tent. To conflate homelessness with Emersonian fantasies about living simply in nature is patently obnoxious and reeks of white privilege. But is it not also reasonable? I suppose the difference lies in the direction of the thought: charac-terizing homelessness as an idyllic experience versus characterizing economic privilege as a collective shortcoming, for which the unhoused experience offers a meaningful perspective.

Is it worth the hustle required to keep my lifestyle afloat? I'm unsure; it depends on the day and how encumbered I'm feeling by the choices I must make to maintain my comfort. It's not simply a question of how hard I have to bust my ass to keep myself financially afloat, but the dissonance I feel with the systems on which I rely to maintain my comfort—fossil fuels, white privilege, labor exploitation.

Kent, however, is pretty clear about where his affinities lie. "There's great freedom in being homeless when you get adjusted to it," he told me. "It's the hardest thing in the world, but once I got to where I was surviving, it was true freedom. I had plenty to eat, plenty of money in my pocket. The world was my stage. I was having the time of my life on Wolfe Road." I was shocked when he first told me this, but some version of that sentiment cropped up again and again in camps I visited. It seemed that the more empowered the unhoused person, the stronger the feeling.

NIMBY–YIMBY TOWN

It was clear that Wolfe Camp's days were numbered, but it was unclear where the residents would go. Cupertino, a city of sixty thousand, does not have a homeless shelter and has but 142 units of subsidized apartments, the cheapest of which are available to households making up to $55,300 annually—not exactly the profile of the folks camping on Wolfe Road. Despite Steve Jobs's histrionics at the city council hearing, Apple ultimately contributed $5.85 million to the city's affordable housing fund as part of the deal to build the Spaceship, which helped fund a nineteen-unit affordable housing complex that opened in 2019, the only such units built in Cupertino in recent memory. Six of those units were set aside for homeless residents who were both senior citizens and disabled. There were 102 unhoused residents of Cupertino according to the last HUD-mandated count, though Kent believes there are at least several hundred street-based residents of Cupertino, and likely many more if you count all the people sleeping in cars and on couches.

Apple, which seems to prefer the white-glove approach to do-goodery, did not send emissaries to the camp on its front stoop. "You would think they would have reached out, considering we're literally right next door," said Troy. Apple declined my interview requests, but a spokeswoman informed me that fruit from the orchards at Apple Park is donated to a Cupertino food pantry. "They're the first company in the world to be worth over a trillion dollars," said Troy. "But have they done a single thing to help us? Lift a finger? Come ask us anything? No. All they see is a nuisance."

For obvious reasons, most unhoused people prefer to camp out of sight. Many of the folks spread along Wolfe Road had been hiding in the bushes around Cupertino for years. One haunt was the bushes around Vallco, a long-dead shopping mall across the highway from Apple Park, which is in the midst of a $4 billion reincarnation into a hybrid condo-office complex with a twenty-nine-acre rooftop park, billed as the world's largest. The Vallco security guards played a game of Whac-A-Mole with the campers—every time they settled into a new spot, a phone call to the sheriff's office was placed. A notice to vacate would be posted, giving the campers the standard seventy-two hours to move. Then the cycle would begin again.

Kent's plan to move onto the sidewalk sprang from frustration and desperation, but it quickly evolved into a scheme to change the power dynamics of the neighborhood. He realized that being in the public eye conferred political leverage, and he moved to capitalize on it. "We knew we were going to be out there in the spotlight," he told me, "but at this point we didn't give a fuck."

Under the glare of public scrutiny, the group's bonds deepened. Jen built a communal patio with soft nighttime lighting and a screened-in shade canopy, a dumpster-dived version of what you'd find at a seaside resort. Dave dumpster-dived some white boards and began facilitating informal meetings for the campers to plot a PR strategy. Troy was in charge of outreach. Kent put up a bulletin board for the display of important documents, such as planning department maps showing that the camp was confined to public property and printouts of their communications with government officials. With all the high-minded citizens coming by, the campers had more food and clothing than they could use, but they wanted something beyond token efforts to make them more comfortable in their misery. They were not interested in a PR-friendly handout, or vague plans—they wanted concrete action, and they wanted to engage with the process, to co-create it. To do so would require pulling back the veil between the haves and the have-nots in Cupertino, and having old-fashioned, messy, time-consuming human interactions. This, however, is not what "helping the homeless" normally looks like.

They had a couple demands: an end to the Whac-A-Mole eviction game and a pathway to permanent housing. "We're making a stand," Troy told me on a Saturday afternoon about eight months into the occupation. Throughout that spring and summer the group had held productive conversations with local politicians, city officials, advocacy groups, the sheriff's office—but not Apple. Surely the company could spare some six-figure change to help its unhoused neighbors get back on their feet. "There's so much money here," said Troy, who sees Apple's lack of engagement in existential terms. "Greed has destroyed countless civilizations—the Romans, the Egyptians, the Greeks. That's what's going to destroy our society. It's disgusting."

I set up a Zoom call with Deborah Feng, Cupertino's city manager and point person on homelessness, who was in regular communication with the city's biggest taxpayer and had invited them to participate in figuring out what to do with the elephant on their doorstep. But Apple does not engage with city staff around homelessness and housing—"ever," said Feng, visibly annoyed. "They haven't come to me with a solution. I'm really open." Having worked in public service throughout the Valley, she wasn't entirely surprised. "Google's not any different," said Feng.

Like many Silicon Valley jurisdictions, Cupertino's city council is dominated by NIMBYs—not-in-my-backyard types—who have strenuously resisted large new housing developments. NIMBYs tend to be older, securely housed folks who got into the market when it was more affordable, raised their kids, and watched their nest eggs balloon in proportion to home values. The YIMBY minority—the folks saying YES! to high-density development in their backyards—tends to be on the other end of the housing stick: younger folks trying to get into the market, for whom decades of ballooning real estate values are a burden, not a boon.

NIMBYs tend to react to any new construction as a threat to their "quality of life" and claim it will bring traffic and change "neighborhood character" for the worse. They can come across as clinging to some sort of 1950s suburban utopia, a farcical and historically racist idea when one's suburb has become subsumed by a diverse twenty-first-century metropolis. Cupertino's mayor, Steven Scharf, an engineer whose LinkedIn profile claims he was responsible for "key design wins at Intel, Compaq, HP, IBM, and Dell," is of the Valley's boomer vintage, and an avowed NIMBY. At his State of the City address in 2019, he said that Cupertino should build a wall around itself and make San José, a much denser city with large communities of low-wage immigrant workers, pay for it. Scharf said he was joking about the wall, but serious about keeping San José's apartment complexes, which thrum with low-income immigrants, from penetrating his city's genteel streets.

The redevelopment of Vallco, the old shopping mall at one end of the camp, is Cupertino's ultimate NIMBY-YIMBY battleground. The $4 billion plan calls for 2,400 units of housing, half of them "affordable"—an earth-shattering number in a city whose last subsidized housing development consisted of nineteen units. But the office space in the development will result in roughly two and a half times as many jobs as housing units, further upsetting the city's skewed housing-to-jobs ratio. A group called YIMBY Action lobbied for more residential units in the proposal, and for a higher percentage at below-market rates. Better Cupertino, a NIMBY group aligned with the city council, filed a lawsuit to stop construction in 2018. In the midst of the kerfuffle, the city fired its city attorney, who then sued, successfully, claiming he had been let go for voicing concerns about the project. Ray Wang, a Better Cupertino member who is also the chair of Cupertino's planning commission, got into it with housing activists on Nextdoor.com: It's time to "save the suburbs from an onslaught of anarchists and YIMBY neoliberal fascists," he wrote.

The campers became a pawn in the fight. For the YIMBYs, they were a symbol of why high-density housing was needed in Cupertino. For the NIMBYs, their presence was a convenient impediment to the Vallco redevelopment, which the courts had allowed to resume—a few months after the pandemic began, a notice was posted at the camp, saying that they had to go because the sidewalk along which they resided needed to be torn out as part of the construction project. The city had already threatened to tear down the camp shortly after it appeared in early spring—a plan thwarted by CDC guidelines stating that unhoused folks should be allowed to shelter in place like everyone else—but the Vallco construction project gave them the necessary political cover to proceed with the sweep. The campers were an impediment to progress! Ironically, they were holding up the construction of 1,200 units of affordable housing. Not that *they* could afford it.

Around this time, Jim Moore, a retired IBM marketing executive, began frequenting the camp. Moore was part of the NIMBY group Better Cupertino. He began advocating at city hall for the campers, whose presence serendipitously aligned with his antidevelopment interests. Moore and his Better Cupertino buddies looked into the construction permit for the sidewalk where the camp was located and determined that it actually pertained to the sidewalk on the other side of Wolfe Road. "The city said they had to vacate because they'd given the property owner permission to work there," Moore told me, "which turned out to be completely and utterly false."

Moore offered to pay for a portable toilet and hand-washing station to be installed and maintained at the camp. City officials said this was not possible because there wasn't space for toilet-pumping trucks to safely park. He compiled photos and other documentation to prove that there was indeed room. "There was a lot of pushback with no evidence to support it," said Moore. After several weeks of pressure, the city relented, installing the equipment on its own dime, along with trash bins that were emptied weekly by the sanitation department. The camp began to feel more permanent.

That summer, Feng, the city manager, formed a task force to figure out what to do about the camp. Camp residents were not invited; Moore and his NIMBY friends were shut out as well—local politicians skew NIMBY, but the bureaucrats do not. There were "lots of misinformation, lies, and stonewalling from the city," Moore told me. "They said we're working on it, but we can't tell you what we're working on." One of the task force's plans, it turned out, was to move the campers to the parking lot of a nearby shopping center. In September, a removal notice was posted at the camp, but the shopping center owners backed out at the last minute, and Feng called off the eviction. In October, a homeless services organization told the campers they had a space for them in a motel they'd converted into homeless housing. This too fell apart, leaving the campers feeling jerked around. "We lost a lot of trust," said Feng.

As the campers relayed the history of the Wolfe Road occupation, I kept getting tripped up on two words I could not compute: "Front Street." It's a term of art they tossed around like it was everyday English—as in "Kent's brave enough to do Front Street," as Dave said one day. It seemed to represent the philosophical underpinnings of their movement, but I struggled to comprehend.

"Front Street is an idea . . ." said Dave, searching for the words that the uninitiated would understand. "The police don't want people forming gangs or groups, and this is Silicon Valley so we have ten million cameras watching us. That's Front Street." I shook my head, still not following. "Front Street is when you're not hidden, so when the police show up, they can't do anything." I raised my eyebrows. "It's when all the public, the ones that hate you, the ones that like you, are *aaahhhhlllllllll* there," he said, drawing out the single syllable in a dramatic grunt.

Eventually I caught the drift. "Doing Front Street" means not hiding in the bushes. It means owning who you are, facing the world on the other side of the poverty veil. It means communicating to that world that your existence is as valuable as, say, Steve Jobs's. "Yes!" said Dave. "When I saw Kent started a camp in front of Apple"—on Front Street, metaphorically speaking—"I was like, this is an amazing opportunity. He's wanted to do this for years."

When Jen and I returned to the camp after lunch one day, we found Kent pacing the bike lane along the tents. He strutted up and down along the curb with his chest puffed out, a sort of territory-marking behavior—the fronting part of Front Street, you might say—that he does in addition to his daily cycling circuit. "You hungry?" said Jen to Kent, pushing her leftover chow mein into his hands.

The wind picked up, swirling the leaves that had started to fall from the ash trees that towered over the tents. It would soon be winter, which is not terribly cold in the Valley, but it is wet. You needed to have your tarps in order. "The rain is coming," said Jen. "I felt it this morning." The camp, however, would not make it to winter.

SWEPT

On a Friday afternoon that fall, I convinced Kent to let me buy him a cup of coffee. We met at Main Street Cupertino, the master-planned town center a block from the camp, a sort of Disney-fied wonderland with too-perfect landscaping and too much Botox. Completed in 2016, it is the closest thing Cupertino, a farm-killing suburb to its core, has to a downtown. Clustered around a central plaza is an assortment of bars, a juicery, a steakhouse, a pasta joint, a Middle Eastern restaurant with nine varieties of hummus, a Taiwanese herbal-jelly dessert place, a Korean corn-dog shop, a luxury apartment building, a Marriott hotel, a big data infrastructure optimization company, a company offering an enhanced haptics feedback experience, one of Apple's satellite office buildings, and a group workout gym, where people strap on branded heart-rate monitors and observe each other's performance metrics on screens mounted to the wall, while striving to accumulate "splat" points.

There's also a Starbucks, where Kent is a regular, though not a very welcome one. He waited outside while I went in. When I returned with the drinks, he was reclining on a bench in the sun as two security guards hovered around him, informing him, with a notable air of embarrassment, that he must leave the premises. Realizing what was going down, I decided to get testy.

"He's loitering," said one of the guards when I began to intervene.

"He's sitting on a bench!" I said, loudly. "Is this not a bench meant for people to sit on? Why can other people sit here, but not him?" Shoppers' heads turned.

"People aren't allowed to play amplified music here," said the other guard. Kent was with his bike, to which he'd mounted a Bluetooth speaker, which was nearly always blasting. Music is a protective bubble that surrounds him wherever he pedals. It's how he stays in his zone. Metal, opera, disco—Kent loves it all.

"I turned off the music," he said, quietly, looking equal parts amused and exasperated.

"He turned off the music!" I yelled.

"He's been asked to leave and not come back today," said the first guard, who then stepped away to confer with his walkie-talkie. He came back a minute later. "There's been complaints," he said. "It's not my decision, I'm just following orders." Kent got up, slowly, without a word, and walked his bike to the edge of the development on Stevens Creek Boulevard. Upon reaching the sidewalk, he cranked the stereo.

Kent gave up gas-powered biking long ago, but he was still a performer. By the time I'd met him, he'd retired his routine of shouting obscenities at Steve Jobs from his bike; instead, he spent his days cycling a circuit around Apple, Vallco, and Main Street Cupertino, putting on a show with his pedal-powered bike. He danced with it; he danced on it; he let people think whatever they wanted about the mask he sometimes wore, while letting his self-confidence blossom behind it. "I love to wake up in the morning, put on that mask, and go right out in rush hour traffic, dancing down the street with my bike," said Kent. "I don't trip about it. There's times I got one butt cheek hanging out—but I'm sweating, with a smile on my face, singing to a song. It's what I do. It makes me alive."

In his motocross days, Kent performed for the adrenaline and adoration; now his shows are more like a spiritual practice. He wants to be seen—not in order to be praised, but to prove something to himself. Like the choice to pitch his tent next door to the Spaceship, his neighborhood cruises are an exercise in taking up space. Front Street! "It's a way to test myself, to learn to be comfortable in my own skin," said Kent. "The more I do it, the happier I am with myself."

For Kent, Front Street is about dignity. He'd found his, and was working to spread that to the collective of the camp. He was constantly cleaning up the place to keep it as presentable as possible and acted as a gatekeeper for who was allowed to join the community—Kent maintains high standards and doesn't tolerate folks who cheat, lie, steal, and cause drama, at least not to the degree found in some camps. As we spoke, he listed the names of the campmates he's closest to—Troy, Dave, Jen, Smurf—and began to cry. "If I became president of the world tomorrow, they'd be . . ." he trailed off, too choked up to finish the thought. "I'm proud of them," he said, after he recovered. "It's hard to be here on Front Street with all the pressure, the media, the people who are angry at us." The community they'd built was the reward for his life-or-death mission to recover his sense of self-worth and well-being. "I've been alone on my deathbed and I don't think anybody deserves that," said Kent. "That's what changed me. I just want to be remembered a little bit by people."

One week before the first pandemic Thanksgiving, Jim Moore, the NIMBY from Better Cupertino, walked down Wolfe Road to deliver some news. He had just learned that the city had a plan to remove the camp—they had arranged for the residents to stay at a motel in San José for six months—on which the city council would be voting at their virtual meeting that evening. Moore distributed the link to the meeting and urged the campers to speak up during the public comment period before the vote. The folks on Wolfe Road were about to find out what policymakers' version of The Fix looked like.

At six o'clock, I logged on to the city's Zoom portal in my apartment and waited for the meeting to begin. A shot of city hall appeared on the screen as a jazzy soundtrack played. The mayor appeared with puffy eyes and a bad camera angle. "Madam City Clerk, can you do the roll call, please?" he asked. The clerk, a woman with crimson lipstick, a black turtleneck, and dark hair pulled back in an aristocratic bun, determined that a quorum of councillors was present.

City Manager Feng, who was overseeing the removal plan, explained to the councillors that normally eviction notices are posted at camps seventy-two hours before the sheriff arrives to do the dirty work. But given the upcoming holiday, she said they would allow the campers two weeks to get out. "Thanksgiving is next week and we know that Thanksgiving means a lot to everybody, whether they're housed or unhoused," she said. "So we decided to give them the time to"—she seemed to be considering her words carefully—"celebrate the holiday."

Finally, it was time for the public comment period. Only a handful of the campers had managed to log in to the meeting; Kent was not among them. Each would have three minutes to speak.

"Welcome, Troy," said the vice mayor, an unexpressive man sporting a black baseball cap and a sparse goatee. "I'm unmuting you now." A surreal moment followed as the raw reality of the camp penetrated the cushy bubble of the councillors in their homes.

"Hello, can you hear me?" said Troy. The whooshing of the traffic next to his tent was audible in the background. "I'm actually one of the residents here at the encampment," he said, rather forcefully. The mayor wrinkled his nose. A few tents down, Dave, Bobby, and Jason were huddled around a screen. "How you doing?" said Bobby, cheerfully, to the councillors, after the trio had been unmuted. "How are y'all?" said Jason.

The city's plan provided the "six months in a stable environment" that Troy asked for, but Dave didn't waste time pointing out the elephant in the Zoom room. "I hear a lot of you talking for us and I don't appreciate that. We have not been included in any of these conversations." He said that many of the campers were unlikely to accept the motel offer, including himself. "We're all very different," he said. "People have different needs." Dave suggested that the councillors come talk to the campers before voting on their plan. "I'd really like you guys to consider working directly with us," he said. "We are willing to talk to you. We're educated. We're very intelligent people. We're not violent."

Dave became increasingly impassioned as he spoke. "A lot of us are out here taking care of the people you lose." Without the support of the camp, "I'd probably be dead," he said. "There's really a lot to think about in this situation." The mayor took a swig from his mug. "It's a homeless encampment in front of the largest and most expensive building in—" The vice mayor hit the mute button. Dave's three minutes were up.

"Thank you, David," said the vice mayor.

The motion passed unanimously, and the next morning a notice to vacate was posted at each end of the camp. A man from a nonprofit group the city had contracted to carry out the relocation walked around with a clipboard asking people whether they wanted to move to the motel. Half accepted the offer.

City Manager Feng had anticipated that this might happen. The city was already setting up a new, sanctioned camp on a nearby side street, away from high-speed traffic. Anyone willing to move there would get a new tent and sleeping bag. Several local companies were chipping in to help pay for the motel and the new camp. The captains of the Spaceship up the road were not among them, however. Nonetheless, the company had no choice but to continue facing the issue—literally. The new camp was being set up in a small city-owned parking lot a few feet from one of Apple's off-campus office buildings, said Feng, just a block from the mothership. "Apple is not happy with me," she said. "But that's too bad."

Raining Solutions

Good news! There's a guy who's figured out The Fix! His name is Gavin Newsom and he's the governor of California. "I don't think homelessness can be solved—I know homelessness can be solved," said Newsom during his 2020 State of the State address. That remains to be seen, but what's certain is that voters have been polishing their pitchforks—housing affordability and homelessness were already the top electoral issues in the state when Newsom was elected in 2018, but by the time the pandemic hit, Californians were pissed. Two-thirds thought he was handling the issue poorly, an opening for conservatives who mounted a recall campaign centered on perceptions that he was soft on the issue.

In deep-blue California, it can be hard to imagine one of the nation's most prominent Democrats being kicked out in the middle of his term. But it wasn't out of the question—just ask San Francisco's former district attorney. He'd been elected in 2019 with a mandate to pursue incarceration alternatives for crimes like sleeping on the street, urinating in public, and drug possession. A couple years later he was recalled from office by a harsh ten-point margin.

"The future happens here first," according to Newsom, who repeats the line like a mantra in his public appearances. It's his spin on an everlasting California trope, in which the state is a progressive trendsetter, whether in the legalization of pot, adoption of electric vehicles, or the kombucha-and-kale-juice lifestyle. In this mythology, the internet revolution could have only happened here, where minds are sufficiently free and open to imagine things like search engines and phones that double as computers (the Valley's military history is conveniently omitted in the myth). Deeply embedded in the state's self-image is the notion of tolerance—freaks and weirdos are celebrated, and people of all races and gender expressions hold hands under the same happy rainbow. The love extends, in theory, to the less fortunate among us. California's social safety net is the envy of liberals across the country, though for many conservatives it explains why there are so many people living on the street—not only are we soft on drugs and crime, we let the tent city degenerates suckle to excess from Uncle Sam's teat.

California has always exported its trends, for better or worse, and the rise of housing costs and income inequality nationally suggests that its tent cities are coming for the rest of America. Given the attitude of the state's housed residents toward the issue, it seems unlikely that tolerance for the tenters will follow. The veneer on California's embrace of diverse lifestyles has always been as thin as a sheet of dollar bills, but as the pandemic ground on, and camps became larger and more visible than ever, along with the ground cover of trash, rats, and hypodermic needles that often accompany them, the fear and loathing could scarcely be concealed. One could nearly see the images of neighborhood blight swirling around with stats on urban crime in the state's collective psyche, a cloud of delusion that spread across the country.

Newsom's most outspoken Republican opponent in the recall election was Michael Shellenberger, the author of *San Fransicko: Why Progressives Ruin Cities*, whose candidacy drew national attention for its hard-line, laser-focused take on homelessness. The book includes fun facts like the 20,933 complaints about feces in the streets that San Franciscans made to a municipal hotline in 2018. Shellenberger also explored the urine crisis: Lampposts are falling over, he says, because of the pee corroding their metal bases. Shellenberger assumes homeless people are to blame, but it doesn't take much scrutiny to come up with a more likely explanation for the prevalence of both number one and number two on San Francisco streets: dogs. There are an estimated 150,000 canines in the city, roughly ten times the number of unhoused residents.

Shellenberger pushes against the prevailing theory for getting people off the streets, known as "housing first," which says that accepting mental health and addiction treatment should not be prerequisites for receiving housing assistance, as it often has been in the past. Many studies have found that compared to "high-barrier" housing programs, participants in those modeled on the low-barrier housing-first approach are more likely to stay housed than end up back on the street. The idea is that as long as a person is dealing with the daily stress of living outdoors, they're unlikely to have much success dealing with the issues keeping them there. Instead, once they have the stability of a home, it's hoped that they will avail themselves of the "wraparound services" provided—drug counseling, group therapy, job training, and so on. Shellenberger sees this as "excessive compassion" and "pathological altruism."

Rather than risk too much compassion, he proposes to use force. "We can get the national guard involved if we need to," he told Joe Rogan, on his podcast, about how he would handle homelessness if elected governor. "If you don't kidnap them, it's very difficult," said Rogan. "I'm not saying you should kidnap people," he quickly added, as Shellenberger chuckled. "But if you don't physically force them into doing something, these people . . ." Here he trailed off and sighed. Shellenberger told him that his version of The Fix revolved around three *P*'s: "More police, more psychiatry, and more probation."

The housing-first approach, though well intended and backed with billions of dollars, hasn't reduced the homeless population in California. "Giving people cheap apartments in some of the most expensive cities on the planet . . . and letting them do drugs there is not necessarily a political winner," said *The Atlantic*, in a profile on Shellenberger titled "The Revolt Against Homelessness," noting that "the problem with housing first is that actually implementing it strains even Californians' progressiveness." Conservative pundits often rant about the "failure of housing first" in California and other blue states, but their actual critique is not that the strategy is ineffective at stabilizing the lives of unhoused people—it's that the government should spend less on subsidized housing and poor people should depend less on the government. The so-called failure of housing first in California boils down to two facts that have little to do with the strategy itself. One: It's extraordinarily expensive to build housing in the state (due to higher-than-average labor costs, heavy-handed zoning restrictions, and other layers of red tape and economic constraints that tend to be less thick in more conservative places). Two: For every person exiting homelessness, there's one or more entering it.

Shellenberger's rhetoric may be unmoored from the reality of homelessness, but it provided a blueprint for exploiting voter resentment about it. Liberal politicians learned to balance affordable housing love—the state's "landmark eviction moratorium," as the governor's office described it, strived to be bigger and better than the renter protections of other states—with the homeless hate that voters demanded. His campaign mantra on homelessness became that it was simply "unacceptable," which could be read two ways: as harm that we bore collective responsibility to repair, or a declaration that the issue would be resolved by any means necessary. The former preserved the veneer of compassion, while the latter spoke to those concerned about excessive compassion.

Newsom was not going to bring in the National Guard, but in the months before the election he pitched a plan to use legislative force to rid California streets of their most visible residents. He calls it CARE Court—note the compassionate branding—which stands for Community Assistance, Recovery, and Empowerment. In the fine print of all the care and empowerment is a system reminiscent of the old-fashioned warehousing approach to mental illness, which both Democrats and Republicans across the country seem intent on reviving. The governor's press release for the CARE Court was an extended oxymoron, in which forcing people to submit to substance abuse and mental health treatment is somehow made to sound like they're selecting a spa package. The program "offers," according to the release, "individualized interventions" called Care Plans, which are not only offered, it turns out, but "court ordered." And if "a participant cannot successfully complete" the program, the government has the option to force them into conservatorship. "We are leaning into conservatorships," said Newsom, who survived the recall.

To demonstrate his determination, Newsom sometimes shows up at encampment removals, raking up trash in front of the cameras. Media coverage of such stunts doesn't focus much on the important fact that the displaced campers will more than likely set up a new trash-strewn camp nearby. Nor do they question whether, given the lack of affordable housing, a more effective strategy for reducing blight might be to simply provide weekly trash bin service to encampments, just like housed people have.

One story I read was so nonsensical it would have been comical, had it not been so sad. It described the governor talking to an unhoused couple at a camp-side PR event with his entourage. The couple explained all the reasons they were better off in their camp than in a homeless shelter—such as the fact that local shelters didn't allow couples to stay together—and how being forced to move their camp destroyed the fragile stability they'd created there. "What you describe is that perverse dilemma," said Newsom, as workers threw their belongings in the trash. "You need that stability in order to then figure all the rest out. We're demanding you figure the rest out before you get the stability. It doesn't make any damn sense." The couple then "piled carts and said they'd move on and find a place to bed down a mile away." The governor "wished them luck," noted the reporter.

Newsom also paid a visit to Wood Street. One morning around 10:30, Monte's friend Theo was snoozing in his van when he awoke to a ruckus outside. "There's all these clean-cut politicians milling around my van fifteen feet away," he told me, as we sat under a tarp at Theo's spot in the Art and Music Camp, one of the sub-camps within the larger Wood Street community. Newsom was there with a posse of advisors, as well as senior officials from Caltrans, the state transportation agency, who were planning a massive sweep of the camp. "How convenient!" said Theo, a hyper-intellectual person with an ironic bearing, who manages to be both comical and deeply serious at the same time. "Caltrans has bully power over us and who put them in charge of our lives? The governor! I could not buy this access with any amount of money in the world. And God puts them right in our lap."

Oakland's Wood Street was politically organized to an extent far beyond Wolfe Camp or the Crash Zone, and outspoken residents like Theo nimbly delivered their pitch whenever the opportunity arose. "I gave him our talking points," said Theo. "I said, dude, if you're gonna sit in meetings with your friends and make decisions about our lives, you need to include representatives from our community at those meetings." Theo began shouting as he relayed the exchange to me. "No evictions, dear governor!" he said. "A moratorium, please, on every fucking displacement or sweep in the state—right now!"

Monte, Theo, and their comrades view their resistance to sweeps as part of a much bigger mission, a revolution bubbling up from the most marginalized communities in America. We are "living the answer to homelessness, and to the social ennui of a materialistic culture in its death throes," said Theo, who views the institutionalized forms of shelter that the government offers not as an interim step toward permanent housing, as their boosters insist, but a stepping stone in the revolving door between prisons and camps. "You tear people out of their network of support. You make it impossible for them to be politically relevant. You isolate them in an internment camp, and then you have a feeder pool into the for-profit slave labor system in the penal colony of California."

STALKING KENT

A couple days after that fateful Cupertino city council meeting I'd flown back to North Carolina, but the following summer I returned with a one-way ticket. I hadn't managed to dig myself out of rock bottom; I'd just spun my wheels in the mud there, like a hamster in hell.

On my return to the Valley, I landed at the Mountain View Airbnb of a guy who oversees the machine-learning data team at Waymo, Google's self-driving car subsidiary. One quirk of living in the Bay Area is that you get used to seeing Waymo vehicles—a Jaguar model covered in Jetsons-esque sensors, including a large button-shaped one that spins on the roof—maneuvering through traffic. My host had little in the way of décor on the walls, other than a large video screen that rotated through images of pleasing natural landscapes, and a series of placards with nauseating tech culture aphorisms, such as "No pressure, no diamonds" and "Never look back. It will hurt your neck." The home was well endowed in the gadget department, however, with a robotic vacuum, smart locks, a smart trash can, a smart showerhead, and a smart soap dispenser. I scarcely saw my host and wondered if he was in fact a robot.

As I wandered downtown Mountain View on my first evening, looking for a place to eat, a delivery robot suddenly appeared in my path; apparently this trash-can-sized contraption on wheels held takeout in its payload. I'd never had such an encounter. As I stared at it coming toward me, the hair on my neck rose, while my heart simultaneously sank. It appeared that the newly minted profession of app-based delivery workers would be short-lived, at least in its humanoid form.

I felt like I fit in more with the campers than the rest of the Valley community. I tried to reconnect with my friends from Wolfe Road, but without a fixed location at which to show up and find them, it was a slow process—unhoused folks often don't keep the same number for long and tend to not be super diligent about returning calls, texts, and emails. I went to the site in front of the Apple building the city had designated for them after the eviction, but there was no sign of any homeless people; apparently the new camp had not taken root. I didn't know where the motel was that some of them had agreed to move to, or if they were still there—seven months had passed since the day the city had promised them six months of lodging. I called the number I had for Kent, hoping he could fill me in.

"Hello," he said.

"Hey, Kent!" I said. "It's Brian. The journalist."

"Ho . . . hold on a minute," he stammered, as though he was in the middle of something.

I waited. And waited. "Kent, are you there? Hello?" Nothing. Eventually the silence went to voicemail, and I realized that all along I'd been listening to Kent's very extended, very mischievous voicemail greeting. I could see him smiling somewhere—he enjoys being off-matrix, and is entertained by the way this positions him socially to those who are not.

While searching for Kent and his Wolves, I dug deeper into the homeless-industrial complex to better understand the reality of existing solutions. The ecosystem of aid for the unhoused entails an extraordinarily convoluted bureaucracy, but the broad strokes are fairly straightforward: move the higher-functioning folks from the street into subsidized apartments, while shepherding the lower-functioning ones into "permanent supportive housing" facilities, where their addictions and afflictions can be ministered to by professionals. The perennial problem is that the number of unhoused folks exceeds the units available in either category, and the pace of people entering homelessness exceeds the pace of construction of units designed to house them.

Wait-lists for subsidized housing are so long that people grow old waiting for their turn at the top. In 2017, the mayor of Los Angeles held a press conference to celebrate the reopening of the wait-list—after thirteen years—for his city's Section 8 vouchers, part of a federally funded program administered by local governments. In 2006, during a rare opening of the Section 8 wait-list in Santa Clara County, where the bulk of the Valley's tech campuses are located, sixty thousand applicants were added in five days before it closed again for fifteen years. Being on a wait-list does not guarantee that you will receive an apartment. Wait-lists for Section 8 vouchers typically place one into a lottery, from which names are drawn as units become available—usually a meager trickle. In 2018, for instance, San José's mayor announced a plan to build "at least" ten thousand affordable units by 2022. Only 901 were built.

In the absence of permanent housing, both higher- and lower-functioning folks are being shepherded into temporary shelter. These come in a variety of flavors: traditional ("congregate" shelters where you sleep in a room of cots or bunk beds, before being kicked out each morning), plus new recipes, like pop-up trailer parks, tiny homes, and low-budget motels converted into dorms for the unhoused. Common to all of these are rules that infringe on residents' basic freedoms, such as the ability to cook, decorate, keep pets, have guests, accumulate possessions, and come and go when they please. Which is why the majority of unhoused folks are unwilling to leave their home on the streets for one of these not-very-homey places.

When HUD sent a team of researchers to San José to examine how the city deals with camps, they found that only one in five people displaced in sweeps were willing to accept the temporary shelter they were offered. Based on my own conversations, that figure sounds rather high. I've found that those most likely to accept shelter are those not yet embedded in camp culture, whether because they are newly unhoused, or because they're experiencing a more solitary version of homelessness, such as sleeping in bus stops and doorways. But once you build a home in a camp, where you have at least some sense of self-determination, there's little motivation to give it up for a place where you likely will not, even if that place has running water and electricity.

Plus, temporary shelter is temporary—it generally comes with term limits, typically three months to a year, during which social workers will attempt to place you in some form of permanent housing. And since that's pretty much like winning the lottery, most residents of temporary shelter eventually get booted back to the street, where they must rebuild their home from scratch. The number who transition from temporary housing directly to permanent housing in California ranges from roughly 20 to 50 percent, depending on the region.

The rise of vehicle-dwelling, by some accounts the fastest-growing genre of homelessness, has led to a new solution on offer at the homeless-industrial complex: "safe" lots. In these sanctioned vehicular camping areas, the rules against overnight parking—the bane of vanlifers—are suspended. Safe lots are typically run by nonprofits, under the direction of local government, and are heavily regulated. You can't just walk in, but I managed to convince the organization overseeing several safe lots in Mountain View—they refer to it as the Lots of Love program—to give me a peek.

It was a chilly November evening when I pulled into an oceanic expanse of asphalt at the edge of the Google campus, where a couple dozen RVs huddled at one end, like a fleet of refugees coming ashore. The improvised RV park boasted a view of Google's newest and most architecturally whimsical office complex, whose roofline looks like a bunch of circus tents stitched together. Otherwise, the scene was pretty bleak: blue port-a-potty, asphalt, more asphalt. The Lots of Love rules preclude patio furniture, play equipment, outdoor rugs, or anything else that might take the edge off. You can sleep without fear of a policeman banging on your door at three in the morning, but unlike the camps I was spending time in, it didn't feel like a place to live.

So I was surprised at how upbeat the residents were about the place. "I feel like a king here," said Abraham, who'd come to Silicon Valley forty years ago from Mexico. In 2007, after working in construction for decades, he'd saved enough to purchase a home. Then the Great Recession arrived; Abraham's work dried up, and the bank foreclosed on the home. He and his wife rented a series of rooms in other people's houses, often doing cleaning and yardwork for the owners to compensate for the portion of the rent they could not afford. Compared to that arrangement, vanlife sounded like liberation—they own their own home once again, and thanks to Lots of Love they can legally park it. Never mind that Abraham and his wife shared 120 square feet with their daughter, two grandchildren, and two dogs. Before the lot opened up, they'd parked with a herd of RVs near Stanford, where Abraham's daughter works as a medical assistant, a solid middle-class job that allows the family to afford their regal lifestyle.

"As long as you follow the rules, no one bothers you," said Abraham, a proud rule-follower, as we shivered in the fluorescent glare of a towering lamppost, a circle of light that dissolved into the merged blackness of asphalt and sky.

Some of the lot's residents were shockingly well off. Jeff, a man with a short white ponytail hanging from the back of his baseball cap, said he ran a thriving construction business with twenty employees. He declined to share his income but assured me that he made "good money." He was there, he said, because he spent his life savings putting his daughter through a top-notch university. He'd moved into a trailer four years back to replenish his savings before he retired, which would have been impossible with his previous mortgage.

Jeff saw Lots of Love as a way out of the housing crisis. "It's not bad," he said. "They should do more of these. Google and Facebook should buy up some property, the city should loosen the regulations and let this happen."

His neighbor, Rouel, a tall Venezuelan man who had recently retired from Lockheed with an enviable pension, shared his enthusiasm. A research scientist who studied "thin-film, single-crystal semiconductors," Rouel envisioned vast new neighborhoods across the underutilized parking lots scattered among the tech campuses along the South Bay waterfront, with areas designated for both tents and RVs. These would be like urban campgrounds, he said, with electricity, water, and garbage collection provided by the local municipalities. In a letter he sent to Mountain View city councilors, Rouel wrote that the Valley's growing "homeless class" necessitated this "new type of neighborhood." Those who "think this is temporary, and look for temporary solutions," he concluded, "may be in denial."

"Is it not also important to address the economic system that has produced this situation?" I ventured. "Isn't that what ultimately needs to change?"

"Absolutely," said Jeff. "But that ain't gonna change." He said it a couple more times, as though I might have needed some help getting it through my idealistic noggin. "It's not gonna change." He shook his head slowly back and forth, giving me an incredulous and slightly hypnotic stare. "It's not gonna change. So you got to think of different ways to live within it. You adapt." I wasn't sure I wanted to adapt to living in a parking lot.

Rouel also agreed with my critique, but he too was resigned to the situation. "At least this way people won't be in tents on the street," he said. "It's something." That it is.

Over time I realized that the folks in sanctioned RV lots, at least high-barrier ones like Lots of Love, tend to be a different breed than those in self-organized camps. Such programs generally require a driver's license, registration, insurance, and a vehicle that is running and well kept, which the "chronically homeless" folks who have been on the streets for years, who generally have multiple layers of trauma, addiction, and mental illness, are often unable to muster. Safe lots are more geared to the newly minted, highest-functioning segments of the unhoused population who haven't yet habituated to camp culture and its inherently subversive nature. I've found that folks who *have* embraced camp culture are often incompatible with tightly controlled living situations like Lots of Love. They tend to be proud rule-*breakers*.

It was also telling that Abraham, Jeff, and Rouel, who had been preselected by my minder for interviews, had such glowing reviews of the parking lot—I have never met any other unhoused person who said the sort of things they said about safe lots, or any other government-regulated shelter.

I eventually found the Wolves. After many phone calls, emails, and Google searches, I learned that the motel rooms Cupertino officials had arranged for them were in a neighborhood on the outskirts of San José, not far from the Crash Zone. I didn't have the exact address, but I learned the street where many of the Wolves were now residing, and it wasn't difficult to find the motel, given the vibe of some of the people hanging out on the sidewalk in front of it. The folks living there came from all over the Valley. When I pulled up and inquired about Kent, the residents said, to my great disappointment, that he had recently moved on.

Formerly known as the Santa Clara Inn, the stucco motel had been rebranded as Casa de Novo by its new managers, Abode Services, one of several large homeless charities in the Valley. As temporary housing goes, Casa de Novo wasn't *too* jail-like, at least not in terms of outer appearances. There was a chill security guard, and I had to show my ID at the front desk to a disinterested employee who wrote down my name, the name of the person I was coming to visit, what time I came in, and what time I departed, and made it clear that no overnight guests were allowed.

It was also against the rules to cook, but that didn't stop anyone. On one of my first visits, I found Walter from Wolfe Camp, who invited me into his room for a burger prepared on his George Foreman electric grill. I was keenly aware that I was complicit in rule-breaking—getting caught with cooking paraphernalia is grounds for a write-up, said Walter, who left his door defiantly ajar, allowing incriminating and mouthwatering evidence to drift outside.

Lesser infractions could also result in a write-up, he said, such as if a guest visited one person's room and then visited another resident without first notifying the front desk person. You also weren't supposed to bring in additional furniture (they balked when Walter tried to bring in an ottoman to store clothes in), a fairly universal prohibition in homeless housing that's meant to prevent the clutter found in camps from developing in taxpayer-funded facilities. But he'd managed to clutter up his room just fine without importing furniture— mountain ranges of empty food containers, clothes, electronics, instruments, and God-knows-what-else had colonized nearly every surface, leaving no space for a guest to sit, and little in which to stand.

The parking lot, however, was barren, and after scarfing my burger I suggested we step outside. The asphalt could have easily been transformed into an inviting gathering area, as the U-shaped arrangement of the motel buildings enclosed it like a courtyard, shielding the space from the street noise. But there was no grilling allowed, no furniture for hanging out—no nothing, other than sitting on the curb and smoking cigarettes, which is what Walter was doing when a handful of other folks from Wolfe Road materialized.

Having gotten to know the tribe in the semiautonomous zone of the camp, it was a little discombobulating to see them living indoors. They seemed cleaner, more bored, less wild. But they were still rebellious. Roger, who seemed less scary than in Cupertino, appeared and got into a debate with Walter about who'd had the most write-ups.

"*I* got that," said Roger.

"No, *I* got it," said Walter. "I got the most violations, bro."

Bobby called out from the second-floor catwalk, lamenting his misplaced teeth. I thought that perhaps I'd misheard and that he'd lost his keys, but no, he clarified, "I lost my dentures." Smurf showed up, and soon a small crowd had formed. I asked how they liked the new digs compared to camp life.

"It's better than a tent," said Walter.

Everyone agreed on that point, and that the food situation sucked. Walter hadn't made his mom's Korean ribs since he left Wolfe Road—impossible on a twelve-inch-diameter electric grill. Troy, of bourbon-glazed pork-chop fame, explained that Abode pledged to provide food to the residents when they agreed to move in, but in practice, "it's not every day." Quality-wise, it was on the level of prison slop, he said, a cuisine many in the group have personal experience with. "I wouldn't feed that stuff to my dog," said Troy, who also has a George Foreman electric grill in his room, plus a portable range top and an air fryer. "I made spicy fried chicken last night," he said. "There's no way in hell I'm not cooking."

Everyone agreed that they'd given up a lot to be there, rather than on Front Street, including political power—their negotiating strength was diminished now that they were no longer blight on Apple's doorstep. "It's better than a tent," said Roger, "but I think we had a little more leverage on the street over there." It dawned on me that their activism had not changed the system, so much as provided them a winning lottery ticket to enter it.

"How are the wraparound services?" I asked, having read on Abode's website that these were provided to Casa de Novo residents. The gang was not impressed. "It's nothing but some donated food and clothes," said Troy, who had recently started working the graveyard shift for Frito-Lay, delivering potato chips. "They've got nothing to help us with our longer-term goals here."

"Charity my ass," said Walter. "Because of us, they got *hella* funding. They got their paychecks because of us."

I pointed out that the promised six months of lodging had passed, but no one in the parking lot knew where additional funding to extend their stay was coming from. And they seemed surprisingly unconcerned about their tenure.

"They're not going to kick us out because we'd go straight back to Cupertino, right in front of the same spot," Walter speculated.

"I'm thinking about going in front of Facebook," mused Roger, who was angry at the company for censoring him online. "I want to know why the hell they're deleting my chats."

I learned that several people had already been kicked out for bad behavior and had gone back to the streets, their location unknown.

Converted motels like Casa de Novo are a central prong in Newsom's plan. During the first months of the pandemic, the state paid for fifteen thousand vacant hotel rooms to be converted to socially distanced shelter spaces. This was branded Project Roomkey, which was soon rebranded as Project Homekey—a long-term plan to convert huge numbers of cheap motels into apartments for the homeless. This was one of the biggest line items in the $22.3 billion homeless and affordable housing budget the state approved in 2021—touted by the governor's office as a "historic" and "unprecedented" expenditure, it was ten times greater than any prior allocation, according to the press release. The state claimed this would fund forty-two thousand units of permanent supportive housing and 7,200 subsidized apartments, slated for "extremely low income" households, among other impressive-sounding promises.

$22.3 billion sounds like a lot until you realize that it can cost a million or more dollars to build one unit of affordable housing in California. Those forty-two thousand units equate to about a quarter of the state's official (vastly undercounted) homeless population, and if history is any indication, the number of units provided will be fewer, and will take longer to build, than anticipated. The 7,200 extremely low-income units equate to less than 0.1 percent of households that qualify as ELI, as it's known in the affordable housing trade. In 2020, there were 972,083 more ELI households in the state than there were ELI units.

Newsom's billions fund a few patches on the tattered net meant to keep low-wage workers from falling into homelessness, but the cash does little to address root causes: low-density zoning, decades of NIMBYism, and most especially, stagnant wages at the bottom of the income pyramid, coupled with historic and unprecedented wealth accumulation at the top. In the first two decades of the millennium, rents in California rose 38 percent, but renter income grew by only 7 percent.

That gap has led to an epically weird situation in the affordable housing realm, which I discovered when I rang up an old friend in Santa Cruz. In the decade since I'd last seen her, she'd established a thriving psychotherapy practice, and with her success, she could finally afford to buy a home, or so I thought. She filled me in on all the giddy details of the cabinets and backsplashes, as well as the terms of the financing—it was a very modest place, she said, but even so, she wouldn't have been able to swing it had it not been part of an affordable housing program.

"Wait, hold up!" I said. "*You* qualify for affordable housing?"

Turns out I did, too, along with many of our middle-income peers, and a growing segment of what would ordinarily be considered the upper middle class. Now that market-rate housing in the Bay Area is a luxury item, many of the roughly two thousand units of so-called affordable housing built in the region each year are occupied by professionals, many of them making six figures. In Santa Clara County, where the bulk of Valley firms are found, households earning up to $266,880 qualify for assistance.

Shortly after moving to Cupertino I met a housing activist whose family lived in a subsidized home. "My husband makes really good money," she said. "$100,000 per year is considered poor in this area." Another housing activist I met told me her husband was the head of respiratory therapy at a local hospital, a job he'd held for eighteen years. I remarked that as someone overseeing the place COVID patients go to have tubes stuck down their throat so they don't choke to death on their own phlegm, I assumed he was well compensated for his work. "We're not in a dire situation," she said. But they are on the waiting list for affordable housing in Palo Alto and have been for nearly a decade. "None has been built, so it's almost a laughable thing at this point," she said.

That upper bracket of affordable housing, needed to keep the professional class solvent, is populated by folks with so-called moderate incomes (up to 120 percent of the area median income, or AMI). This limits resources that can funnel down into low-income (up to 80 percent AMI), very low-income (up to 50 percent AMI), and extremely low-income (up to 30 percent AMI) housing. ELI units—needed to house the masses mowing lawns, cleaning toilets, and preparing chopped salads for the securely housed class—compose roughly one in ten subsidized units in California. All of which explains why those at the bottom of the pyramid are increasingly found living in RVs, cars, and tents, rather than in so-called affordable housing.

I learned from the folks at Casa de Novo that while I was away in North Carolina, the Wolfe women, Yesenia and Jen, had received a blessing from the gods: apartments of their own. As did a couple of the camp's senior citizens—including Kent! But no one knew his new address, other than that it was somewhere on Leigh Avenue. After a little Googling, I discovered that Abode operated a brand-new senior housing facility on Leigh Avenue—presumably the spot.

I tried punching his name into the shiny new intercom outside the front door of the building, but a guy walking by told me it had never been set up. I banged on the door until a security guard came out, but he said visitors were only allowed in the building in the company of residents, and that, no, he could not go tell Kent that I was here to see him. I once again tried calling him, but apparently he'd given up his number. *"Hola?"* said the new owner. Walter told me that Kent had joined Facebook, so I tried messaging him there—crickets.

One day I chatted up a resident named Alfred, who was working on his truck out front, and asked if he knew Kent. "Oh," he said. "You mean that guy who's always on his bike?"

"Yes!" I said.

He didn't know which apartment was Kent's and didn't seem too keen on the idea of accompanying me into the building to track him down. "It's like jail," said Alfred, who used to live in the Jungle and was thinking about fixing up his old cabin by the creek there as a "kick-back spot" for when he needs to get away from the tyranny of permanent supportive housing and the tentacles of its wraparound services.

The more I failed at finding Kent, the more I wanted to find him. I became a fixture on the sidewalk in front of the Leigh Avenue Senior Apartments, where I would sit in my car as often as possible, hoping to catch him coming or going. I'd often visit Rudy at the Crash Zone, swing by Casa de Novo, and then park in front of Kent's place for a while, killing time by returning emails and researching the homeless-industrial complex on my phone. Sometimes I'd check his Facebook account to see if he'd posted anything new. His first-ever post, a photo of himself in the Guy Fawkes mask at Casa de Novo, had been that winter. This was followed by a photo of just his chest and torso, shirt open, his tanned skin glistening with sweat. That spring, he posted a photo of a young freckled boy with a crew cut—himself, I assumed, looking like he'd just walked off the set of *Leave It to Beaver*, earnest and innocent. "I will always miss these times," he wrote. "I was the baby. The youngest. For a brief time I was well-loved and protected."

I could see from his Facebook feed that he'd moved into the apartment the week before I arrived back in California. In a video tour he'd posted of the yet-to-be-furnished space, I saw his balcony, bathtub, and walk-in closet. "It's mine," he said, without emotion, at the end. A couple days later he wrote: "I got a brand-new home 48 hours ago. Still not one person has come by." Over the next couple weeks, he posted nearly one hundred times, ranting and raving about how awful Facebook is, how shallow our world is, how annoying online dating phishing schemes are, and how lonely he was, all peppered with bucket-loads of random raunch, like, "Turn on a blowtorch, stick it up your sphincter and enjoy."

In Kent's angst, I sensed desperation. His online vomit fest ended tenderly. "If you need somebody to love," he wrote, "I'll be somebody to love." His account then went dormant.

Kent's building is sleek and modern, with a rooftop courtyard and therapeutic gardens. As permanent supportive housing goes, it's A-class. On an October afternoon, I was sitting in my car in front of it when a guy with an unbuttoned dress shirt walked by.

"Kent!" I yelled.

A few minutes later I was touring his apartment. It wasn't clean, but it wasn't carpeted with detritus like many of the rooms at Casa de Novo. Kent still spent his days scavenging for recycling and dumpster scores, but now that he was housed, it was as much out of habit as necessity. He described to me in great detail the adventures involved in transporting his four flat-screen TVs, in various states of disrepair, to his new home by bike. He'd also taken up leisure activities, such as hitting golf balls into the ponds along the Los Gatos Creek Trail, which runs near his place. He'd gotten to know some of the folks who camp along it. "I'm kind of jealous because they've got these big old five-acre chunks of land along a beautiful creek," he said.

As Kent told me about his new life, he seemed lost somewhere between melancholy and ecstatic—he was more comfortable, less vital. He appreciated the apartment, but he missed his old life. "It was true freedom, one that this stripped me of," he said. "I'm grateful I have a place to shower and eat, but I've gotten soft." His torso was still tan, but no longer sculpted. "I've gained sixty pounds!" he said, exaggerating.

Abode touts itself as an organization based on the principles of housing first. But one thing I learned about housing first is that while they may not disqualify you for insobriety, they are highly selective about who gets keys to the limited number of subsidized apartments—it's generally the highest-functioning folks. And there is nothing to say that they won't kick you out—maybe not for drug use per se, but definitely for some of the behaviors associated with it. You have to have your life fairly together to remain in these places, which Kent fortunately does. But they're not for people who are going to invite their heroin addict friends to stay for weeks on end, light fires in the trash can, defecate in the communal lounge, run down the hallway naked, and punch the security guard, which are not unrealistic scenarios for what would happen if you stuck the lowest-functioning members of unhoused communities indoors. They will throw you right back out on the street, if not in jail or a psych ward.

The informal, peer-based social service systems of camps, however, can attenuate the behaviors of their most dysfunctional residents—not make them disappear, but contain them, take the edge off, reduce the harm. Policymakers and social service providers like to go on and on about housing first, housing first, housing first, like it's some sort of cure-all. But in my observation, it's a solution for only a tiny portion of the unhoused population. Homelessness is much more complex than that.

WORLD-BRIDGING

One of my first acts after settling in at the autonomous car guy's Airbnb was to join Hinge, a dating site that's supposed to be different than the others. I didn't want to *actually* date anyone; I was just curious, in an anthropological sense, to understand the online dating phenomenon. The first person I connected with was Samira. She turned out to be the only person I connected with—we're now married. The year after the worst year of my life would not be worse after all.

On her Hinge profile, Samira listed her occupation as "founder." Given my journalistic focus on the evils of Silicon Valley, I imagined a date of stimulating debate, if not provocative fodder, for my book. I didn't take it seriously; getting into a relationship with a "founder" was not something I envisioned for myself. As it turned out, the biotech company she'd founded hadn't yet attracted much investment, so she wasn't the sort of founder with lots of zeros on her net worth. And I was surprised to discover one thing we had in common: Samira was all over the tech-as-evil space. As a side project, she'd conceived and produced a major documentary film about the dark sides of her own industry—and the world's first genetically engineered babies, in particular.

We quickly settled into a life together, in which I had a foot in two worlds. I took Samira to camps, of which she was terrified—we visited Wood Street on our third date—and she took me to somewhat frightening parties where nearly everyone seemed to work for a household-name tech company, with salaries that allowed them to purchase those $3 million bungalows. I found it awkward in such circles to answer the question *So what do you do?* Upon hearing my reply, the conversation would often become strained. "My employer does not allow me to talk to the press," people would say, and slowly inch away.

Through Samira, I suddenly found myself in the backyards and back rooms of the tech world, observing what happens when the Valley's highly paid brains get together. There's clearly a disconnect between their way of thinking and the camp way of thinking. Still, the Valley's wealth and brainpower were an enormous resource—if only it could be hitched to solutions that actually worked.

I met a couple with high-level positions at Google, who were fortunate enough to live in walking distance from work—at one of the Valley's last remaining mobile home parks, Santiago Villa, which against all odds has held out on a tiny slice of real estate surrounded by the Google campus. Santiago Villa is the only residential community in the neighborhood, unless you count Lots of Love, which is a few blocks away, and the RV dwellers parked on the street. When Santiago Villa opened in the sixties, it was intended as a low-income community for seniors. That it exists at all today feels like evidence of a benevolent God—one can imagine the real estate pressure bearing down on the place. The couple told me their combined salary is in the seven-figure range, but they bought their mobile home for $90,000. As a result, "we have more money than we can reasonably consume," said the husband.

They didn't want me to use their real names, said the husband, who I'll call Jack, "because one could easily vilify our position of being wealthy but using low-income solutions as either taking advantage of low-income solutions or reducing the supply of low-income solutions." He estimated that Google employees made up somewhere between a third to a half of Santiago Villa residents. When they first moved there in 2011, the monthly rent for the concrete pads where people park their mobile homes was around $850; when we spoke, in 2021, they said it was up to $2,500.

Jack works on a robot research program at Google geared toward a class of robots designed to replace low-wage service workers, like janitors and burger flippers. He seemed to sense what was going through my mind: Google's going to make a whole lot of money in the process of making low-wage workers homeless. "The current philosophy on the project I'm on is not so much about replacing people," he said, "it's actually about enabling and magnifying human capability." *Really*? I thought, trying not to say something rude. He wanted very much to convince me that these robots would result in increased prosperity for those at the bottom of the wage pyramid. "The low-skilled worker," he continued, would be empowered "to upskill through the robot. So José, who's flipping burgers today, all he needs to run the robot that flips burgers is the ability to know how to flip burgers. You can get the exact person with that exact skill set to begin teleoperating a robot, to train it and eventually to oversee it, just as José could oversee a line of burger flippers."

I sensed Jack's IQ far exceeded mine, but something about his spiel didn't add up. While upskilling might in theory result from his robot project, it seemed far more likely that a restaurant owner would hire a computer guy to manage the robots, or at least a restaurant manager—basically someone whose career trajectory is aligned with such things already—thus leaving José out of work. Jack admitted it was possible that all might not go according to plan: "If José has difficulty upskilling to teach other burger flippers, then yes, he may not be able to upskill."

He also admitted the obvious fact that even if José stayed on to oversee the robots, the other burger flippers were definitely out of a job. But Jack had a solution for them, too. It would be just like when the tractor was invented, he said, and suddenly the masses toiling in the fields were liberated. "Now technology enables one farmer to do the work of one thousand farmers. That does mean lesser jobs in that particular domain. But that means that there's more capacity to do more high-value work elsewhere. So everyone who would have been a farmer now has decided to become a car mechanic. Or decided to work at a bank, or do something else that has higher value than harvesting seeds from the ground." This did not sound like a particularly realistic—or sincere—plan to mitigate the potential social upheaval catalyzed by the robots.

The couple was very into vanlife and dreamt of going fully nomadic. They sometimes worked while camping in one of their two RVs, which they occasionally parked at the office as well—"It's basically a really nice nap room," said Sheila. Jack said that part of the vision for the robots, which could be managed from anywhere in the world with a solid internet connection, was to allow their operators to experience the joys of remote work. Furthermore, the decoupling of workers from places would help ease the housing crunch—José could move back to Mexico, for instance, where his California wages could buy him a mansion. "That presumably should put less pressure on the housing market" back in California, said Jack.

Though I suppose if José was one of the many restaurant workers living in an RV on Crisanto Avenue in Mountain View, he would only be freeing up a parking spot, and the point would be moot. It would also be moot if instead of José managing the robots remotely from a mansion in Mexico, he was laid off because a guy in India was hired for the job. I'm not sure which scenario is more likely.

I still had one more question for the couple: Why, with their seven figures, were they choosing to live in a mobile home? Were they minimalists, averse to conspicuous displays of wealth? I eventually teased an answer out of them. It seemed to be, in part, a nerdy tendency toward maximizing efficiency. "There's certainly a stigma associated with both mobile homes and RVs that I thought was irrational," said Jack. "I didn't really care so much about what other people thought. I cared about having a nice place that was reasonably affordable." It was also a good investment, as he often tells his buddies who cashed in on their stock options to purchase a home, as is common in Valley circles. "The housing market has done very well, but the tech stocks have all done extraordinarily well," he said. "So they would actually have more wealth had they done this path. When I describe my living and working situation to my colleagues who are also in an extremely wealthy class, they often respond with envy."

The majority of unhoused people I've gotten to know are deeply skeptical of the standard remedies for homelessness, which can feel as though they're designed to get them out of sight and back into an economic system increasingly divided between those lunching on chopped salads in the glare of their computer screens and those making and delivering the salads. For many of the campers I've met, it's easier to imagine them pioneering a post-capitalism world order than taking a job at an Amazon warehouse.

As a half-joking experiment, I once opened an AI text-to-image program, called DreamStudio, and plugged in the term "homeless camp of the future." The crystal ball of this particular AI, I discovered, prophesies ethereal tentscapes bearing yurt- and tipi-esque aesthetics. In some of the images, the structures were situated along pleasingly meandering bodies of water; in others, the tents appeared as hipster accoutrements to New Age cityscapes. Overall, they evoked a harmonious integration of people, cities, and nature. Is this the evolution of cities in a coming Age of Enlightenment? I wish I was *that* optimistic.

As awkward as it is to admit it, I was moved by the images. They spoke to what I was hearing from the oracles in the camps: a version of The Fix based on the transformation of unintentional homelessness into an intentional alternative to the status quo. The vision for The Fix set forth by policymakers, in contrast, has more of an adult daycare vibe: institutionalized blandness for folks deemed incapable of regaining dignity, or simply too disenfranchised to demand it.

Tiny homes are the newest, sexiest trend in temporary shelter—in the eyes of their boosters, that is—but these are not the utopias you see on Instagram, with modernist touches and smart window shades that adjust themselves to maintain comfort while minimizing energy consumption. They have more of a barracks vibe, with rows of pre-fab sheds plunked on asphalt lots (some are literally garden sheds that can be found at Home Depot), where they are monitored by guards and often enclosed behind barbed wire fences. This sort of design thinking tends to be a turnoff for a demographic with a high rate of incarceration. When the city started building tiny homes on Wood Street, I managed to convince the security guard to let me take a peek inside the uninhabited structures, white-walled boxes whose sterility felt eerie next to the colorful chaos of the camp next door.

Tiny-home villages are an enchanting idea, one whose allusions to simplicity and communalism would seem to align it with The Fix that flows from the space between unintentional and intentional homelessness. But a tiny-home community designed and managed by its residents, which is basically what homeless camps are (some more intentionally than others), is night and day from the government-sponsored versions. The latter certainly take the freedom, and the fun, out of camping.

OXYMORONIC

There are those in the Valley who cling to the OG Valley paradigm—more tech is the answer—but there's a growing subculture in which it is fashionable to rail against the hand that makes your bank account fat. These folks are super interesting, both in terms of political analysis and psychoanalysis.

One day, while watching drone footage of the Apple Spaceship on YouTube, an image climbed up the right side of the screen, where the suggested videos live, and caught my eye. The YouTube algorithm apparently thought I'd enjoy a Doobie Decibel System jam session, livestreaming at that very moment. When

I clicked on the image—a drawing of a raccoon with a joint in its mouth—four masked and socially distanced musicians appeared on the screen playing a cover of "Let's Go Get Stoned." I was one of forty-two souls tuning in as they performed a set list of sixties anthems, including "Ticket to Ride" and "We Can Work It Out." They also have original tunes, like "Couple of Puffs," in which the singer croons, "No matter what, no matter when, on cannabis you can depend."

These lyrics were not penned by a bong-worshipping fifteen-year-old, but by an acquaintance of mine: Roger McNamee, a venture capital guru whose social network includes members of the Grateful Dead, the US House of Representatives, and the Valley elite. He was at the table when Larry Page and Sergey Brin presented Google's vision for world domination to a group of early investors, and later when Jeff Bezos pitched Amazon. Bill Gates was a co-investor in one of his early funds; he used to jam with Paul Allen, the other Microsoft founder, back in the early eighties. McNamee was a close advisor to Zuckerberg during Facebook's fledgling days, but when people started blaming the industry for the rise of the Orange-Faced One, he joined the bandwagon and published *Zucked*, a self-congratulatory treatise on how the Valley is destroying humanity.

Among his music world friends, who include T Bone Burnett and Bono, McNamee is known by his stage name, Chubby Wombat. His wealth is such that he's hired top-tier musicians, including a Jefferson Starship guitarist, for his backing band, with whom he has toured in the range of one hundred cities in a year. I was acquainted with him because I'd profiled him for *The New Yorker* back in the pre-pandemic years when the media decided the tech industry was very, very bad. The main thing I'd learned about Wombat is that he's a walking oxymoron. For instance: his band played for the Occupiers of Zuccotti Park in 2011, not long after his firm invested $210 million in Facebook. "Silicon Valley's most obnoxious, sanctimonious caviar socialists have found their poster boy," wrote *Gawker*, about Wombat, at the time.

Wombat is no anti-capitalist—he just likes it in moderation. To be fair, moderation to a venture capitalist like him might look different than it does to ordinary folks. But he's adamant that people like himself are best positioned to fix what the excesses of capitalism have created. "Who better to criticize than the people who participated in it?" he asked when I interviewed him over breakfast with a friend during his book tour. The friend, Jim Balsillie, a tech billionaire turned Valley-hater, told me that folks like him were important allies of more hardcore activists. "So when someone like Roger or me says, here's how we share this issue, it allows those people to be better heard. They can say, 'We're not raging socialists, because, look, there's a capitalist over there.'"

When I moved back to California, I called Wombat in hopes he could put me in touch with some of the Valley folks in his orbit to interview about homelessness. I was particularly thinking of Marc Benioff, the CEO of Salesforce, who Wombat has been friends with for more than thirty years. Benioff is of the breed who's not afraid to deride fellow billionaires for clinging to their riches, and he's made throwing money at homelessness part of his philanthropic brand. Wombat was restrained in his praise: "I think Marc's heart will always be in the right place, but his business interests have become juuuuust a taaaaad conflicted," he told me, belaboring the vowels for effect.

A couple years before the pandemic, Benioff had supported a ballot proposition in San Francisco to tax large companies in order to fund programs to help unhoused people get off the streets, which Jack Dorsey, the CEO of Twitter at the time, opposed—a stance Dorsey took to Twitter to express. Eight minutes later, Benioff bit back.

"Hi Jack. Thanks for the feedback," he wrote. "Which homeless programs in our city are you supporting?"

"Marc: you're distracting," Dorsey replied.

The proposition passed, buoyed by the $7.9 million that Benioff and his company, the biggest employer in San Francisco, donated to the campaign. The same year, at the ribbon-cutting for Salesforce Tower, the tallest building in the San Francisco skyline, Benioff promised to corral $200 million from his buddies "to get every homeless individual off these streets." He'd already put $66 million of his own toward the cause, including $30 million to fund a UCSF research center, which conducted the recent state census on homelessness and has pledged to study "the root causes of homelessness and identify evidence-based solutions to prevent and end homelessness." The center has been contracted by various government agencies to evaluate homeless services programs and has launched research programs on topics like basic income, rent subsidies, and vehicular homelessness. But in terms of root causes, they steer clear of calling attention to income inequality, the excesses of capitalism, or other hot-button issues.

Benioff may be rhetorically and financially engaged with the issue, but there's not even a whiff of a notion that the solution might lay beyond the reach of philanthropy. Nor can one imagine him putting the brakes on the train of profitability should a homeless camp happen to appear on the tracks, which is exactly the scenario that arose during the construction of Salesforce Tower and the adjacent Salesforce Transit Center. The old transit center on the site was home to an extensive community of unhoused people, who are conspicuously absent from the new, gentrified incarnation, with its lusciously landscaped rooftop, known as Salesforce Park, where Samira and I once strolled among the giant sea dahlias, dragon trees, and baboon flowers. Tiny, the *POOR Magazine* and Homefulness cofounder, was there when the transit center community was evicted, and she wrote an open letter to Benioff to let him know what it was like. "50,000-watt lights bored down on the vast ground floor of the terminal, a huge drill/crane whirred, grinded, and burrowed into the marble surface in a terrifying volcano of construction and destruction," she wrote. "At the strike of 11pm, the construction and Cal-trans workers made their final call. Everyone must leave. I was still coaxing José and Jack, and Annie and Miss Melissa and so many more to consider leaving before the cops and anti-social workers arrived on the scene to forcefully evict or incarcerate them. But most people had become paralyzed with absolute terror and were unable to move, much less speak or leave the building."

Tiny told Benioff that his $30 million donation seemed to her like a "$30 million public relations campaign." His research program? "It's more of what I call, About Us Without Us," she wrote. Tiny had been pushing tech companies to redistribute their wealth directly into the hands of poor people through a Tech Reparations Fund, administered by Homefulness, and she suggested in her letter that Benioff contribute to it instead. She did not receive a reply.

Tiny's Tech Reparations Fund never took off. Tech companies throw huge sums of money at the homeless problem—there's a competition among the state's neoliberal lawmakers and CEOs for who can throw the most—but they prefer to do it through other sorts of funds. In 2019, Facebook and Google each pledged $1 billion to the cause; a few months later, Apple upped the ante, pledging $2.5 billion. The funds are to be distributed across the state over a series of years, but when you drill down into the details, they look a lot like revolving loan funds—a small percentage of the money is in the form of grants that don't have to be repaid, but they're not, for the most part, giving the money away. Google, for instance, put some of its $1 billion of housing money into the TECH Fund—the acronym stands for Tech, Equity, Community, and Housing—which garners up to 2 percent interest for the investors.

Leigh Avenue Senior Apartments, where I staked out Kent for months, was the first TECH Fund development to be completed. The grand opening was attended by the mayor of San José and other local dignitaries; Kent was invited to speak. "You should have seen it," he recalled. "I fucked them up. They had a host and his first question to me was, *It's pretty hard out there, huh*? And I said, *Hold on, hold on.* I said, *Well, yeeaaahh. But it made me who I am today. And I like me today. So it's OK*. And everybody kind of *oooh*ed on that."

The PR event had a clear message: The system is working. The politicos and nonprofit administrators behind the homelessness solution industry use stories like Kent's to reinforce their mantra: "The solution to homelessness is housing," which they valiantly plaster across social media and eat-your-vegetables op-eds. *Duh*. But also: In the same way that the sense of home does not equate to a roof over one's head, the solution to homelessness is much more complex than housing. I think it's a question of how we relate with people who don't fit in, who behave in ways we wish they wouldn't, who suffer, who are alone, who are dispossessed. In regions where the rent is high, those folks are more likely to be housed than in regions where the rent is low. But housed or not, they are the same person.

In that light, homelessness is not the distant reality that many of us imagine. Its underlying gestalt is baked into human civilization, its manifestations rarely farther than arm's length. You don't have to be in the orbit of poor, mentally ill substance users to have a nexus to homelessness. That weird kid who got picked on in your fifth-grade class? You knew him in a sense, but you didn't really know what was going on inside him. There's a higher-than-average chance he ended up on the street, as with all of those whom the status quo cannot contain. Even if they don't become chronically homeless, they compose part of the cloth from which homelessness is cut.

If we're honest, we can admit that intractable ills like homelessness, loneliness, bigotry, and polarization aren't cured with bigger datasets, more funding, and better policies. They're a product of norms entrenched through generations of human relationships—broken ones. If we're honest, we can admit that the most pragmatic remedies are the skills, and the willingness, to mend them. Skills like listening without judgment; building bonds across pain by acknowledging our own imperfections; resisting the patronizing temptation to "fix" people, and instead providing them with the necessary time, space, and resources—not just financial ones—to move in the direction that the human spirit generally desires: toward a sense of belonging, purpose, wholeness.

World Building

One foggy summer's eve, my phone rang in the middle of the night. The first time I ignored it. The second time I rolled over and listened to the voicemail that had been left. It was Monte's mom, Cynthia. I'd met her briefly a few days before because Monte's brother, Butchie, had died, and she'd flown in from Louisiana. She was calling because Monte had just been arrested at a traffic stop. "I don't even know if he's going to be home for his brother's funeral," she said on the voicemail, calmly, but in a manner that felt like she was forcing herself to hold it together. "My back is against the wall. I absolutely don't know what to do. I don't know how much more my heart can take."

Another one of Monte's brothers had died eight years earlier while in police custody. He was a drug dealer who had become a quadriplegic after being shot in the back during an altercation on the street. He continued to deal from his wheelchair and one day was picked up by the police, with whom he'd already had a long relationship. He apparently swallowed the drugs, and, in his family's understanding of the events, the cops tried to force him to regurgitate by squeezing his windpipe. He lost consciousness as a result and started having seizures. Cynthia told me that he was brain-dead by the time the cops brought him to the hospital. Another brother had taken a trip to Africa years ago and was never heard from again. Now Butchie, Cynthia's only other child, was gone. No one had mentioned a cause of death, and I didn't pry, but I understood that he was a drug user and that seemed to say enough. I'd set up a GoFundMe to cover funeral expenses, and I guess Cynthia felt like I was a safe person to call in a moment of desperation.

Butchie had been homeless for years, though he'd recently gotten a subsidized apartment in Berkeley, the sort of building where formerly homeless folks

live side by side with people in market-rate apartments of identical quality—
wealth redistribution at work. Apparently he rarely slept there, using it mainly
as a place to play video games. Monte said Butchie was more comfortable living
on the street. Cynthia had been staying there, and when Monte got out of jail a
few days later I went over with some food to share. They'd mostly emptied the
place of Butchie's belongings, and Cynthia looked extremely exhausted. Mother
and son were in an argumentative mood, which reminded me of the way my
mom and I sometimes nitpick on each other. But just like with my mom, even
in the irritation there was love.

"He's full of grief and he's full of anger," Cynthia said, in a wizened grandmother's voice, about her son. "He's full of unanswered questions." Monte was
very resistant to the idea of becoming housed—he didn't feel ready, and he felt
like he needed the community on Wood Street, and that it needed him. "He
cares for other people more than he cares for himself," said Cynthia. "I tell him
all the time, LaMonte, you have to learn how to love every part of you before
you can love anybody else."

The food seemed to help everyone feel a little better. Monte slipped into
a bashful childlike mode that I'd never been privy to, saying "yes, ma'am" in
response to his mom's urgings, rather than arguing back. After a while Cynthia
began to open up. Her story was like a map for Monte's.

Cynthia, who comes from a Louisiana family of modest means, came of
age in Berkeley in the late sixties. She wore flowers in her hair, the whole bit.
She was part of that great experiment in American anarchy, which in Berkeley
found its geography in People's Park, a couple acres of land downtown near
where Telegraph Avenue dead-ends into the university. Using eminent domain,
the university had bought the property and cleared the houses on it, with a
plan to build sports fields and eventually student housing; but the plans were
delayed, and the land sat empty for a couple of years. In the spring of 1969, a
call went out in *Berkeley Barb*, a local underground newspaper, suggesting that
community members come together to make a park on the derelict land. One
hundred people showed up and turned the place into a slice of hippie heaven.

"It was freedom," Cynthia told me. "You could express yourself—or not.
It was heavily spirited. They weren't harming anybody. The people just really

blended. It didn't matter what color you were, what your background was. People's Park was wide open arms for anybody."

They didn't have permission, but that was also the point. After a few weeks of free love, Ronald Reagan, then the governor of California, sent in the highway patrol. Thousands of hippies gathered to defend the space against the cops. A few days later, Reagan sent in the National Guard. Tear gas was sprayed from helicopters. At one point, thirty thousand people assembled in protest; one bystander was shot and killed by the police, and scores were injured. The authorities managed to wrest back control of the park, fencing it off from public use. But a few years later, after protesters liberated it in an overnight battle with local police, the university backed off from their development plans. For decades, it was a gathering place for freethinkers who, over the years, were increasingly likely to be homeless. People's Park was probably the closest thing to hobohemia to have emerged in the modern American era—there were destitute homeless people and housed radicals and semi-intentionally homeless radicals, and it was difficult to draw clean lines between them.

During one of the many periods of tension between parkies and the police, a teenage anarchist named Rosebud Denovo broke into the chancellor's residence in 1992 just before sunrise with martyrdom on her mind. She had been living between the park and a camp in the Berkeley Hills and was already on the police's radar after a copy of *The Anarchist Cookbook*, a bomb-making manual, had been found in her possession, along with explosive materials and crossbows. In the chancellor's house she carried a machete and a note that said, "We are willing to die for this piece of land. Are you?" The police shot her to death.

During her People's Park days, Cynthia discovered the Black Panthers. She doesn't have a militant personality like her son, but she was drawn to their philosophy of helping the poor. Cynthia volunteered with the group, distributing clothes and whole chickens. "That was my first exposure to people being homeless and hungry," she told me.

She soon found herself on the other side of the situation. After meeting Monte's dad, a longshoreman at the port in West Oakland, they both became addicted to drugs. When Monte was still young, his parents transitioned to the street, while he and his brothers went to live with his grandmother, and later a foster family. The foster family didn't work out, and shortly after Monte returned to his grandmother's house, she died. Monte was a teenager at the time. "They practically were raising themselves," said Cynthia. A local drug dealer took Monte and his brothers under his wing, employing them to sell his wares, but also serving as a father figure. "He took very good care of them because he knew the parents were addicts," said Cynthia. "He made sure they went to school and they had clothing and all that."

When Monte was in his mid-twenties, long before he became homeless and got hooked on meth, his mom moved to Louisiana, where she had family, and got clean; she's been sober ever since. She spends part of each week handing out food and clothes to her unhoused neighbors and helping them however she can. Cynthia did the same when she was on the street herself. "There were a lot of elderly people that were homeless, and it seemed like I was the one to make sure they ate and would take them to take showers and make sure they got clothing and stuff," she told me. "Even in homelessness, I had a ministry, I had a calling."

Cynthia had visited Wood Street several times, and while she was impressed with the community, she didn't see it as the savior that Monte did, which is the source of many of their arguments. She'd rather see him get sober and come live with her. She cares deeply about the politics of homelessness, but that's not what got her sober and housed—that she attributes to God. Cynthia has become a devout Christian. "I don't know, Brian, if it's going to ever get better," she said, "until God comes to re-create us again."

How do homeless folks envision The Fix? In a multitude of ways. But the gestalt is to re-create the world, or at least create their own world within it. Because they don't have many resources for world building, the results are generally humble. Often, the new world doesn't get beyond the confines of thought. Tiny has gone further than any homeless person I've known with her new world, but it started much less tangibly. It started with art.

After becoming homeless, she and her mother hand-printed T-shirts with "horrendously cute little brown bears" and sold them on the Venice Beach boardwalk in LA. Then Dee designed "a kind of post-modern Zoot suit" prompting such a buzz on the boardwalk that they launched a fashion line called Street Clothes, which was advertised in *Playgirl*, sold in avant-garde boutiques, and even, for a brief moment, at Macy's. The clothing business quickly went nowhere, but Tiny and Dee's ambitions evolved instead into street-based performance art, which commented on their poverty with tongue-in-cheek satire, while also attempting to make a buck. One routine, called "The Depressed Box," involved a cardboard sign that read, "We are depressed. For $1 per minute you can help us not be depressed." In Tiny's early teen years, they moved from LA to the Bay Area, where they squatted in an abandoned building and staged a show-slash-installation called "The Art of Homelessness." This included "docent tours" through their reality, such as the reality of Tiny's "intimate relationship with a space heater," as she put it, the building's sole source of warmth: One time she fell asleep curled a bit too close to the heater and woke up to find that her skin had melted onto it. "The process of extracting one's own skin off burning metal is one of the most disgusting things a human being can do," she wrote.

Tiny and Dee rubbed elbows with established Bay Area artists like Ellen Zweig, and Pamela Z. Articles were written; radio interviews were given. In Tiny's twenties, more than a decade after becoming homeless, she and her mom began to parlay their creativity into a sliver of stability. With the birth of *POOR Magazine* in 1996, they managed to attract grant money, hire staff, and rent an office and an apartment. Their artsy friends helped raise funds and lent technical expertise. *POOR Magazine* was conceived as an edgy art and literary magazine, but it was also overtly ideological, the public forum through which Tiny and Dee developed their theories of "poverty scholarship," which is centered on the idea that the ultimate experts on poverty and homelessness are those who have experienced it. The magazine embodied the notion that poor people should tell their own stories, make their own media, and claim political power in the process.

This was still the case a quarter century later when I met Tiny at Rudy's camp in the Crash Zone fields at the end of the SJC runway. Three times a week, she and her crew drive a route through the Bay Area to distribute food and supplies to camps, conducting brief interviews for RoofLESS Radio as they go. Along the way, they invite folks to come to one of the weekly writing workshops at Homefulness, part of a seven-days-a-week roster of outreach, events, and activism. Thursdays at noon they distribute food and supplies in their front yard, followed by their "Community Newsroom" at one—further fodder for the group's radio shows, podcasts, and publishing. Once a year, they lead book-writing workshops for poverty scholars who get serious about their craft. POOR Press, their publishing arm, has released more than four dozen books in the two decades since it grew from the trenches of *POOR Magazine*, ranging from poetry and memoir to practical guides, like *How to Not Call the Po'Lice EVER*. These may be purchased, along with radical merch—coffee mugs and hoodies emblazoned with slogans like "Mama Earth is NOT for Sale"—at poorpress.net.

Tiny and Dee's political consciousness had hatched years before. Tiny didn't have a junior high diploma, much less the resources to attend college, but she and her mom occasionally audited classes in women's studies, African American studies, and La Raza studies at San Francisco State University, where thinkers like Angela Davis and bell hooks sharpened the deep-left radicalism that grew organically from their lives. Fifty years ago, Black people in this country were not given credibility as experts on the Black experience. Twenty years ago, trans people were not given credibility as experts on the trans experience. In that light, homelessness is one of the last frontiers of the civil rights movement, and Tiny is ahead of her time.

One day, while perusing the mind warp that is *POOR Magazine*'s online archives, I came across Tiny's review of the film *Nomadland*, which had just won three Oscars. She was not kind to *Nomadland*. While Tiny found the film "artistically powerful," she slammed it as another episode of "Hollywood's ongoing dedication to performing poverty, disability and homelessness to feed the ever-hungry, ever-exploitative film, media and akkkademik industries." Tiny traces this tendency back through Western literary history, "from Dickens to Steinbeck," and she insists that "these aren't our stories told by us, for us, and more importantly, for collective liberation. They are fodder for the ruling class and the Charity Industrial Complex."

I read the *Nomadland* critique just before my first interview with Tiny, which made it clear that if I wanted her to be a major character in the book, I'd better not come across like I was writing a Silicon Valley version of *Nomad-land*. I told her I'd read the review and appreciated how "fierce" it was. I said this was not going to be a book about top-down solutions, but an exploration of the homelessness crisis told through the voices of those experiencing it, with wealth redistribution and bottom-up solutions as central themes. I explained that I, too, was tired of poverty journalism steeped in the voices of so-called experts, who get paid to pontificate on solutions that fail to produce meaning-ful change, while rendering those experiencing hardship in a one-dimensional way, designed, consciously or not, to invoke pity, rather than empowerment. My goal, I said, was for readers to see the book's characters as the multidimen-sional human beings they are—people with talents and dreams, who simply lack the fertile soil needed to make them grow.

"I appreciate where you're coming from," she said. "Everything that you're saying I teach as a poverty scholar." Tiny said she appreciated that I wanted to confront my "byline privilege." I said I looked forward very much to learning from her what that meant. "Thank you for being open to that answer," she said. "Because people such as yourself have been lied to a whole lot about access and privilege and authorship, and what is grist for the story mill, and how you deal with it in a way that does not perpetuate the violence of about-us-without-us"—a phrase she sometimes wields as a noun, like a blunt and barbed rhetorical object.

I felt I had earned some sort of humility badge and was basking in Tiny's approval. It was all going so very well. Until it wasn't.

I knew Tiny could sense that my actions and choices in life did not always embody my socialist ideals. I felt she wanted to give me the benefit of the doubt, but that she was also looking for the holes in my façade. I was asking her to trust me with her story, and she was telling me all the reasons that people like me can't be trusted to tell the stories of people like her. The dam broke when I explained the vision I had for my book tour. Rather than put myself on a pedestal, as authors normally do, I imagined sharing it with Kent, Rudy, Monte, and other poverty scholars. Instead of me lecturing, the audience would listen to them; if there was a panel discussion, they'd be the panelists. "My idea is to put *them* onstage to tell *their* stories," I told Tiny. "I would be there too, but not as the focus."

"So, I'm going to stop you," she interjected. "Because that's more exploitation. We don't give a fuck about telling our story over and over again. What for? So that you could sell more books? No. Uh-uh. Fuck that."

I told her that's not what I meant. "I guess where I was coming from," I ventured, "was something I got from you"—avoiding the about-us-without-us trap, leveraging my privilege to open doors for those with less, and so on.

"I get it, I get it," said Tiny. "I know you're trying to move with a loving heart. But you didn't understand where I was going with that. Where I'm going with that is not that you put us on a stage for trauma porn and excitement for a book party. But that you actually use poor people theory. And listen to our instructions. And call in the people who are sweeping us, who probably will not join you on that stage because they don't want to take accountability." She softened for a moment, but then her voice rose again. "I don't got to tell no rich people my story again. I've done that too many times for somebody else's profit. Intellectual property is the only property us poor people have."

For Tiny, part of creating a new world has been to smash old narratives and midwife new ones. Media is one venue for this—the tabula rasa of the next generation's brains is another.

She runs a school at Homefulness called the Deecolonize Academy, named after her mom, Dee. I visited on an overcast afternoon after the minuscule school, which Tiny assured me is official and legitimate in the eyes of the state, had let out for the day. The sole classroom is also Tiny's living room, which contains several computers, couches, and a terrarium that houses Don Juan the Low-Income Lizard, a learned-looking bearded dragon who had a cricket leg sticking from his lips. Quarters are tight. The school kitchen is also Tiny's kitchen. To get to the bathroom, you have to walk through her bedroom. A loft above doubles as the Homefulness office and a bedroom where three teenage boys sleep, the academy's first graduates. One of them, her son, Tiburcio, helps to teach the younger students. They study the usual subjects, write about their life experience, and take field trips that consist of participating in protests and visiting camps with the Homefulness posse.

The school-slash-Tiny's-quarters shares a somewhat dilapidated bungalow with two additional apartments housing other Homefulness residents.

Another resident lives in a garage-sized outbuilding next to the bungalow. These structures sit in the shadow of four townhomes, clumped together in a three-story stucco monolith that occupies a big hunk of the narrow lot, which is sandwiched between cheap motels in one of Oakland's poorest neighborhoods. There's a large mural depicting the residents on a wall facing the street, but otherwise the beige townhomes are not outwardly remarkable. However, the decade-long effort to build them—housing funded by the "radical reparators" of the Homefulness Solidarity Family, with nary a penny of nonprofit money—most definitely is. On my first visit, the paint was still fresh. The group was awaiting a final occupancy permit, held up by a requirement to build two extra parking spaces that its mostly carless members did not need. In response, Tiny had put out a call for the $30,000 needed to satisfy the "permit gangsters"; the funds were trickling in. The building process was an opportunity for students of the Deecolonize Academy to learn the math required to raise a wall, the practical skills of carpentry and plumbing, and the civics lessons inherent in dealing with the Oakland planning department.

As Tiny and I strolled through the yard, a multigenerational tribe of currently and formerly houseless folks bustled about, unloading food and supplies, shouting about this and that, keeping busy with the work of being homeful. Chickens foraged beneath fruit trees planted along the driveway, while the "therapy goats," as Tiny calls the pair living outside the back door of the bungalow, bleated in their pens. The scene felt like a grittier urban version of off-grid "intentional communities" I'd visited in the wilds of Northern California during my back-to-the-land days. But don't get the wrong idea, said Tiny: "This ain't some kind of cutesy, gentri-fucked, hippie-utopic dream." It's more like a landless people's movement, she said, citing the Zapatistas, South Africa's shack dwellers movement, and the MOVE organization in Philadelphia as inspiration.

Dee, who passed away five years before the property was purchased, seems to be the biggest inspiration, however. Homefulness—the name of the first issue of *POOR Magazine* in 1996—was her vision. Geographically, it was the inverse of Kent and Rudy's return to their home zone upon becoming homeless. Homefulness, by some cosmic coincidence, came into existence on a block where Tiny and Dee were once homeless: a stretch of MacArthur Boulevard where, decades ago, they sometimes slept in their car.

At Homefulness, Dee is not just an inspiration in the token sense that people refer to their deceased relatives as inspirations. She's more like a living presence, a ghost that everyone, not just Tiny, interacts with. I first recognized this when a resident named Izrael gave me a tour of the facilities. As we entered the metal shipping container that houses the Homefulness radio studio and library, he made a series of cutesy utterances that sounded as though he was being affectionate with a cat lounging off to the left, in front of some bookcases. As my eyes adjusted to the dim interior, I did in fact see a cat—a statue of one, anyways. At first I couldn't really understand what Izrael, who's from Mexico and has a strong accent, was saying. But then his falsetto baby-kitty speak suddenly clicked in my ears: "Heeeeyeee, Mama Deeee; ohhhh, Mama Deee-eeee; howwww are yooouuuu?" The statue turned out to be a cat-shaped urn holding Mama Dee's ashes.

SWEEP NOT

Implicit in the new worlds that the unhoused are building, or at least dreaming of, is a sense of self-determination. In the world we live in, one's degree of agency is often proportional to one's bank account—money can't buy happiness, but it can buy an address, legitimacy, credibility, and the ability to put ideas into practice. Wood Street Commons shows what's possible with virtually no fiscal resources, but there's an even more basic resource that prevents unhoused communities from progressing: permanence. Without being able to remain in one place, it's difficult to develop the stability required to move ahead in life, whether your goal is to build a new world, or simply get a job and get back to the existing one.

Which is why the first step toward The Fix, from an unhoused person's perspective, is to stop the sweeps. As a camp grows larger and more organized, its mission inevitably becomes intertwined with the idea of resisting eviction. It's a constant threat—John told me that before settling on Wood Street, he was being swept once or more per month. Compared to evicting housed people, evicting homeless people is a labor-intensive process, one that has spawned a burgeoning, if little-known, industry.

Each morning in America, people wake up, go to work, and carry out the business of removing homeless people from their dwellings. Some are professionals working for city agencies; others are employed by nonprofits; cops are typically involved. These folks are the overseers, the decision-makers, the enforcers. Those who do the dirty work—bulldozing tents, tossing people's belongings in trash trucks, picking up syringes and bags filled with diarrhea—are typically employed by private contractors, who pay wages that in expensive real estate markets like the Bay Area make them highly vulnerable to finding themselves on the other end of the sweeping business.

Large West Coast cities generally have hundreds of camps, and they routinely sweep one or more each day. Those who are swept typically have nowhere to go. They expend tremendous energy and resources to reconstruct their camp nearby, if not on the very same site. The cycle repeats. The impact of sweeps has not been thoroughly studied, though data collected in Boston showed that hospitalization and death rates increased significantly among encampment residents after being evicted from their camps—researchers found that overdoses rose 30 percent, for instance.

In the fall of 2021, while my friends from Wolfe Road were getting reacquainted with indoor plumbing, the Crash Zone became a case study in the horrors of the sweeping industry. The community had known for some time what was coming and had made efforts to leverage their visibility, à la Wolfe Camp, even staging a demonstration that was written up in local media. "Hell no, we won't go!" shouted the thirty or so protesters as they marched down Coleman Avenue, a thoroughfare that ran from the camp to the airport. There was a rally with calls to "claim your power"; talk of "illegal search and seizure" during sweeps circulated in the crowd. They held signs that read "Destination: Nowhere," which poked fun at Destination: Home, one of the Valley's largest homeless charities. Residents refer to Tucker Construction, a local company contracted to conduct sweeps, as Fucker Construction.

Caltrans spent $36 million to clean up 1,262 camps in 2020, a tenfold increase from the decade prior, just within the state right-of-ways that compose its jurisdiction. The sweep of a single two-hundred-person camp in Los Angeles cost taxpayers an estimated $2 million, just for police forces. Local politicians boasted that nearly all the displaced residents had been placed in motels and other temporary shelter, but a follow-up study conducted a year later found that only five had made it to permanent housing, while six had died; the majority were presumed back on the streets. According to a 2019 audit, San José spent $4.9 million on encampment closures in the preceding fiscal year, but only $740,000 on outreach and engagement efforts in camps—efforts intended to connect unhoused residents with housing and social services.

I sent out dozens of public records requests to better understand the nature and scope of camp eviction spending, which I estimate to be well north of $100 million per year in California, just for private contractors. I found individual contracts with Caltrans worth up to $26 million. Even tiny Santa Clara, a suburb of San José on the other side of the airport from the Crash Zone, had a $1 million contract with Tucker, despite having documented only 264 unsheltered residents at the time. Comparable sums are spent on city employees, including the droves of police that accompany eviction workers—lest a camper resist, or in case contraband is found. During the Crash Zone evictions, there were generally a dozen or more officers on hand.

In the hundreds of documents I reviewed from public agencies involved in sweeping across the state, I found that the companies receiving contracts occasionally include local construction outfits like Tucker, but it's primarily large environmental services firms. These firms specialize in cleaning up hazardous waste and responding to public emergencies, and they tout their ability to work in dangerous environments as part of the pitch for their sweeping services. Communications I obtained between the Los Angeles County Public Works Department and Ocean Blue, a company claiming to have cleared out more than three hundred encampments per year in Southern California, revealed bizarre marketing claims. "Blood spills and trauma scenes are everyday occurrences for Ocean Blue," the company wrote, stressing how experience with cleaning up things like plane crashes translates to encampments. "Because of our specialty in handling . . . feces, urine, vomit, needles . . . we now perform homeless encampment cleanups."

A page in the Ocean Blue files stamped "! CONFIDENTIAL" featured photos of people in hazmat suits picking through encampment debris and discussed some of the alleged dangers of the work: "Homeless people have different personalities and mental illnesses and can be aggressive." Ocean Blue also purports to be sensitive to the complex politics and shifting legal landscape surrounding their work. "Among burglaries, illegal drug proliferation and class-action lawsuits, municipalities are held accountable to their respective approach towards homelessness," they stated. "Ocean Blue approaches each homeless encampment differently depending on the client's needs . . . whether it be to segregate 'life-essential items,' or using heavy equipment to quickly dispose loads of garbage." In other words, they're happy to take extra care with personal property, or just bulldoze it, whatever the client prefers.

It seems to be a lucrative line of work—I found a purchase order for Tucker, covering just the six-month period when the Crash Zone sweep began, that was worth $1.425 million—but not necessarily for the workers. I learned that fourteen members of Tucker's camp cleanup crew had sued the company in 2019 for failure to compensate them for all hours worked, among other labor violations. The workers were awarded a $325,000 settlement; a separate city audit resulted in $105,000 in restitution. I assume most needed every penny to pay their rent: "Some of them have been unhoused," a city employee overseeing Tucker's work at camps told me.

An ongoing series of lawsuits has attempted to balance the right of the unhoused to occupy public space with other public interests. One of the most significant cases since *Martin v. Boise* was filed in San Francisco in 2022, which resulted in a yearlong citywide injunction against sweeps. But the issue remains a legal gray area. Homeless advocates won a similar federal injunction in Phoenix, where residents of a camp called the Zone at one point numbered more than one thousand, but shortly thereafter a state judge issued a conflicting ruling at the behest of local business owners. The latter case ordered the city to enforce the sort of "nuisance" laws that the former painted as criminalizing people based on housing status.

Local authorities have become adept at clouding their sweeping in legal gray areas and shepherding it through loopholes, making it more difficult to mount a successful case. *Martin v. Boise*, for instance, requires that shelter be offered before forcing an unhoused person off public land, but it doesn't specify what sort of shelter, and cities know that most folks aren't going to accept an offer of a night in a roomful of bunk beds in exchange for their hand-built homestead. During the Crash Zone sweep, local shelters were generally maxed, but that didn't stop the sweeping of several hundred people—the requirement is merely to offer shelter; it doesn't matter if people accept it.

I contacted the San José city attorney's office and the police department to ask how, given *Martin v. Boise*, the sweep was legally justified: They said shelter was being offered to every camper who "engaged" with the nonprofit service provider contracted by the city, a group called HomeFirst. I contacted Home-First, which is known in the camp as HomeLast, to ask what "engagement" looked like and got some boilerplate in return: Their "outreach teams" regularly visit the site to "get those interested into shelter." Most of the campers I spoke with said they'd engaged with HomeFirst and expressed interest in shelter but were not willing to go to a congregate shelter. I did meet one person who'd accepted a tiny home and heard about a woman with a newborn baby who accepted the offer of a motel room, though I was told that the rest of her family was not allowed to join her. Signs posted at the camp encouraged residents to call HomeFirst's hotline for housing help, but when I called it went to voicemail, which was full.

At the camp, I met Rudy's friend Scott, who enjoys tormenting the sweepers by reminding them of their lack of humanity. As we strolled the Crash Zone fields, he introduced me to a couple of the cops who patrolled them, with whom he was on a first-name basis, and told them about my book.

"Is this the worst camp in the Bay Area?" one of the cops asked me.

"What do you mean by that?" I said.

"Filth," he said. "The dirtiest." Scott assured me that these particular cops were relatively cool, unlike the one walking toward us—Officer Hoopes—who was infamous in the camp for meanness.

"I don't like Hoopes," said Scott to the other cops, loudly, so that Hoopes could hear. "He's got a stick in his ass."

"Oh, stop it," said the first cop. "Hoopes is nice, you just got to get to know him."

Hoopes greeted us, but Scott cut him off: "Hey, we're not talking to you, Hoopes."

Before Scott became homeless and lost his teeth, he was the clean-cut son of an early Valley entrepreneur. When he was growing up in the seventies and eighties, his dad's company made circuit board components. This was the era when the *silicon* in Silicon Valley—a blue-collar place where silicon chips and other electronics were manufactured—had a physical reference. By the time Scott was old enough to work in the family business, the manufacturing had moved overseas, ushering in the white-collar version of the Valley, and hollowing out the middle class. After his dad died, the business fell apart and Scott started partying too much. A meth addiction cemented his transition to the Valley's vehicle-dwelling communities. When I met Scott, he was living at the edge of the Crash Zone in an RV he acquired through great duress after his previous RV, stuffed with everything he owned, including his father's ashes, was impounded—and later demolished, he said—for being illegally parked.

Back when Scott was growing up in the Valley, the semiconductor workforce "was women of color, mostly immigrants—hunched over tables with magnifying glasses, assembling parts, sometimes on a factory line, sometimes on a kitchen table," according to Louis Hyman, author of *Temp: The Real Story of What Happened to Your Salary, Benefits, & Job Security*. Long fingernails were one of the most important worker traits, he writes, "so that they could more easily maneuver the components onto the circuit boards." On the streets as an adult, Scott found himself in the company of former semiconductor assemblers. "A lot of the old-timers told me they used to work in the tech sector, and when their jobs got shifted to China and India, they ended up living in motor homes," said Scott. "I would tell them about what happened with my motor home and they'd go, *Scott, this shit's been happening since the seventies. The worker bees here got thrown out like trash.*"

After we left Hoopes and his buddies, Scott spotted a HomeFirst vehicle and tried to engage with some outreach. "Hey! Hey!" he shouted, running after it. When we caught up with the car, the HomeFirst employees filmed us, while Scott filmed them. He told them about my book, and they instructed me to contact the HomeFirst media person, who I'd already spoken with. "We're not allowed to give out any information," they told me.

"What about me getting information about safe parking?" said Scott, who'd been attempting to secure a spot in an RV lot the city promised to set up for vehicle-dwellers at the Crash Zone, which had yet to materialize. They were familiar with his game, a walking satire of uncomfortable questions, and drove off while he was mid-sentence.

Later, Scott accosted a couple other HomeFirst employees, who were not yet hip to his antics. As they listened earnestly, he explained that the city had told him "that you guys are doing extensive outreach right now. I'm down to the final hour and I don't have a safe parking program," he said. "Where do I take my RV? What options do I have?"

The HomeFirst employees told Scott about a church group that would soon be opening up a safe parking program. "They don't have it now," said one of them, "but you should call and get on the waiting list." Scott said he was already on their waiting list, among others. "Are you OK going to a shelter?" the guy asked. Scott said he'd called around to shelters and had been told there were no beds available—"It usually takes about a week," the guy admitted—but that he would like to have the option as a last resort. "I just need to know what I'm looking at if I need to make a decision—because they could kick that door down and arrest me for trespassing."

In the many days I spent observing sweeps at the Crash Zone, I became convinced that egregious violations of constitutional rights were the norm. Apart from the Eighth Amendment violations associated with sweeps—cruel and unusual punishment—federal courts have found that sweeps also risk running afoul of the Fourth Amendment, which protects citizens against the unreasonable search, seizure, or destruction of personal property. Whether the Fourth Amendment is violated or not depends on how "property" is defined. Cities have generally interpreted it narrowly—they'll hold on to your wallet and laptop, but not your shack and the entirety of its contents—a stance that continues to be tested in court. One settlement between unhoused residents and Caltrans awarded $5.5 million to the plaintiffs for loss of property but stipulated that moving forward, the agency was only required to preserve items deemed to be worth more than fifty dollars, or weighing less than fifty pounds. Later, in the case of *Garcia v. City of Los Angeles*, a federal judge ruled that size does not matter: Every mattress, couch, and shack, no matter the monetary value, must be preserved.

To me, it seems obvious, both legally and morally, that we should not be destroying the meager possessions of unhoused people. But I understand that it is immensely impractical to store huge numbers of rickety structures that would collapse into rat's nests of tarps, bungee cords, and two-by-fours if you tried to move them, along with the entirety of the items in and around camp dwellings, which tend to be extensive. Cities point this out in court cases as justification for why they refuse to do so. Leaving the homes of unhoused residents intact doesn't seem to occur to them as an option. This impossible predicament points to an existential rift between a world in which tent cities have become the norm and what is convenient for cities and their constituents. It suggests that a paradigm shift—a new way of looking at labor, land use, and social norms—is in order. The unhoused empowerment movement has some ideas about what that might look like, but we are not listening. Instead, cities wiggle around the court rulings, which the judges responsible for enforcing them have limited ability to uphold on a day-to-day basis. The end result of all the sweeping, in my observation, is that homelessness becomes more entrenched.

I began asking everyone I met at the Crash Zone two questions: Were you offered shelter before being evicted? Did you lose any belongings in the process?

On the property destruction front, the first line of legal defensibility is for the sweepers to ask the unhoused resident what they would like to take with them and what they would like to leave. Many do not know their rights and assume that they will have to surrender any belongings they cannot move, allowing the sweepers to say that they did so voluntarily. But most often there's a negotiation process, in which the unhoused resident makes a pile of stuff they want to keep as the sweepers throw everything else in dump trucks. The clock is ticking during this process. They may come by and say you have until tomorrow, then give you an hour warning, and then hover over you as you drag the last things into your pile. Eventually you have to move your pile, setting off another series of deadlines about when that must be gone—or else it, too, is going in the garbage truck. This approach preserves the veneer of due process, which is codified in the Fourteenth Amendment—also frequently cited in court cases involving unhoused folks and their property.

Guided by due process principles, local authorities often post notices of an impending sweep at least seventy-two hours in advance. But in my observation, the verbal negotiations involved in carrying out sweeps are ad hoc, arbitrary, and ever-shifting. Around 9:30 one morning, I found Mr. Fujio, a Crash Zone elder, standing next to a small pile of his possessions. He said the workers had agreed to give him until the end of that day to move, but instead they showed up when he was asleep at 7 A.M. and immediately began throwing his belongings into a trash truck, including his tent and the pallets he slept on. Within about fifteen minutes, his camp was gone. Scott, who lived next door to him, showed me a video in which Mr. Fujio can be seen pulling a purple tarp and a blue water bottle from the cloud of dust kicked up by the workers as they raked up the last scraps of his home. He was waiting there hoping someone with a vehicle would help him move his remaining possessions a couple hundred yards, so that he would be safely out of the sweep zone. Otherwise, Mr. Fujio, a former restaurant owner who said he still works part-time as a "restaurant helper," would have to start schlepping. "I can't do that," he told me. "I'm getting old."

A couple hours later I encountered Gabriella, who worked as a dishwasher in a restaurant, as she frantically pulled her belongings from a series of piles destined for the landfill and added them to crates and boxes stacked on a few small carts and a U-Haul dolly. "I spent the whole weekend putting everything that I wanted to keep on something that had wheels," she said. "So I told them, anything that has wheels, do not touch." But while she was away from her spot for a few minutes helping a friend, some of the agreed-on keeper piles had been consolidated with non-keeper piles that were in the process of being loaded into a trash truck, including one that had the key fobs for her car and her daughter's car, which she said will cost $200 to $300 each to replace.

Like most everyone I've met in the camps, Gabriella had experienced the physical and emotional upheaval of sweeps many times. "You feel devastated, you feel in a rush, you feel like your whole world is coming to an end," she told me. "It's not so much the loss of the material things, but that they are the only things you own."

The sweepers' second line of defensibility is a promise to store belongings that residents have not been coerced into surrendering. The city's contract with Tucker includes instructions for storing property in sweeps, which state that "if there is any uncertainty regarding whether an item should be thrown away or stored, it should be stored. . . . Unless an item is trash or poses an immediate threat to public health or safety, it should be retained for storage as potential personal property." The notices to vacate posted throughout the camp defined storable items in very different terms, however. Nothing "dirty" would be kept, they said, which anyone who's ever been in a homeless camp knows is most everything. Same with anything "broken or disassembled," which likewise encompasses a high percentage of possessions belonging to folks whose shopping happens largely in dumpsters.

The flyers further specified that the broken and disassembled items not to be stored include "bike parts, pallets, or wood or other metal parts." Piles of bike carcasses are ubiquitous at camps, because residents' mobility often relies on cobbling together parts from multiple nonfunctioning bikes—tinkering with one's rig is both a practical necessity and pastime, and the most skilled bike mechanics can turn their expertise into a business. Pallets, wood scraps, and metal parts? These are essential resources as well. Pallets are upcycled into walls and bed frames. Metal equals money at the recycling yard. A scrap of wood can cook dinner, warm your toes, and invite company into the glowing circle of its embers, keeping the cold of loneliness at bay after dark. In the camps, the value of a discarded two-by-four cannot be understated.

City attorneys may be able to convince judges that dirty, broken, and disassembled items are trash, rather than property, but the premise does not comport with the reality of camps. Even items that clearly fit cities' own descriptions of what will be stored are routinely trashed. The Crash Zone eviction notices gave instructions for where to pick up confiscated belongings, which were to be held for ninety days. One option was to call, which I did on behalf of a man named C. L. who said that during the sweep he'd lost tools that he used to work on cars ("tools" are specifically named as an item to be kept). I provided the location and date on which they were lost, as the notices instructed, and about a week later received a call back: C. L.'s tools could not be located.

Another option for retrieval: go to the HomeFirst shelter on the other side of town and tell them what you lost in person. I went with a couple residents, Theresa and her partner, Dave, who'd lost many items of value, including an intact bike, which is listed as an item approved for storage. The people at the front desk had never heard of any such storage policy. Back office people were consulted—they'd never heard of that either. The back office people made phone calls to higher-ups, who said we should contact Tucker. Tucker said to call the city.

The city had a weekly Zoom meeting with several homeless advocates who were helping residents cope with the eviction and find new places to camp. The advocates had to sign something saying they wouldn't speak with the media about the contents of the meetings, but one of them broke ranks and told me that the city had acknowledged to them that nothing from the Crash Zone sweep was being stored. One day I walked by a Tucker worker sitting in his truck on a break, so I asked if the company was storing anything from the sweep—he shook his head.

All this time, residents were telling me they'd noticed that during sweeps the most valuable items often got loaded onto trucks that were not the usual trash trucks. They said they had intel that the workers were taking their shit and selling it, and that at least one Tucker worker had been seen hawking items from the camp at a nearby flea market. I didn't put much stock in the rumor at first, but residents insisted. One day, C. L., the man who'd lost his mechanic's tools, pointed out a pickup parked at the edge of the camp, loaded to the gills— one of the thieves, he said. I ambled over and casually struck up a conversation with the guy sitting in the cab, a middle-aged Latino man. The bed of his truck had high sideboards that concealed most of its contents, though I could see the neck of an acoustic guitar protruding from the top.

"Where are you going with all this stuff?" I asked.

"I sell it at the flea market," he said.

"Do you work with the cleanup crew?" I asked.

"Sometimes," he said.

"People here think you're taking their stuff," I said.

"Sometimes," he said.

"Do you take their stuff and sell it?" I asked.

"Yeah," he said. "They throw it away. I can make a little money. That's good for me."

As the Crash Zone sweep moved into fall, rain muddied the process. One drizzly morning I came across a camper named José, whose camp was next to a small side street that divided the current sweep area from the yet-to-be-swept area. As he dragged some of his belongings across the street to safety, Tucker workers were tossing others' items into a trash truck. José was limping and wearing only one shoe, which was only half on. I started filming on my phone, as I normally do in these situations. But as the rain picked up, my blood began to boil. To keep it from erupting through the top of my head, I stopped filming and started helping him move his stuff. The workers seemed confused by this. They stopped loading the trash truck and stood around watching us instead. After a few minutes, one of them joined. Soon, the whole crew was dragging José's stuff across the street in the rain.

I've found that sweepers occasionally help campers move stuff, which seems like the least they could do, but it's rare. After the last of José's possessions were moved across the street, I asked the supervisor of the encampment crew if they'd ever done that before. "We're just a vendor, we do what we are told," she said.

GAME ON

They came for Rudy on a Wednesday morning in late October. I arrived at his camp just as the army was staging their positions. Garbage trucks pulled in alongside a squad of police cars. Tucker employees stood around leaning on their rakes. Face-masked city employees—from an agency called BeautifySJ, which is tasked with cleaning up camps—hovered with clipboards. Crash Zone residents milled around, offering Rudy words of support and taunting the cops, one of whom unfurled red police tape around the crime scene of his camp. I tried to pass as a friend of Rudy's by helping him move suitcases jammed with his belongings onto a cart. Before long, a cop told me I needed to get on the other side of the red tape.

The BeautifySJ employees knew that Rudy knew his rights and that he was not going to surrender his turf without a fight. The key to holding onto one's camp, I learned that day, is to irritate the city into submission. You have to make yourself such a pain in the ass that they question whether it's worth the trouble to remove you. It's a huge help if there are journalists present and bystanders with cameras. Even better if you can competently cite the relevant jurisprudence that calls the legality of what's happening into question. Many lawsuits have arisen from sweeps, and it's clear that city attorneys advise staff to tread carefully when they encounter resistance.

A supporter asked Irma, one of the BeautifySJ employees, if Rudy would be arrested. "I'm trying not to," she said, her fingers unconsciously fidgeting with themselves. "I don't want to," she repeated, earnestly. "I don't."

Another supporter approached and informed Irma that Rudy's Teenage Mutant Ninja Turtle—a four-foot-tall figurine—was very important to him. "Let's put the ninja turtle aside," said Irma, motioning to a worker, who moved it outside the police line. The plastic reptile stood watch as the battle unfolded.

Because Rudy was resisting, they'd called in a sergeant, whose name was Rick. Rudy explained to Rick that according to San José municipal code 17.02.070, a court order was required to evict him (I later determined Rudy's legal analysis was incorrect in this instance, but it was a valiant effort nonetheless). As Rudy read the code, Rick slouched his body and face into an increasingly irritated expression. Finally, he held up his hand to stop the traffic of Rudy's monologue.

"Here's the thing," said Rick. "What I know is this: I have a job. My job is not to be an attorney. My job is to be a police officer."

A little earlier, as the army amassed, I'd called Scott to let him know it was prime time over at Rudy's place, and as Rick paused to consider his line of attack, he came running over, arriving out of breath. Rudy, Rick, and the other cops had been standing just inside the crime scene tape, while the rest of us hovered within earshot outside it. But suddenly, the crime scene tape was on the ground, ripped open, and Scott was on the other side of it. Hoopes, Scott's least favorite officer, who was standing with some other cops nearby, leapt to action.

"Excuse me, sir," said Hoopes. "Sir! Hey, that red tape is up for a reason! Can you back up, please, and step to the other side?" Scott ignored him.

As Hoopes tied the ripped ends of the tape back together, Rick motioned Rudy farther into the crime scene, away from prying ears and cameras. Rudy refused to follow. Scott, as usual, was filming. "I'd prefer to be right here where he's recording," said Rudy.

"These are obnoxious distances," said Scott, regarding the taped-off area, a blob shape maybe seventy-five yards in diameter.

Rick again raised his hand in an irritated, dismissive gesture. "Scott, you know that I don't do things that aren't right."

"I know," said Scott, who had previous experience antagonizing Rick. "But you're setting a perimeter right here so you can talk to him farther away where I can't film the interaction."

Rick raised his hand again, his body language even more irritated. "Scott," said Rick. "Ughhh . . . ," he groaned. "I'm not engaging with you right now."

"I know," said Scott. "You're not."

Scott told him that "I'm a guest at Rudy's house right now."

"No you're not," said Rick. "This is not Rudy's house."

Rick was beyond annoyed at this point. "Scott!" he said, threateningly, and then instructed Rudy to move farther inside the tape and away from the crowd.

"I prefer to stay right here," said Rudy.

"OK, that's great," said Rick. "I would prefer to not even be here at all. But we have to do this. So, here's the deal. They're going to remove your property. They're going to—"

Rudy interjected: "No, they're not."

"Yes, they are," said Rick.

"No, they're not," said Rudy. "If you can show me a law," he continued, "that says they can take my things without—"

Rick interrupted him. "No," he said.

"Yeah," said Rudy. "I want you to show me that."

"No," said Rick. "I don't do that."

"Why?" Rudy asked.

"Rudy," he said, gritting his teeth and clenching his facial muscles. "My . . ." He couldn't seem to find the right words. "Shhh . . . stop talking. I've heard your . . ." He sighed. "Rudy, you can sue in court. You might be a millionaire in court, but right now, today—"

Scott jumped back in, yelling: "Yeah, Rick, and I might have been a millionaire after they fucked me out of my motor home and every fucking thing I owned."

"You might have been," said Rick, shrugging sarcastically.

"Maybe when they took my shit and my father's ashes . . ." Scott screamed.

"Scott, why are you yelling at me?" said Rick, in the taunting tone of a guy in a bar ready to pick a fight.

Because, yelled Scott, "you're going to sit back and let this shit happen."

"No, no, no," Rick corrected him. "I'm going to actually advocate for it to happen, because it's supposed to."

Four officers from San José's Mobile Crisis Assessment Team, part of a Black Lives Matter–era program to encourage de-escalation over the use of force, had been observing quietly from behind their sunglasses. Eventually Rick and the other officers persuaded Rudy to come talk to them next to his tent, away from the crowd. Scott followed them, and, after further bickering, they tolerated him filming the interaction from about ten feet away, with the Crisis Assessment guys standing between Scott and Rick like a politician's security detail—stoic expressions, hands on holsters.

Outside the police line, I struck up a conversation with a plainclothes officer named James, who told me that he'd helped to establish the Crisis Assessment Team. I told him I thought that Rudy's only crisis at the moment was being surrounded by an army of people intent on destroying his home. "Rudy doesn't really have mental health issues," I said.

"We all have mental health issues," said James, with a good-natured chuckle. "I know I do."

"I mean he doesn't have severe mental health issues," I said. "Though he might after this."

James told me how he completely understood that sweeping solves nothing. "It makes it worse," he said. "It would be lovely to have the ability to be like, *Hey, we have a place for you right now, let's get your stuff and go.* As opposed to, *Here's a card, now it's going to take us a year to get to you.*" But James told me that letting the unhoused choose how and where to live was not realistic. He'd encountered many who had no intention of moving indoors and rejoining society. "They refuse because they're more comfortable here," he said. "It's really a hard thing to have to be the one to have to force it to happen."

Meanwhile, the negotiations between Rudy and Rick went on and on. I could make out only the parts that were yelled. "This is illegal search and seizure!" Rudy shrieked at one point, referencing the Fourth Amendment. "I'm going live on TikTok!" he threatened later, holding up his phone.

Finally, about five hours after the army arrived, it began to make the motions of departure. Rick decamped to his squad car and lit a fat cigar. Scott followed him there, his face glowing—Rudy had won the day. It was not clear exactly why they didn't drag him away in handcuffs, but it was clear that his refusal to cooperate was the key to victory.

"Too bad you didn't get to arrest me today, Rick," said Scott. "You working tomorrow?"

"I hope I got better things to do," said Rick, sardonically.

"Well," said Scott, as Rick started the engine. "It's good seeing you."

"Scott," said Rick, extending his hand. "Take care."

Scott walked away, leaving Rick's hand in the air.

Infiltration

It's hard to rebuild the world from scratch with no resources. Local land use regulations and cultural norms are further impediments—anarchic tribes of highly dysfunctional people cobbling together roughshod villages are unlikely to be welcomed in most neighborhoods. Tiny managed to do it in part because she was able to take the sharpest edges off the anarchy and dysfunction. Homefulness doesn't invite people in off the street unless they are willing to commit to sobriety and not cluttering up the place with mountains of trash and dumpster scores—rules superficially similar to those of institutionalized housing programs, but radically different in terms of who has power and agency. She runs a tight ship and has a superhuman capacity to steer that ship through the oceans of bureaucracy and naysayer-infested swamps that stand between a revolutionary vision and its implementation, despite lacking many of the technical skills normally required for the endeavor, not to mention her ongoing process of trauma recovery. Also, while the idea for Homefulness emerged during Tiny's houseless years, she didn't embark on the practical aspects of the vision until she'd pulled herself out of homelessness. It's hard to change the world when you're living in a tent, numb on narcotics.

Plus: The Solidarity Family, Homefulness's network of donors and supporters, has her back. There will need to be millions more like them if the unhoused empowerment movement is to succeed. How are the unhoused acting on their values? What are they doing to help themselves? More than building autonomous villages, they're working on the necessary prerequisite, which is to attract support for the cause. They're becoming activists. John broadcasted live from Wood Street on Instagram nearly every day. Rudy called city hall incessantly.

A network of "homeless unions" are spreading across the country, composed of a mixture of unhoused residents and their most aggressive advocates—hobohemias are making a comeback.

These folks stage protests, file lawsuits, and put their bodies in the way when the sweepers roll up with their bulldozers. A group called Where Do We Go? Berkeley mounted a final stand to defend the camp in People's Park, which required a militarized police operation to squash. The Berkeley unhoused community, which Tiny and the Wood Street folks next door in Oakland are closely connected with, is extraordinarily militant. The university knew that a simple fence would not keep them from recolonizing People's Park, so they created a fortress by stacking shipping containers two-high in a line around the property, allowing them to, five decades later, break ground on those student dorms. The Where Do We Go? Berkeley crew then pitched tents on the lawn at city hall, with one word each of Where Do We Go painted on four of them, forming an illuminated sign when they lit up the insides of the tents at night. They keep getting swept but regroup quickly and set up in another high-profile location in the city. They have even published a "Guerilla Encampment Manual" to guide other groups inspired by their approach.

These and countless other groups across the country spend their waking hours talking to anyone who will listen about their reality and the parts of it that the media and policymakers are not paying attention to: that sweeps are counterproductive; that unhoused communities are perfectly capable of helping themselves; that unhoused folks have some thoughts about the situation that might be of value to the rest of us.

Tiny is unwilling to soften her message or attempt to make it more palatable to the masses. But she is a cunning and calculating coyote when it comes to getting herself in front of audiences that will be made uncomfortable by her sermons. Beyond cash, Tiny's deeper ask of the Solidarity Family is to leverage their privilege to provide access to the levers of political power—her relationships with academics, for instance, have brought her to podiums at Stanford, UC Berkeley, UCLA, Columbia University, and other hallowed halls. Her most impressive act of subversiveness, however, was getting herself invited to Talks at Google, the company's esteemed lecture series, whose YouTube channel has 2.4 million subscribers.

Tiny's Trojan horse at Google was an Irish chap named William. As a college student in Dublin, William had interned at Google, and he'd been working for the company ever since. He was one of those people you hear about who work for giant tech companies by day while dabbling in antithetical activities on evenings and weekends. William did a stint for Google in Hong Kong during the period when Edward Snowden fled there, and because of his ties in the world of subversive techies, he found himself caught up in the greatest hack in history (he managed to keep his role out of the media and away from his bosses' attention, and that's all that he'll allow me to say publicly about the matter). A couple years later, he transferred to the HQ in Mountain View, where he rode to work on a Google shuttle bus, the sort Yesenia of Wolfe Camp piloted.

"I was doing policy comms, defending the company," William told me in his backyard in Berkeley. "I was the one on background with reporters, explaining things like Google's tax position." I'd often interacted with folks like him when working on stories slamming the tech industry. "According to somebody familiar with the matter?" said William, raising an eyebrow suggestively as he mocked newspapers' awkward language for anonymous sources. "That was me. I was the person familiar with the matter. I did it all over the world for Google. I was good at it."

Around this time, he came across Tiny's memoir, *Criminal of Poverty*. After devouring it, he reached out to see how he could be of assistance. "I found myself going into work nine to five and living that life," said William, "and then in the evenings I'd get off one of those big shiny spaceship busses and spend from 6 P.M. to midnight helping Tiny." He applied the skills of his day job—crafting tweets, writing press statements, editing video for social media—to promoting *POOR Magazine* and Homefulness. "I found myself helping people who didn't have power to get it, even though my full-time job was to get more power for Google. I was creating the problems we were protesting."

Employees can nominate anyone for Talks at Google, but William knew he'd have to package Tiny just right to make her sufficiently palatable to the folks in charge. He thought that his friend Kim-Mai Cutler, a well-known tech journalist who had become a venture capitalist and housing advocate, would be the ideal wrapping. The plan was to nominate Kim-Mai and Tiny as a pair—the former would interview the latter onstage. "All the Google techies would have read

Kim-Mai's blog in TechCrunch," said William. "She's got a lot of fans in Google, so having her as the moderator kind of sanitized it a little bit and got it through the application process."

Google had no idea what they were getting into, nor did Kim-Mai. "I don't think she had a full understanding of exactly . . ." said William, trailing off.

As the employee nominator, William was supposed to be present at the event to introduce his guest. But when the day came, he happened to be out sick, which wasn't entirely coincidental—he'd contracted trigeminal postherpetic neuralgia, which causes unbearable pain in the face. William attributed it to the stress of "this double life I was living," and it indeed got better when he left the company a few months after Tiny's talk. Because he was at home in excruciating pain, William called a like-minded coworker and said, "Hey, can you step in for me tomorrow, and just host this thing?" She agreed. "And also, I need to tell you that something might happen after the talk. But you can't know that it might happen," said William. "She was like, *Okaaay?*"

Tiny arrived at the Googleplex in her go-to outfit for bourgeoisie events: a tattered, neon-orange prison jumpsuit, along with black gloves, dark shades, and a baseball cap, from which her preternaturally straight hair hung like a golden sheet. Tiny was not there to do an interview. This was to be a performance. She commanded the room, in an uncomfortable sort of way. Kim-Mai, who fidgeted with her fingers and at one point let out a nervous laugh, could barely get a word in. "I'm from LA, and so I believe, like my mama always would say: Hollywood is in everything, even the revolution," said Tiny. "It doesn't have to be boring. For all y'all out there watching, stay at the edge of your seat."

Tiny began by explaining her racial identity to the audience, which is confusing for the uninitiated—though outwardly white, Tiny claims African and Indigenous heritage via her Black Puerto Rican grandfather, who she says carried the blood of the Taino, the Indigenous group present when Europeans arrived on the island. Her "colonizer dad," as she refers to the wealthy psychiatrist who left Tiny and her mom to fend for themselves when the marriage fell apart, diluted her gene pool. "I'm part of the mestizo nation," said Tiny, falling onto rhyme. "I am a poverty scholar, that houseless mama, that houseless daughter. All those people you don't want to see, never want to be. Look away from me—what you gonna do, arrest me? I'm in your ci-*teee*. I'm a poverty scholar, and I rock my jailhouse attire cuz me and my po' mama did jail time for the poverty crime of being houseless in this occupied Indigenous holler. I am a poverty scholar, the melanin-challenged daughter of an Afro-Boriken mama, without whom there would be no me."

Tiny's public speaking gigs typically include an extended self-intro such as this, including a long list of shout-outs. There was a shout-out to William for "doing what we call infiltrating-his-access." There was a shout-out to "my fellow welfare queens Laure and Queenandi and Junebug, and so many of y'all out there on the street right now struggling with barely staying alive. Shout-out to the Muwekma people, on whose land we're humbly standing, the ancestors, the First Nations, and to my Mama Dee." For Tiny, these machinations each embody a key element of her belief system—eldership, interdependence, redistribution of privilege—and lay the groundwork for the paradigm-shifting soliloquy that follows.

She told the Googlers her story of becoming homeless at the age of eleven, leaving school to take care of her mom and enrolling "full-time in the school of hard knocks." She talked about being on the run from Child Protective Services, as she and her mom went to extraordinary lengths to keep their family intact. She told them about getting arrested and spending several months in jail—for unpaid parking tickets and other motor vehicle violations—at the age of eighteen. "I ended up being put in jail for the act of homelessness—shout-out to all our brothers and sisters inside," she said. "I had to do my time. For what? For not having access to a roof? What an oxymoron."

She slowly started to prime the audience for her ask—Tiny doesn't interact with people of privilege without making redistribution part of the conversation. "What I want to talk about in this space, because I know there's folks with resources watching, is the way that people with resources changed our life," she said. Tiny told them about Osha Neumann—the lawyer who helped her get out of jail, later becoming a father figure—and the gift that he gave her. To satisfy the court's mandate of three thousand hours of community service, he arranged for Tiny to write about her life, which led to a published article, and eventually to her memoir and POOR Press. "The fact that I was listened to, that

I was heard, was actually life-changing," said Tiny. "As it is for everybody. But for me, I'd felt silenced, I felt like a bum; I'd internalized all the ways people think about poor folks."

Then she told them about the landlord who offered her and her mom some flexibility on the rent—"A revolutionary act," said Tiny. They'd been evicted umpteen times, a constant cycle between short-lived indoor living situations and the street. Finally, they caught a break, which allowed stability to sink in a little deeper. "I don't believe in the buying and selling of Mother Earth in the first place," Tiny told the Googlers. "But I want to say to folks watching who might have rental property that there are little things you can do to make change." She told them about Iris Canada, a centenarian in the Homefulness orbit who had recently been evicted, and then died shortly thereafter. "She was evicted because the landlord sold her building to, you know, to folks who had more money. So what can you do about that? I hate to say it, but if you're making big salaries here, then you, by default, are involved in the removal of poor folks and have a responsibility for reparations."

Tiny moved into even more provocative territory. She spoke a little louder. She began to let her anger show. "They call us the homeless problem. I'm your homeless problem, folks. Right here, right now. And I'm telling you there's a solution. Like for instance, if you're an executive and you have four or five condos, or you have a vacation home and a regular home—do you really need all those homes to live, to take care of your family, to be safe and to thrive?" Anticipating the pushback likely swirling in the room, she added, "There's a mythology that if you give people money, they'll just be lazy. Actually: no. They'll just be OK."

She suggested to the Googlers that they were in a uniquely powerful position to do something about the sweeps in their neighborhoods. "I know it's a controversial issue, but I want to say that you as employees can do blogs and talk and share and conversate in your own communities about stopping that removal and criminalization," she said. "With the RV dwellers that are getting criminalized and cited and harassed here, you can actually begin a conversation with them. They're humans. If you as a Google employee does something, your voice is more important than us protesting or speaking to the mayor or fighting for decriminalization. Your voice matters more than ours."

Finally, Tiny signaled that her talk was coming to an end and she would soon release her students from class. "When I say I have a PhD in poverty, I'm partly joking. But I'm also real," she said. "When we say poverty scholarship, what we're saying is, put us at the table. Because no matter how many times you did a $200,000 study about homelessness and poverty, it did not give us a home. And no matter how many times you put us in jail for being homeless, it did not make us homeful. And so actually what we need to do is start recognizing that folks in poverty have the knowledge to solve our own problems," she said. "Because otherwise you're just talking about us without us."

After the talk ended, Tiny labored through the necessary pleasantries with Kim-Mai and then walked to the parking lot where a dozen or so of her fellow poverty scholars and welfare queens were waiting in a van. The crew convened in the quad outside Charlie's Café, an enormous food court where Googlers enjoy their legendary free lunches. Being the lunch hour, it was packed.

The powers that be at Google didn't know this, but Tiny's public appearances typically include a group component, which is part ritual, part protest. It involves deafening drums, scantily clad men dressed in three-foot-long feathers, the incantation of various forces of nature, and a fair bit of screaming. As the Googlers munched, their conversation was suddenly drowned out with a penetrating drumbeat. Tiny's ideas about redistribution, politely proffered during her talk, were repeated as high-volume demands.

"There were like two thousand employees who heard the first part of our reparations demand," Tiny told me. "By the fourth demand, a siren went off and all of the employees stood up at the same time, literally, and left. It was very creepy." They were soon surrounded by more than a dozen security guards wearing taut black shirts and earpieces. "They circled us like an army," said Tiny. "They were screaming at us. It was very surreal and powerful and scary all at the same time."

William was at home in bed when the calls started coming in—from Google security, from his boss, from Tiny. Tiny wanted him to tell the company that she was an invited guest. The company wanted him to tell Tiny to stand down. "They were like, there's this motley crew of crazies screaming you need to give us reparations. Only a few miles away people are living in tents, but they were very upset that their lunch was being ruined," William told me. His superiors interrogated him for hours. "My boss was like, did you know about this? I was like, I knew about the talk—I lied to the company. I'm pretty sure I would have been fired if they'd found out that I had organized a protest on Google's campus."

Tiny and crew eventually skedaddled. A few months later, William quit and formed a cooperatively run firm called the Worker Agency, which does PR for tech industry labor groups like Gig Workers Rising and the Alphabet Workers Union. "Inviting Tiny was a little bit of a fuck-you to that whole situation, my way of pushing my coworkers to reckon with reality," he said. He later heard from colleagues that the Talks at Google team got a thorough scolding. "A big marketing director was like, how did this woman get through the cracks? We need a post-mortem, we need to hold people responsible." In the end, it was decided that the video of Tiny's talk would not be published online with all the other Talks at Google. "This was their punishment to Tiny," said William, rolling his eyes. "They were like, now we got her!"

Tiny posted her own video on YouTube with highlights from the day. It begins with a young Black boy in the back of Tiny's hooptie telling the camera, eagerly, that "we're going to Google to get our money, and also to get housing for the poor people!" After the aborted protest, they continued their agenda for the day, which included the SillyCon Valley Stolen Land and Hoarded Resources Tour, a tech-themed edition of a recurring ritual—part performance art, part fundraising—in which they knock on doors in wealthy neighborhoods and have what are often very awkward conversations.

The video concludes with a clip of Tiny knocking on a door in a leafy neighborhood. A young white boy cautiously opens it. "Is your mom or dad home?" Tiny asks.

"No," he says.

"Oh, OK. Would you do us a favor and give this to them?" Tiny asks, handing him a flyer. "We're having a conversation about people distributing extra resources for folks who have nothing on the street."

"OK, thank you," says the boy.

"Thank you so much," says Tiny.

"Have a good day," says the boy.

SYNCHRONICITY

Tiny reminded me of my grandmother—wild, angry, righteous, entertaining, uncompromising, and so eccentric that at times it was difficult to connect with her. In her prime, she was a well-known housing advocate in Manhattan. My grandmother's core cause was always housing, and like Tiny, she saw it as a baseline bulwark from which to strike out at other forms of injustice. By the time I was born, she'd blossomed into an omnivorous activist, railing against nukes, Vietnam, racism, and every brand of oppression, military aggression, and corporate malfeasance she could find the time for. I grew up vividly aware of her reputation as an old lady who didn't fuck around—a reporter once remarked that she "has the look of a kindly young grandmother and the fighting spirit of a lion with an ulcer"—a vibe she managed to project even as dementia slowly consumed her. In 2012, at the age of ninety-seven, she appeared in a MoveOn .org get-out-the-vote video produced by Michael Moore. "I want the Republican Party to know, if your voter suppression throughout this beautiful country enables Romney to oust Barack Obama, we will burn this motherfucker down," she said, nearly growling, to the camera. I remember her telling me later that she was a little embarrassed about the f-bomb. Yet she dropped b-bombs like rain. "Son of a *bitch*!" she would rant, about anyone on the wrong side of her cause du jour.

My grandmother was arrested dozens of times, including at the age of ninety-one when she attempted to enlist in the military at the Times Square recruiting office—a protest organized by the Granny Peace Brigade, of which she was the figurehead. The grannies were acquitted after an awkward and at times hilarious court appearance that drew national media attention. Witnesses recalled my grandmother banging on the recruiting office door with her cane after it had been locked to keep the grannies out. They then parked themselves on the sidewalk outside and refused to leave. The judge asked my grandmother why she sat down at the recruiting office. "I was tired," she drawled in her North Carolina accent, with an extra layer of country bumpkin earnestness.

My grandmother's name was Marie, but I called her Granmarie. My family visited often from Atlanta when I was growing up. I remember her apartment as a happy, bustling place, always with a steady stream of eccentric visitors, a sort of ongoing party over which my grandmother presided. One could count on being regaled with tales of her crusades beginning at the five o'clock hour, when she'd pour a gin and tonic and set out bowls of Chex Mix and other salty snacks to "nosh" on. She had a red velvet couch, long as a Cadillac, where I would sit, quietly noshing on pretzels, rapt, as she held court on her travails against Harlem slumlords, or perhaps reminisced about Dr. King's speech at the March on Washington or the 1968 student protests at Columbia. She told us stories about the leftist Latin American militants she'd harbored in her apartment and her long friendship with the Black Panthers. She once organized a fundraiser for the latter in the swank Central Park West apartment of Leonard Bernstein, the famous composer, which became the basis for the infamous Tom Wolfe essay, "Radical Chic."

Tucked high in one corner of the living room was a poster featuring the body of a lion with a photo of her head pasted onto it: "Marie M. Runyon—The Lady Is a Fighting Lion," it read. This was her campaign poster from when she ran for New York State Assembly in 1974. She was elected, a white woman from southern Appalachia, to represent the Black and Puerto Rican community of West Harlem. In a documentary made about her life years later, she said it was a group of local Black leaders who'd urged her to run. "You know perfectly well I'm not about to do that," she recalled saying. "That would be a very racist thing for me to do. I ain't gonna try to put no Black official out of his business— unless of course he's a son of a bitch. They said, *Yeah, but this guy is.*" She ran well to the left of her African American opponent—"If Malcolm X came along, I'd gladly step aside and work for his election," she'd told the *Times.*

My grandmother devoted much of her time in the legislature to exposing the racial politics of mass incarceration, which both then and now forms a direct pipeline to the housing-insecure population. She would sometimes show up after hours at upstate penitentiaries for surprise inspections "to see what the *hell* was going on in there," I remember her saying once during radical story hour. One time she helped organize a sit-in at the governor's office to demand clemency for a Black Puerto Rican Muslim anarchist who had been jailed on trumped-up charges engineered by the FBI. The governor acquiesced, and she swiftly hired the man as an aide.

I wanted Governor Newsom to acquiesce. I wanted to show up at his doorstep and demand that he stop the sweeps, like I knew my grandmother would. I wanted to dedicate myself uninhibitedly to the cause, but I didn't have my grandmother's conviction. I didn't have her rage. I hadn't lived through what she had. I didn't really know what it was like to be a single mother in 1952 with no income and facing eviction. My back has never been up against those sorts of walls. I felt like I lacked the necessary source of power to do the work. Or did I? I'd touched rock bottom, too. Maybe that's what rock bottom is for.

My grandmother operated on an uplifting principle: While those at the bottom may be exploited by the ruling class, they are in fact more powerful—and more fun—than their oppressors. I loved that she cursed and danced in a Michael Moore video and partied with the Panthers. I once saw a news clip of her at a protest hurling faux dung at a cardboard image of then-Mayor Rudy Giuliani—a scary, big-headed caricature, with "Ghouliani" written below it—whose broken-windows policing policies antagonized the unhoused. "His handling of homeless and other vulnerable people is beyond the pale," she shouted at the reporter. "He has no heart, only a head—and a big head!"

Like Tiny, my grandmother raged against the machine with verve and self-possessed style. She wore shirtwaist dresses and homemade earrings fashioned from bottle caps and subway tokens—a beret, trench coat, and crimson lipstick if she was going out. A *Times* columnist noted a décor in the "early radical" style after visiting the apartment for a legendary party at which my grandmother unveiled her 671-page, heavily redacted FBI file, a gift of the Freedom of Information Act. Her front door was plastered with a patchwork quilt of bumper stickers: *Fur Hurts*; *Greenpeace '93*; *It's the Guns, Stupid.* One wall of the hallway was lined with corkboard, to which hundreds of political buttons were pinned in a rambling mosaic: *Amadou Lives* (in honor of a victim of police brutality); *Viva la Raza* (the rallying cry of striking Chicano farmworkers); *Girls Say Yes to Boys Who Say No* (the slogan of the Draft Resisters Peace-Chick Support Squad). The living room held a museum-worthy collection of revolutionary posters: the Panthers, Malcolm X, the Soledad Brothers, Che Guevara, Emiliano Zapata, Mother Jones. One tattered poster bore Russian writing and an image of a hammer and sickle. Another dated from an anti–Vietnam War rally she'd helped to organize at Madison Square Garden. I remember wandering those walls for hours, a red-headed boy with geeky glasses and a bowl cut, trying to figure out what it all meant, and to understand my place within it.

I wasn't really thinking about my grandmother when I embarked on my mission that fall in Cupertino—I was thinking about evil tech dudes and how I was more interested in understanding the people who cleaned their toilets than I was in understanding them. But in the camps, I felt my grandmother's ghost trailing me. I'd grown up with an aversion to the idea of congregating in the street and screaming about change—perhaps because this was such a big part of both my grandmother's and my mother's identities, it was inevitable that it would not be part of mine. I didn't like the aura of negativity and burnout that I saw around activists. But the camps awakened me to the realization that fighting for the underdog, even if you don't succeed, means *the world* to those folks—and that the act itself can transform their lives. When you're at rock bottom, nothing means more than another person reflecting your value back to you—not just telling you that you're worthy, but consistently demonstrating it. I know this from my own experience at rock bottom, when I ached for someone to do that for me.

Carried by that feeling, I've evolved, slowly and with great discomfort, from journalist to activist. It started with giving money and supplies to the unhoused folks I met. Then I ghostwrote a series of op-eds for friends on the street. Later I followed a convoy of unhoused cyclists to protest homeless policy at the Capitol in Sacramento. I began to contemplate putting my body in the way of the police conducting sweeps. I motivated myself with the idea that activism doesn't have to be all doom and gloom. Screaming at people can leave one feeling lighter. The revolution, as Tiny said, can even be entertaining.

Tiny made me realize that I cannot be a bystander, that social change is a product of the cumulative process of personal transformation and the actions one takes as a result. What are homeless people doing about their situation? They are convincing people like me to join their cause. I guess it wasn't *so* hard, given the grandmother I grew up with. I know she would have lavished her Southern honeyisms on Tiny, and Tiny would have vibed it up with her, had they met. But there is more to the story of Tiny, my grandmother, and me than a quaint commonality. As I continued in search of The Fix, our stories began to converge in ways I couldn't have imagined—beginning on Morningside Drive in Manhattan, where my grandmother lived for sixty-four years.

When my grandfather left, my mom and grandmother stayed for a while with family in the Appalachian Mountains of North Carolina, where my maternal ancestors are from. Later, back in Manhattan, my mom's crib was housed in the closet of a friend, whose older boys "terrified" her, she said. Then they crashed with another friend, who lived in subsidized housing in Flushing. The agencies that run subsidized housing tend to be very strict about not allowing live-in guests. In the camps, you often hear stories about someone "getting housing," which then becomes a crash pad for their fellow campers—grounds for eviction. In my mom's case, it was she and my grandmother who got kicked out. "Someone called the housing authority on us," said my mom.

Fortunately, they did not complete the descent to "unsheltered" homelessness on the street. In 1954, when my mom was four, my grandmother got a job that allowed her to move into an apartment on Morningside Drive, on the outskirts of Harlem, where the rent was cheap. They didn't have any furniture at first, so "we sat on paint cans instead of chairs," my mom recalled. They slowly built a life, but in 1961, when my mother was eleven, they received an eviction notice again—not for lack of rent this time, but because the landlord wanted to demolish the building. The landlord turned out to be their neighbor, Columbia University, hidden behind a shell company, which had given eviction notices to the residents of seven buildings they owned next to the campus. Columbia's ongoing expansion, and the gentrification that's followed, is a long-festering blight on relations between the Ivy League school and the Black community of Harlem, which lies just to the north.

This time, my grandmother refused to leave. She fought the eviction tooth and nail, organizing countless protests, which were often colorful and creative, such as the time she and her crew blockaded the building with the help of gray-haired women from the neighborhood sitting in rocking chairs. To defend herself and her neighbors facing eviction in court, she learned to "practice law without a license," as she was fond of saying. The fight to preserve her apartment went on for decades—literally. The university boarded up windows and let the place fall into disrepair; heat and hot water could not be relied on. Over time, all but about a half-dozen tenants of her building succumbed to Columbia's pressure tactics and left. My grandmother kept going and made her fight much bigger than Columbia. She helped spearhead a movement across New York to break into vacant apartments so that unhoused families could take shelter. In 1977, the year before I was born, she founded Harlem Restoration Project, an organization that employed formerly incarcerated folks to fix up what she called "slumlord" housing—privately owned buildings the group purchased and managed cooperatively with the tenants.

My grandmother eventually won—in 1996. During her "Forty Years' War" with Columbia, as the *Times* referred to it, she metamorphized from a home-maker with a Southern accent into the hardened activist I grew up knowing, living proof that direct and persistent action makes a difference. Tiny led me back to the seed that my grandmother had planted.

On a spring day in 2022, I opened an email from Tiny, and as my eyes crept across the words on the screen, the hair on my neck rose: She was organizing a protest in the neighborhood around Columbia University. Included in the email was a small map showing the route. It ended on Morningside Drive, a couple blocks from my grandmother's old apartment. Tiny was planning to conclude the tour at this particular location because it's the home of the university president, who she was hoping to have a word with. The president's house is at the top of a cliff that rises above Morningside Park, a gentrified relic of the city's ice age geography. There's an overlook there, where a small group of my grandmother's closest friends and family had gathered to disperse her ashes into the winds above Harlem, as she wished.

KNOCK KNOCK

On a sunny summer day in Manhattan, Tiny and her posse walked up Broadway to 116th Street, where the laureled iron gates of Columbia University are found. Tiny's head was completely covered in red bandannas and black shades, as per usual. And as usual, a scantily clad man with a drum and an enormous feathered headdress was at her side. Tiny held a container of smoldering herbs in one hand and a rattle in the other; she and some of the others had rattles attached to their ankles as well. As they walked, the rattles rattled. Drums were beat. Fragrant smoke was smudged. Vibes were disseminated.

For decades I'd crossed the Columbia quad through these gates as I walked from my grandmother's apartment to the subway, or to get groceries. Columbia was her hood, these gates its most prominent landmark. Once the tribe was situated, a battery-powered PA was flipped on. As a few passersby stopped to gawk, Tiny performed her standard slam poetry intro. Tibu, her college-age son, then grabbed the mic and explained to the steadily growing crowd that they were gathered there today for a "gentrifuckation" tour.

"Gentri-FUCK-ation tours 'r' us!" the group then shouted in unison.

The tour intro was tightly choreographed; the tone was extremely pointed. "We are demanding," said Tiny to the crowd, as the drummer broke into a penetrating rhythm, "that they give at least one of their hundreds of buildings back to the houseless folks who are currently being swept violently like we are trash. This is an emergency."

When thinking of gentrification culprits, universities aren't top of mind for most folks, but Tiny and my grandmother share a special vitriol for the real estate interests of academic institutions. Columbia wasn't successful in evicting my grandmother, but roughly ten thousand of her neighbors, 85 percent of them Black or Puerto Rican, were displaced during her first decade in the neighborhood. Tiny had been a central figure fighting the displacement of the camp in People's Park by UC Berkeley, but her issues with academia reach beyond the gentrifying forces of universities and into the core of poverty scholarship theory, where the links between capitalism, individualism, and the desire of eighteen-year-olds to leave home—a manufactured one, in her view—reside. To the "families who might be listening," she said, "uncolonize your mind from the idea that your child is going to learn more by leaving their home and traveling eight thousand miles away and spending money on rent and housing when they had a perfectly good home where they left."

Tibu then blew on a conch shell, initiating a lengthy series of prayers to the four directions, among other incantations, after which the group drummed, rattled, and smudged its way down to Hogan Hall, a dorm located on a residential street at the edge of the campus. The air tightened as the posse entered the heavy wooden doors and filled the lobby with their paradigm-shattering presence. Students continued to enter and exit the building through the smoke and ruckus, most of them pretending not to notice the intruders. At first I was shocked that people didn't stop, stare, and gossip among themselves, but then I remembered that this is Manhattan, where it's normal to behave as though the mentally ill homeless person screaming next to you on the subway does not actually exist. For many of the students, coming home to eccentrically dressed people carrying on in the lobby may have felt like just another day in New York.

I found myself feeling sorry for the security guard behind the plexiglass-ensconced front desk, a young Black man who didn't seem particularly culpable and probably wasn't paid enough to be housing-secure himself. His facial expression—irritated, with a touch of fear—suggested that his day had suddenly been ruined. The drumming and rattling faded out as Tiny approached him.

"Is the house manager on site?" she asked, casually, as though she had an appointment.

"The manager of what?" the guard replied, taking out his earpiece.

"This is a dorm, right?" said Tiny. "Is the house manager on site?"

"Not that I know of," said the guard.

"Um, could you find out?" said Tiny, gently. The guard wanted to know what they wanted the manager for. "Just to demand reparations for housing for the people who were displaced," said Tiny, as if she was discussing the weather.

"You can't . . ." said the guard, stopping mid-sentence, befuddled about how to respond.

"We can't what?" said Tiny, innocently. "Can they just come down? It will take two minutes of their time."

The guard picked up the phone and called someone who said Tiny could take their complaint to the hospitality desk at Hartley Hall, which was inside the campus proper.

"Oh, OK," said Tiny, as she chewed on the idea of going inside the heavily policed campus, which she quickly determined was not a good idea. "We can't do that because we're poor people," she said. "We don't have an option."

The guard was still on the phone, struggling to explain what was happening to the person on the other end. "They're poor and don't have a option," he said, in a hushed tone. "It's a whole bunch of 'em," he whispered. "They're homeless."

A higher-ranking guard arrived with a couple backup dudes. This guy was huge, and the way he pushed out his gut as he strode slowly and deliberately through the crowd said that he was not in a mood to fuck around.

"Nice to meet you," said Tiny.

"How can I help you?" said the guard.

Auntie Francis, a close friend of Tiny's with a long history in Oakland's Black Panther circles, piped up: "We're here to offer the medicine of redistribution."

"So," said the guard, a middle-aged Black man, "this is a dorm. You're not allowed access in here."

"We just wanted to speak with the house manager and give them our proposal," said Tiny.

"Yeah, um, we can't let you in the building," said the guard.

"Even though it's just a dorm, it's a branch of the removal and eviction of hundreds of people," said Tiny. "So it's important."

"Do you have access to the internet?" the guard asked. He suggested they communicate their concerns to the university via email, which was of course not the point.

"You're a resident of New York, I'm assuming," said Tiny. "Have you seen the evictions that have been caused by dorms?"

"I'm not too familiar with that," he said. "Have you reached out to the city of New York?"

"Yes we have," said Tiny. "The mayor right now is sweeping houseless folks by the hundreds. It's not OK."

"Right," said the guard.

Tiny told him about Homefulness and suggested he look it up online. After further fruitless back-and-forth, the posse rattled out the door.

Finally, the crew arrived at the residence of Columbia's president. The four-story home, built in 1912 with eight bedrooms and quarters for seven servants, was once the residence of Dwight D. Eisenhower, who was the president of Columbia when he decided to run for president of the United States. As we crowded around the building, posse members discussed its current resident, Lee Bollinger, the highest-paid university president in the country, who, despite residing in a university-owned mansion, had recently purchased an $11.7 million apartment on Central Park West with his multimillion-dollar salary.

"How does one person have a house like this?" said Tiny. "It's an apartment building!" She knocked and waved at the doorbell camera. "Hiiiii!" she said, peering through the tiny glass window in the door. "Oh my God, there's a pool back there!" said Tiny, making a sound of disgust in her throat like she'd just swallowed a fly.

The president's house is at 60 Morningside Drive, about 1,500 feet up the road from my grandmother's apartment at 130 Morningside Drive. Demographics can change seismically over the course of 1,500 feet in the neighborhood around Columbia, known as Morningside Heights, a historically white neighborhood that lords over Harlem from atop a cliff, with the long green sliver of Morningside Park in between. My grandmother's end of Morningside Drive is where Harlem officially begins and the student housing gives way to the General Ulysses S. Grant Houses, a massive low-income development that broke ground around the time my grandmother moved to the neighborhood in the fifties.

This was the era of "urban renewal" in urban planning circles, when "slum clearance" was official government policy. Seeing that the tenements of Harlem were spilling in Columbia's direction, the university's president at the time launched a plan to buy up real estate in the neighborhood to prevent this "greatly feared invasion," as he described it. The plan was overseen by none other than David Rockefeller, a grandson of John D. Rockefeller, and one of Morningside Heights' most aristocratic residents. The idea, as described in a *Times* piece titled "The Cancer of Slum Housing Mars the Face of Morningside Heights," was to halt the organic, community-driven expansion of "slums" with a neat and tidy warehousing model ruled by the New York City Housing Authority. My grandmother found herself in the middle of the conflict, geographically and otherwise, though her allegiances were 100 percent on the Harlem side of the line.

At the president's house, Tiny made a fuss about a new seventeen-acre, $6.3 billion expansion project, the largest in the university's history, which will displace an estimated five thousand residents once complete. The state has permitted Columbia to use eminent domain—the most bludgenous tool of gentrification, which the university has a long history of wielding—to force people out. University lawyers were able to prove in court that the area in question was "blighted," which New York law permits as justification for eminent domain—a relic of the slum clearance age.

Nobody answered Tiny's knocks at the president's door, but there was a number to call posted there. "This is a message for the president," she said to the voicemail box that answered. "We weren't able to get in, but we're here to propose radical redistribution and community reparations, and that the president actually give back their oversized monolithic house so that houseless people can live in it instead of getting swept." She raised her voice. "And so that the evicted people from the dorm-industrial complex at Columbia can actually be housed! Because this house actually can house hundreds of people." Thunderous drumming punctuated her point.

Tiny continued again in a softer voice. "We noticed that there's a really nice yard in back too, so we could actually build other houses in the back. Myself and Auntie Francis could also do a food giveaway. So anyway, you can call us if you want more information," she said, leaving her number. "Please consider coming to a session of People Skool, mister president, our degentrifuckation and decolonization seminar. *Ometeotl!*"

Another ceremony closed out the tour. Tiny asked, as she often does, if anyone would like to honor their ancestors. I'd told her about my grandmother, of course, and she'd invited me to share something about her during the gentrifuckation tour—I figured this was the moment. As I told them a bit of my grandmother's story, the posse drummed and rattled to accentuate my points. For a moment, I felt like part of the tribe. I concluded my speech with the news that my grandmother had passed away a few years prior at the age of 103, and that we'd spread the last of her ashes from a cliff top above the park, just across the street from where we stood. As we emptied the urn into the wind, a magical thing happened, I said. It was mid-afternoon on a crystal-clear late fall day. The sun was beginning to drop in the sky. Around it, a circular rainbow suddenly formed. I later learned this is a rare atmospheric phenomenon, called a sun halo. We interpreted it as a manifestation of my grandmother.

"What's her name?" Tiny asked when I finished the story, even though I'd told her before—naming ancestors out loud is one way she keeps her relationships with them alive.

"Marie Runyon," I said.

"*Ibaye!*" she shouted.

I didn't know what that word meant, but it pointed to another bizarre convergence with Tiny that would soon come to light.

Piercing the Veil

How can homelessness be fixed? Bombarding unhoused people with free stuff is the lowest-hanging answer to the question. At Wolfe Camp, I'd watched as the donated goods piled up along the sidewalk faster than the campers could consume them: cases of fruit, fifty-pound sacks of organic rice, Hefty bags of day-old pastries, cartons of underwear, bags of shampoo. "It's overwhelming sometimes," Kent once told me, as he swept the sidewalk in front of his tent. As if on cue, a woman pulled over in the bike lane and honked—the sound of a delivery. Kent hustled out to the street and returned with his arms full of bags. "That happens probably thirty times a day," he said. "A group came by the other day to make a list of what we need, but I couldn't think of anything—they said they weren't taking no for an answer," said Kent. "It's where a lot of the garbage comes from. We don't need five hundred loaves of bread, but we accept everything because it's important for people to see this."

Handing over an armful of groceries can open the door to a conversation, which then opens the door to a more transformative step: getting involved in the lives of our unhoused neighbors.

During the months I spent stalking Kent, one relationship that began with a journalistic basis was becoming more personal. I'd first met Bobby on Wolfe Road as he tinkered with a pile of bike parts. That day he'd inhabited his 49ers hoodie like a turtle shell, mumbling semi-coherently and fading away at times, his body retracting into itself, fetus-like. "Did you hear that?" he asked at one point. I asked what he meant. "Like the sound of glass breaking," he said.

I didn't speak with him again until I saw him at Casa de Novo, the San José motel converted to homeless housing, where he was in a much better space. I got to know Bobby as a goofy, klutzy, impossible-not-to-love child inhabiting a man's body. He said he'd gotten hooked on meth in the seventh grade when he found his parents' stash on the dining room table. It was unclear whether he had a mild developmental disability, or perhaps brain damage from four decades of drug abuse, or if he was simply trapped in his seventh-grade self. Walter said he thought Bobby was "on the spectrum—maybe Asperger's." I didn't ask. At Casa de Novo, Bobby immediately appointed me as his friend, a relationship that he inched in the direction of caretaker. Most folks I've met on the street are shy about asking for help, but Bobby has no such filters. He constantly asked me to buy him things and take him places, which invariably led to chaotic adventures.

One day I agreed to take him to the laundromat, not realizing that the volume of his dirty clothing would completely fill my car from floor to ceiling. He became very excited, prancing and dancing around his room as he stuffed every bag he could find with clothing and spilling a drink on his laptop in the process. Then he spilled detergent on the floor of my car. Bobby enjoys listening to Christian heavy metal on a Bluetooth speaker at an extremely high volume, inasmuch as the people around him will tolerate it. I tolerated it all the way to the laundromat. There were no employees visible at the laundromat, but after a while I politely suggested that the other patrons might not appreciate the music at that volume, after which he instructed me to finish his laundry so he could sit in my car and continue to groove out to his tunes. I discovered all sorts of interesting things among his clothes, including a padded bra and a dog collar. Several hours later we made it back to Casa de Novo. Bobby was ecstatic. I was exhausted.

Another day he took me for a tour of the Jungle, the San José megacamp, where he once lived. I convinced him to leave the Bluetooth speaker in his room, but instead he brought two phones and listened to different Christian metal songs on each one at the same time. "God gave me two ears," he said with a grin.

"May as well use them," I replied.

We stopped at the Walmart down the street from the Jungle so I could buy him stuff. He told me about how he used to "fill up the cart and push it right out the door and down to the camp." He said usually no one attempted to stop him, except one time he did get busted and did a stint in jail. After meeting some of his friends who still lived in the Jungle, Bobby asked if I would take him to a thrift store and buy him a video game system. I agreed, on the condition that we could find a used one for cheap. Bobby enlisted the help of his phone.

"Hey, Google," he said. "Hey, Google!" he repeated, at a higher volume. "Can you hear me?"

"I can hear you loud and clear," said Google.

"Hey Google, where's the nearest thrift store where I can buy an Xbox?" he asked.

This actually worked. Google didn't seem to have a local inventory of used video game systems, but it did supply the numbers for several thrift stores, which Bobby called until he found one with a good selection of video game systems. Half an hour later we were on our way back to Casa de Novo with an Xbox in hand. Bobby said he'd previously had a video game system in his tent and had found it transformative. "I think if we had one over there where we're at, it would help us to communicate, to socialize, to come out of our shell," he said. "Coming out of your shell is a beautiful thing. I've come out of mine several times."

For months at Casa de Novo, Bobby seemed very much out of his shell. He is a fanatical Jesus-lover, which he expresses in a way that moves me to tears. He can barely care for himself, but he's determined to care for those in need. When he's in a good space, he travels the Valley's camps, spreading the gospel. "Whenever I'm with somebody who is having a hard time, I don't leave them until they've got some semblance of a grip and they have their heads a little higher," he told me. "I give them a little glimmer of, *Hey, you're not alone. I'm here with you.*" This is how he serves God, and in turn God sends people to do the same for him when he needs it. "God sent you to me," he told me. "Like a guided missile."

Bobby's fiftieth birthday was coming up, and I asked Samira if she'd join me in taking him out to lunch. He'd been telling me for weeks that he'd really like it if someone gave him a red electric guitar for his birthday; we gave him a card with some cash, so he could find one he liked. He seemed very overwhelmed about the lunch, and when we got to the restaurant I had to convince him to leave the large container of whiskey and coke he'd brought in the car. As we ate, he recounted a series of childhood memories, such as how his mom used to pull her hair, and that time she threw an ashtray and "it went like an arrow into the wall." He became increasingly fetal as lunch progressed, back in his shell, his voice diminishing into a semi-coherent mumble. It wasn't the goofy, fun-loving Bobby I'd been telling Samira about, but his other half.

Even as I remained convinced that forming direct relationships with the unhoused is an essential facet of The Fix, I remained unconvinced about my capacity to handle the other halves that every highly traumatized person has. I know they're simply amplified versions of the other halves that less traumatized people have, but I struggled to know where, or how, to create boundaries. I chose not to answer the phone when Bobby called in the middle of the night, and after doing so a couple times, he stopped. That boundary felt pretty clear. How much of my time and money to devote to unhoused friends, and to which ones, was less clear.

The merging of my personal life with the professional task of writing a book created plenty of stress. I became less afraid of venturing into camps, which did not comfort Samira. I occasionally floated the idea of inviting an unhoused friend over for dinner, which terrified her—then they would know where we lived, and who knows what bad things that might lead to. I was more concerned about how them seeing the home we'd moved into, with its sweeping views of the Golden Gate Bridge, might change the dynamics of my relationships. As long as they only knew me on their turf, it seemed easier to maintain the notion that we were more alike than not. I believe devoutly that we are, but I felt it wouldn't take much to make an unhoused friend question whether that notion was a façade. I wondered if they actually believed it to begin with, or if they just appreciated the company, rides, and meals out that I provided.

Rudy, for one, often seemed unsure. When I told him where I lived, he became slightly agitated. "Ahhh, one of the rich areas," he said. "I bet you go home to a nice house every day and your girlfriend has dinner ready on the table." I didn't know what to say. "Has this changed you?" he asked. "Do you think about us when you're falling asleep at night?"

Samira was supportive, but she also forced me to question my assumptions. Were these relationships not primarily transactional? Could I really trust the people I met on the streets enough to let them into my personal life? Even if they have good intentions, haven't some of them done bad things? Do they even have the ability to prevent themselves from doing bad things when under the influence of substances or mental duress? How well do I really know these folks? Not very well, I had to admit. But how could I if I didn't open up more?

Around this time I was invited to participate in an event organized by an affordable housing advocacy group in Palo Alto. I was to be interviewed onstage by a local pastor who'd founded a homeless services organization in the area, which was working with the Chan Zuckerberg foundation to build a factory producing modular homes for low-income folks. I was high on my horse at the time about the idea of getting to know one's unhoused neighbors, and I steered my response to every question in that direction. The pastor lauded my passion to break down those barriers. But he told the audience that as someone with a great deal of experience working with the unhoused—far more experience than myself—that he did not recommend wandering into local camps. It simply wasn't safe, he said. I clarified that I wasn't encouraging schoolchildren to take candy from the guy asking for change on the corner, but I thought somewhere on the spectrum between that and looking away when you pass a homeless person there was an opportunity for radically transformative relationships to emerge.

This was met with a mix of excitement, bewilderment, and hostility in the audience. It turned out that a woman on the board of Abode (the homeless services organization behind Casa de Novo) was present, and she made sure to tell the event organizer afterward that I was off my rocker. The organizer, whose father has been homeless, told me she was glad I'd made the audience uncomfortable and said that as someone who is deeply embedded in the world of homeless mega-charities, she thought that the paradigm shift I proposed was at odds with their "neoliberal leanings." The most beautiful moment of the day occurred when an older man stood up and said that he completely agreed with what I was saying and had in fact invited a homeless man to live with him for a time. He didn't seem like some radical leftist, just an old rich guy in Palo Alto who was lonely and woke up one day with a logical thought: Why not share his home with someone who didn't have one?

Forging one-on-one relationships with unhoused neighbors may be an ideal solution, though I admit that most people aren't going to see it as a practical one. I found myself wavering on the idea. Who am I to think that I could take care of someone at the bottom end of intergenerational trauma and poverty, suffering from multiple layers of addiction and psychosis? There's a reason we use taxpayer dollars to pay people to do that. It's an enormous burden to bear.

I also came to recognize that most of my relationships with the unhoused were based on their aspiring, inspiring, up-from-rock-bottom sides. I gravitated to these qualities and away from others. More and more I had to acknowledge that my unhoused friends mainly shared those parts of themselves and kept the others under wraps, if only out of shame.

They told me constantly about the ubiquity of theft in their world—from stores, from housed people, from each other. People generally didn't say that they themselves were thieves; if anything, they "used to" steal. But I sometimes wondered whether "dumpster-diving" referred only to actual dumpster-diving, or if it was a euphemism that alluded to other forms of "ownership transfer," as one unhoused friend referred to his bike theft habit, which he assured me was a thing of the past, despite the high-end bikes I often saw lying around his camp. I noticed that some unhoused friends had an awful lot of dumpster-dived items that were, to their alleged amazement, unearthed in original packaging. Bobby had an extraordinary array of electronics, including eight phones that I counted at one point. He was always losing and breaking them, but he said not to worry, because he could "get them for free at T-Mobile." It seemed unlikely that the lying and cheating and con-artistry I heard about in camps was never conducted by the people I got to know, and exclusively by those I did not get to know.

And then there are the drugs. Most folks gave me the impression of being more or less clean, or at least on the cusp of recovery. One day at Casa de Novo, Walter took it upon himself to set the record straight about the Wolfe crew. He said everyone in the community stayed up all night doing meth. Even sweet Jen? I asked. "Everyone," he said. What about clean-cut Troy? "Troy shoots heroin," he said. "If they're not doing meth, they're doing something else." I thought that Kent was getting clean, I said. "He's just trying to clean up his image," said Walter. I felt doubt creeping in.

LOVE IN THE AIR

Could my unhoused friends be trusted? Was I actually making a difference in their lives? Was I unconsciously engaging in poverty porn? Wood Street Commons proved to be a useful laboratory for reconciling the doubts that arose from my relationships with the unhoused folks I'd met.

There was a constant stream of nonresidents at the camp, some of whom were such a frequent presence, and fit so naturally in the environs, that a casual observer would be hard-pressed to identify who lived there and who resided in the land of the housed. I came to think of Wood Street as a single community, in which housing status was a blurry and unimportant delineator. "We help to dissolve the invisible barrier between the housed and the unhoused," Theo told the Oakland officials in his emancipatory address.

One of the camp's most decadent parties occurred one evening in late August, when I was still a new face on Wood Street. It was hosted by Amelia, a friend of the camp, who advertised the event on her Instagram feed as "a landmark evening of consciously crafted food, cocktails and community," teasing a series of photos that were pure Napa—intimate outdoor rooms bedecked with twinkling strings of patio lights and large wicker baskets sprouting head-high bouquets of wild fennel and pampas grass—but staged at John's compound. "This will be the grandest, weirdest, most mystical dinner party ever held," she wrote.

Amelia was a sports journalist turned digital nomad who had fled her corporate newspaper job and had been blogging her way through West Coast encampments, chronicling homeless communities along the Guadalupe River in San José and at Skid Row in Los Angeles, where she periodically returned to host street-side barbecues that bumped with music and booze. Her Instagram account is a collage of beachside meals in Baja, comic asides about vanlife— think pee buckets—and photos of receipts for tents and hot dogs purchased on behalf of her homeless friends. Amelia's followers have donated tens of thousands of dollars for camp residents, and she scrupulously documents how the money is spent.

As guests poured in to the Wood Street party, the quotient of dyed hair and designer spectacles grew. Janani Ramachandran, a state assembly candidate running on a campaign to address the housing crisis—she lost but was later elected to city council—took selfies with residents as an aide hovered nervously in business attire. A few journalists mingled. The smell of sauteed shrimp melded with barbecued brisket; unshucked corn steamed on another grill. Amelia—tall, slender, and self-possessed—mixed cocktails behind a makeshift bar in black slacks, a classy blouse, and heels.

What might have looked like voyeurism on Instagram—"I'm in love with this community," Amelia gushed a couple days before the party—looked very different in real life. She'd been living at the camp in her cargo van, named Bertie, for a month and had become a trusted member of the tribe, hauling trash, fighting off the rats, and resisting the city's threats to remove the camp. "From the beginning she was all-in and balls-to-the-wall with us," Theo told me.

In an outdoor kitchen, LeaJay and Kye chatted about drugs and love as they tended to giant pots of pasta and potatoes that burbled atop a series of camp stoves. "It wasn't until I dated a user that I really moved into that, like, harm reduction thing," said Kye, a recent UC Berkeley graduate who got a $25,000 university grant to build a community garden at the camp, including "wicking beds," which irrigate themselves. "Like, I'm going to restart your heart and that's what matters most at the moment," they continued. "We can't moralize it." Hip-hop beats and the chatter of several dozen partygoers competed with a discussion about the meaning of "demisexual" and the difficulty of finding bisexual people to date. "There's a Tinder and a Grindr, but they don't have a Binder," joked LeaJay, a heavily pierced camp resident who wore a T-shirt that read, "I Am a Strong Black Queen."

As the sun set, the crowd settled into lawn chairs strewn about a small clearing. Amelia emceed. "There are fewer walls here," she told the crowd. "You have to connect, because you rely on your neighbors."

Residents took turns passing the mic, telling stories of their journey from housed to unhoused, explaining why the city's homeless services are of little use, and making it known that what they'd really like is to have some municipal funds to help make the camp's fledgling infrastructure more permanent. The housed world tends to assume that unhoused people want what they have, a script the campers sought to flip.

"I like it here because I'm not alone," said John, Monte's dreadlocked neighbor, who was dressed in an orange linen shirt, khaki shorts, leather loafers, and aviator glasses, lenses removed. "The people I care about are out here," he said. "It really works—it's simple." John, who worked as a chef before becoming homeless and had overseen the evening's menu, suggested that their lifestyle had value to the outside world—"We can spread what we're doing here to other places, so people can fill that void inside of them"—and said, with a trace of a smile on his lips, that he'd like to monetize it: "We could make so much money!" He continued, more seriously. "If people want to experience this, just come out here and spend a weekend with us. We'll pop a tent up for you, or you can stay in the lounge area on a couch. You can see the raw us; we can talk."

Messiah, a camper wearing a gold chain and a fedora, grabbed the mic and launched into a monologue about the downsides of the housed world. "They ain't free," he said, in a husky preacher's voice. "They was born in a box and they went from there to another box—a baby crib. They went to elementary and high school in a box. Started college in a dorm box. You get out there, you're living life, trying to find yourself—then you get a job and go back in a box." Life in the camp was like an antidote to the limitations of the housed world, said Messiah. "Here is no boxes. Everything is 360 degrees, like the sun, the moon, and the stars. Alpha and omega." He noted that on Wood Street, "you got to walk past his house, my house, and his house to get to they house, so you get to know everyone. How many of you guys live in a neighborhood where you don't even know your neighbors?" The result of having escaped the anomie of the housed? "We happy," said Messiah.

It felt almost like a political speech. "So am I homeless?" he implored. "Because I don't live in a box? God provides me with everything I need. And a lot of shit I don't need." The crowd laughed, some more comfortably than others. His message for politicians concerned about the growth of homeless camps was this: "We gonna do what we wanna do—you can assist us, or move the fuck out of the way!" He paced the impromptu stage as he expounded on his roots in the Black Power movement. "Imma Panther, baby! Y'all understand? I was born with a fighting spirit burned into my chest!"

Amelia lit a cigarette and cracked a Miller High Life as she listened, and nestled into the arms of Moose, of the Moose Pit Café, a strapping resident of Persian descent. She later waxed poetically about their love affair on Instagram. "Moose and I walked the back road at night, balancing atop the concrete K-rails," she wrote. "We held hands. We heard gunshots."

The camp became a bit of a lovefest, which, as love often does, produced both beauty and chaos. One day I found Zelda, a tattoo artist, painting a mural at the camp entrance—sinuous tree branches on which tiny homes sprouted alongside the leaves—and struck up a conversation about what drew her and others to Wood Street. While she lived in an apartment at the time, she'd once lived in a camp in San Luis Obispo, just for fun. She was among the regulars at Wood Street and had gotten involved with Nick, a fellow volunteer who was part of the camp band, the Commoners, which performed at camp events and jammed on Sundays at the weekly barbecues. "Homeless people are really real," said Zelda, puffing on a spliff. "I don't get that genuineness from people who have to work within the matrix. I'm sure that's why you're out here, too." I nodded, sheepishly.

The volunteerism at the camp had a strong hipster flavor, which had solidified early in the pandemic when a group of housed folks banded together to distribute green juices, herbal remedies, and organic food from a white van they piloted down Wood Street. Then they started building things, mounting a GoFundMe campaign that netted more than $80,000 to construct a community kitchen, bathhouse, guest cabin, free store, and health clinic, where one could obtain both immune-boosting tinctures and Narcan. All of this was constructed out of "cob," an adobe-like construction material with a hobbit-village aesthetic, which formed quite a contrast with the rat-and-needle vibe. There was even a cob pizza oven and an accompanying cob "moat"—think sushi boat restaurant, but for pizza. The cob structures formed a mini-neighborhood in the camp, which came to be known as Cob on Wood.

The Cob on Wood volunteers put on outdoor film screenings, including *V for Vendetta* and *Dope Is Death*, a documentary about an acupuncture-based opiate detox program developed in the seventies by members of the Black Panthers. There was a weekly open mic night and regular clean-the-camp parties, sometimes followed by free massage sessions. On any given day, visitors would likely find a handful of volunteers hauling off junk, helping to repair camp infrastructure, or just hanging on the couches beneath a canopy of stretchy white fabric—an event space, soundstage included. Regulars included a psychedelic NFT artist known as Supafray, who pledged 10 percent of proceeds to the cause, and local hip-hop musician AshEl "Seasunz" Eldridge, who has performed with Erykah Badu and will.i.am, and also offers sound baths and other multisensory ceremonies through his Soulestial Church Band.

Sometimes I questioned the value of what the volunteers brought to the camp. One event I attended was billed as a healing circle—"Come repair your heart and spirit," said the flyer. When I arrived, a guy with a man bun whose shirt said "passionate about compassion" stirred a giant vat of soup. Others chanted around the fire, made prayer ties, and smudged themselves with a smoking goblet of herbs. I didn't recognize any of the participants as residents of the camp.

Many of the volunteers on Wood Street referred to their work as "mutual aid," a term coined by the Russian anarchist Peter Kropotkin at the turn of the twentieth century, which reemerged as a buzzword in the era of Black Lives Matter and pandemic-induced poverty. Rather than rely on top-down solutions from the government and nonprofits with seven-figure budgets, the ethos of mutual aid is neighbors helping neighbors—ideally with those in need defining what is helpful or not—and dissolving boundaries between givers and receivers. "Solidarity, not charity" is the movement's slogan.

Tiny, who played a sort of wise elder role on the Wood Street scene, takes a more circumspect view. "Most of these mutual aid workers are folks who have never missed a meal," she told me. "I say this with love, but they think they're doing way more than they're actually doing." However, "their presence does matter," said Tiny. "If there weren't these hipster-artists doing a Burning Man village down there, the city probably would have bulldozed the whole fucking place already."

Race is an elephant in the conversation. The vast majority of the volunteers were white, as were the reporters who regularly descended on the camp. Theo, a relatively new white resident, had a tendency to act as camp spokesperson when outsiders were present, which the camp's long-time Black residents chastised him for. In an effort to rectify the situation, Theo once posted a YouTube video explaining that some members of the Wood Street community wondered how things like fancifully designed mud huts were going to help them. They "felt that was colonialism all over again, that the rich housed people said, oh, there's free land here, we can do what we want, and we can"—he flashed air quotes—"help the homeless."

Despite my confusion about how to integrate myself with the Wood Street community, it was crystal clear to me that it was going to take a coalition of housed and unhoused—however messy—to fend off the bulldozers that were coming.

Camp residents can be fiercely protective toward outsiders, including members of the media. The cuteness of a hobbit village in a homeless camp proved irresistible to the press, resulting in a string of stories that tended to center the narratives of housed volunteers more than the campers. In the midst of it all, a YouTube personality named Nick Johnson published a forty-one-minute video about the camp, featuring an extended interview with Monte, which has racked up more than seventeen million views, superseding his previous most popular titles, "America's Poorest States" and "The Absolute Worst Ghettos Ever Seen." The camp's message had reached the masses, but perhaps not with the sort of framing they might have hoped for.

I'd generally felt welcomed in camps, but the atmosphere on Wood Street was more charged. "You need to get the fuck out of here," said a resident who walked by one day as I sat alone, taking notes at a table next to John's place. I looked up, startled. "Yeah, I'm talking to you," he said, and kept walking. John later told me that the guy is not fond of white people.

The camp's volunteers found themselves dodging angst from multiple directions. Zelda, who can afford rent in Oakland because of her parents' financial support, described the standard critique as, "You rich kids are coming in and just making this your playground. I do think about that because, you know, on one level, that's true," she said, puffing on a spliff. As the manager of a couple of the camp's social media accounts, Zelda sometimes responded to attacks, such as a post from a user named candypinkspaceship: "Can anyone tell me in the like hella months these people have been out gentrifying/hippie shitting on this homeless encampment how many people have gotten any real help toward a long term solution? The focus could be on bringing them inside."

"In my opinion, people are a little too sensitive," said Zelda. Most of the feedback, she said, was positive, if misguided. "Everybody's like, oh, you're helping them. And I'm like, they're helping us. We're learning."

Other critiques originated from residents. Monte told me that some of the volunteers had a tendency to impose their own vision, rather than offering support for resident-driven projects, and described a wave of pushback within the camp as a result. "Don't just come and do things—ask us," he said.

Xochitl, an early volunteer who spearheaded green juice delivery and was one of the core organizers of Cob on Wood, said the deluge of media attention after the first structures were built led to a deluge of donations and a sense of urgency to expand—too quickly, perhaps. "In retrospect, I think that some of the critiques that people have of Cob on Wood might be different had we been able to just slow down at that moment." Organizers offered to pay residents to help build the structures, yet "there was always a challenge in getting residents to participate," said Xochitl.

"She opened Kmart inside of our Bloomingdale's and tried to hire us as employees," said Monte. "I'm like, no, we don't want to work for you."

The UC Berkeley–funded garden beds did not see much use, and winter rains caused mud to slough off some of the cob structures. When I arrived at the camp, the project was in course correction mode. "We had all these lofty goals about what Cob on Wood could be," said Xochitl. "I've really tried to come into a space of acceptance and to learn from the mistakes that we've made. This work is really hard."

It was clear, however, that many residents valued her efforts. When there weren't outsiders hosting festivities at Cob on Wood, the facilities were well used. Lydia, a resident who oversaw the cob health clinic, for which she received a hundred-dollar weekly stipend, viewed the discord as part of a meaningful learning process. "There's a lot of hurt feelings about how the money is getting used, and who's deciding all that stuff," said Lydia, a cofounder of the Oakland Drug Users Union. "The priorities have been a little out of order."

At the healing circle I attended, the only resident I spotted was LeaJay, whose RV sat a few feet from the drumming and dancing. She peeked out from behind it and absorbed the scene with a perplexed grimace. "Xochitl was hella fucking annoying at first," she told me. "It was like, here she comes with that nasty-ass juice." But they have since become dear friends. On LeaJay's birthday, Xochitl took her to see *Black Panther: Wakanda Forever.* When LeaJay decided she was ready to kick opiates, Xochitl organized a series of healing ceremonies for her—a year later she was sober and had moved into Homefulness. LeaJay, who received one hundred dollars per week to manage the cob kitchen, told me that the hipsters hanging out at Wood Street may have made for some awkward encounters, but she saw their presence as a reflection of one of the residents' biggest goals: "We're pushing to be treated like humans, to not have the stigma of homelessness on us so much," she said. "Because that's an ugly, ugly jacket."

Being in community is hard even when you have a lot in common with your peers. Forging bonds across differences is a mountain most people would rather not climb, despite the magnificent view from the top. On Wood Street, I saw that the relationships between residents and volunteers were, for those that stuck with them, transformative. Like a marriage whose early stumbles become the raw materials of selfless devotion, it's the commitment that matters. The more vulnerable the person on the other side of the relationship, the more steadfast commitment is required.

There are perils at every step, such as a man who skulked by me one afternoon at Wood Street with an eighteen-inch knife held behind his back, as though he was looking for someone. I heard gunshots on multiple occasions. A resident in the depths of opioid addiction showed me the wall of his RV where he'd scrawled the names of his friends who had died. Administering Narcan is a basic civic duty in the camp. Fire is a constant threat. Amelia, the nomadic journalist, woke up one morning to find the camp's event space, just a few feet from her van, ablaze. The arsonist holed up in Moose's shed, refusing arrest. The situation was eventually resolved with a small battalion of police, some of them bearing sniper rifles, and a robot of the sort used in hostage situations.

But it was interpersonal tensions that brought Amelia's stay to an abrupt end. "Something happened," she later explained to her online followers, without elaborating. "The fragile sense of safety and security I had enjoyed there had been removed." Bertie was barely running at the time, and she found herself with a different experience of vanlife: "It felt weird and cruel to be apart from my adopted home but still stuck in Oakland, languishing alone and sick from a cold on an unfamiliar street."

Zelda gave Amelia a tattoo before she left—a tableau of the camp that stretched from armpit to elbow, with the Sixteenth Street Station in the background and the white canopy that presided over the event space in the foreground. Not long after, Amelia moved to Argentina, where she wrote me a moving email about her time on Wood Street. "We talked about our fears, and our sadness, and our hopes and our joy. We talked about really hard things, and really personal things and really honest things. We talked to each other in a way that most people in the outside world do not, because for the most part people at Wood Street weren't afraid of judgment from their neighbors." Wood Street, she wrote, was "a place where others could let their deepest selves unfurl, and I could as well."

I was impressed with Amelia's ballsiness. Living in a homeless camp for four months is about as hardcore as journalism gets. I hadn't yet spent a single night in a camp but decided it was time. I planned a four-night stay at Wood Street, inviting my friend Joe, a tough-as-nails street photographer who'd spent a decade documenting Skid Row in LA, to join me. Joe slept in the minivan he'd converted into a tiny camper, and I slept in the back of my car. For privacy, I brought a farmer's market tent canopy, strung blue tarps around it for walls, and backed into it like a garage.

One evening we sat around a campfire at Moose's place, which had recently received a garden makeover, complete with a head-high fountain. A couple of well-fed rats scampered across the patio, like cats coming out to play. "We try to stay out of their way," joked Moose, who boiled a kettle on the fire and passed around hot cocoa in cups he'd made moments earlier from sliced-open water bottles. Whiskey went around the circle, too, followed by a meth pipe; Joe and I passed on the latter. The crew dug into the midnight snack Moose whipped up over the fire: a stir fry of chopped cabbage, ramen noodles, and egg.

Monte joined us and struck up a conversation with Joe about childhood camping trips with their fathers, which soon turned into a conversation about their childhood traumas. Joe opened up about how he's still haunted by his mother's alcoholism. "Sorry to hear that," said Monte, who told Joe about a recent decision he was proud of: "I just acquired a pistol, but I took it back to the person that I acquired it from. I felt like I wasn't responsible enough to handle it."

"I'm glad you did that," said Joe. At this point, the two men were finishing each other's sentences. "I feel like saying that you guys are homeless is kind of a stretch—"

"We're not," Monte interjected.

"Because this is your home," Joe continued. "It's just that they're not accepting your idea of what—"

"Home is," said Monte.

They embraced. "Bring it in here," said Joe. "I can't not hug you right now." Joe said such moments are why he hangs out in homeless camps. "I love stuff like this. I find it very, uh, therapeutic."

MATCHES AND FUEL

In the summer of 2022, the Wood Street lovefest devolved into a crisis. Caltrans, which has jurisdiction over the majority of the land, announced they were gearing up for a massive sweep. At the time, fires were breaking out in the Caltrans portion of the camp an average of more than once per week. Residents maintained that most of the fires were the work of one or more pyromaniacs, but this person or persons seemed to be so feared that no one dared rat on them. The fire department didn't seem interested in investigating, and it was a convenient pretext that gave Caltrans the necessary political cover to bulldoze the place. The last straw was an enormous fire that shut down the MacArthur Maze for several hours.

The camp, with the help of pro bono lawyers, sued to prevent the sweep. At 10 o'clock on a Thursday morning, residents and supporters gathered in front of a laptop at Cob on Wood with Brigitte Nicoletti, a lawyer with the East Bay

Community Law Center, who was leading the litigation. They had a Zoom hearing scheduled in response to their request for a temporary restraining order to stop the sweep. Their lawsuit named the city, the surrounding county, Caltrans, and Governor Newsom himself as defendants. Representatives for each appeared in the Zoom portal, along with a federal judge, William Orrick, who sat in front of an enormous bookcase with row after row of perfectly aligned legal volumes. With his wire-rim spectacles and brown hair parted on the side, he projected a stern, unflappable bearing.

Several residents took the virtual stand. The first was an older white man named Kelly Thompson, who everyone on Wood Street called Mr. Kelly. He is known around the camp for having a working truck and a willingness to tow nonoperational vehicles and RVs—which house a large percentage of Wood Street residents—when called on. Mr. Kelly is one of the highest-functioning residents, but he was so overcome with emotion when he appeared in front of the laptop that he struggled to get his words out.

"Take your time, Mr. Johnson," said Orrick, visibly moved. "Take a breath."

After several attempts, he finally managed to speak. "I've been trying to rebuild my trailer and having to move constantly has been real difficult," said Mr. Kelly. "It's very difficult having to pack and move every two or three months and then find a place that's secure enough to spread my stuff out so that it's out of the house so I can work on the trailer." He said he'd practiced his speech the night before, but now it wasn't coming to fruition. "I don't know where I'm going with all this," he said.

"So, Mr. Thompson," said Orrick. "This is what I get from what you're telling me: You would like to remain where you are, that moving is a burden to you, and you're unsure of what will happen if you are forced to move. Is that basically what you're telling me?"

"You put it in much better words than I have," said Mr. Kelly.

Next up was John, Monte's close friend and neighbor, and the de facto co-leader of the camp. John was in the hospital with some sort of infection and appeared on the screen with his head covered in a white bandage. But he spoke forcefully.

"My experience over the years of being homeless and being moved constantly is that you never can get a foundation," he said. "There will be loss of belongings, of housing, vehicles. Some people work out there and would lose wages. But more importantly," he continued, "they're communities. They're people that know each other. They stay at these places because they feel safe there. We provide resources for one another, we take care of one another. We cook meals. We provide bedding. We provide shelter, tents, clothing, conversation. What I noticed though, through these evictions, is that the agencies come through and basically rip apart these communities with no solutions, no alternatives." He paused for a moment to catch his breath. "I'm in the hospital, so if evictions go through then all my stuff is lost and gone."

Orrick was smiling slightly as John continued his speech. He seemed tickled to be speaking to this homeless man with a head bandage. John kept talking and talking.

"Mr. Janosko, you have said quite a lot," Orrick interjected at one point, letting out a little laugh, which for a guy with such a heavily buttoned-down demeanor felt like an unbridled giggle.

"I hope I've gotten something across," said John.

"You've done an excellent job, Mr. Janosko," said Orrick.

Stephen Silver, the lawyer for Caltrans, said that the agency was sympathetic to the residents' situation, but that the constant fires posed an even greater threat to their safety and well-being, and that of the general public. He produced photos of the recent fire that had engulfed the highway overpass, noting how close it was to enormous tanks of flammable gases at a wastewater treatment plant next door to the camp. Had the wind been blowing the other way, he explained, the flames might have reached the tanks, potentially causing an epic explosion that could have killed many residents. "This is simply a potential catastrophe that cannot be tolerated," he said in a grave tone.

"That potential catastrophe I suppose has been there for the last six years," Orrick retorted, clearly unimpressed. "Would that be true?"

"That would be true," Silver replied.

Nicoletti, Wood Street's lawyer, pointed out the obvious fact that fire prevention and eviction were not the same thing. Couldn't they find a way to prevent the fires, which the residents weren't happy about either, without kicking everyone out? "Caltrans still could be coordinating with residents to provide trash removal," she said, as an example, thus reducing the fuel load.

"There has been no evidence that Wood Street residents have been involved in these fires," she noted. "The burden on Caltrans placed by these fires, and also the risk to public safety, can be mitigated," she continued. "But the risks to the plaintiffs of irreparable harm if they are kicked out of Wood Street without anywhere to go cannot be mitigated immediately. It's a life-and-death situation here for folks."

"What is the plan?" Orrick asked Silver, the Caltrans lawyer. "Where specifically do you expect that the plaintiffs will be able to go? How will they get there? What are the plans with respect to storing property?"

Silver said that those details were the city and county's responsibility. "We don't do that ourselves. We coordinate with them."

Orrick asked the lawyers for the city and the county the same questions. Jamilah Jefferson, the lawyer for the city of Oakland replied that, "there have been conversations and some level of coordination, but . . . I am unaware of the actual specifics."

After some back-and-forth it became clear that the city, county, and state had scarcely spoken about what was going to happen to the evicted residents. There was tension in the air among them. The city had been working on a plan to move the campers into tiny homes, but they hadn't yet begun construction. Both the city and county representatives seemed irritated that Caltrans had suddenly announced a massive sweep with a few days' notice and seemed to expect local authorities to spring into action to take care of these people. Both said they did not have the resources to do that. The city's shelter system was at capacity, for starters.

"I understand that everybody wants to wash their hands of this particular problem," said Orrick. "That's not going to happen."

Cases involving sweeps are often brought in federal court because they are often based on violations of constitutional rights. In this case, Nicoletti had thrown a constellation of legal offenses into the filing, including the First, Fourth, Eighth, and Fourteenth Amendments, as well as citing potential violations of the Americans with Disabilities Act. One of those, the crowd at Cob on Wood was delighted to discover, seemed to stick for Judge Orrick: the Fourteenth Amendment, which guarantees the right to due process. In particular, Fourteenth Amendment jurisprudence includes the "state-created danger" doctrine, which Orrick said would be impinged by the eviction—by kicking people out with a few days' notice, the state was subjecting them to a litany of peril.

"Caltrans and the defendants have allowed this encampment to exist," said Orrick, "and with five days' notice wanted to evict everybody without a plan, as best I can tell, about where the residents of the encampment would go. That's a problem. And a state-created danger." Caltrans had done "a lot of hand-waving about getting help from the county and the city," but in reality, said Orrick, in a scolding tone, "there is *nooo* plan for any of that."

Orrick issued a temporary restraining order to prevent Caltrans from proceeding with the sweep. He set another hearing date a month later for the parties to reconvene. In the meantime, he said that the city, county, and state needed to come up with a viable relocation plan if the eviction was to move forward.

It felt like a victory, but that feeling was short-lived. When the parties reconvened a month later, they presented their plan, which to me sounded very thin. The city had freed up forty shelter beds for the roughly two hundred people estimated to be displaced by the sweep. Caltrans said they would break up the sweep into three phases with a two-week pause between each one, so that not everyone would be displaced at once, theoretically reducing the strain on the homeless services system.

Orrick accepted their plan. Apparently, from a legal perspective, a state-created danger could be mitigated with sufficient due process. And apparently forty beds and an elongated timeline was sufficient.

The battle was on. Monte, John, and many of the camp's other core organizers were not subject to eviction because they lived in an area of the camp that was on city-owned land. But as Monte likes to remind people, their motto is "all or none"—they planned to defend their neighbors.

I got there before dawn on the first day of the sweep. As the sun came up, Caltrans officials, highway patrol officers, and about fifty laborers working for a contractor called Marinship began assembling at one end of the camp, along with a platoon of heavy machinery. Eventually, the army of evictors began marching down an unpaved Caltrans service road that runs beneath the overpasses, toward the area that had been designated to be swept first. There's a point where the service road passes through a low concrete wall, creating a bottleneck where the army would have to narrow down to fit through the roughly twelve-foot-wide opening—the perfect spot for a blockade.

Monte suddenly appeared, wearing a cowboy hat and boots, and just before the army reached the bottleneck he began filling it with shopping carts, busted furniture, mattresses, and other items pulled from nearby refuse piles. Residents and volunteers—about thirty housed allies had shown up—pitched in, and within twenty minutes the road was blocked with a giant pile of trash. People parked vehicles next to the trash heap to further block the path and climbed on top of them to berate their evictors. A standoff ensued as news crews, including one circling overhead in a helicopter, filmed.

Monte, in a fit of rage, screamed at the police. "There's a ton of you guys out here—with weapons! What the fuck! We're homeless people." He delivered the lines with an actor's cadence. "You have guns on the side of your hips—you fucking bullies! How about we come sleep in your backyard? Because you're pushing us to nowhere."

At one point I sat with him and Henry, a resident wearing a ski mask, as they lashed together three-inch-long spikes—"nail bombs," they called them, which they intended to sprinkle in the road to puncture the tires of the sweeping equipment and cop cars. "At this point, it is war. It is not a peaceful thing," said Monte. "Without making people uncomfortable, change doesn't happen. It's time to make them uncomfortable."

The residents' show of force was impressive, but they were massively outnumbered and out-resourced. The Caltrans workers bulldozed through the blockade and used giant forklifts to move the vehicles that had been positioned in their path. Two residents who refused to move were arrested.

The media, for the most part, treated it as a spectacle, rather than a serious protest. I, however, was inspired. Monte's rage felt just, his performance authentic. It seemed to me like this was a battle that could be won. The courts tended to agree, in principle, with the cause. And having witnessed it firsthand, I knew that most people, if they could see what I saw and feel what I felt, would be supportive. The question was how to bring them into the fold; I wanted very much to dissolve the veil on a bigger scale. It's not enough for a few hipsters and activists to mix with their unhoused neighbors—they need you.

There was a moment in the chaos that day when Monte calmed down and took a smoke break. He'd built another trash barrier, this one nearly eight feet tall, at a gate that formed a bottleneck at the other end of the service road. Caltrans eventually bulldozed that one, too. But before they did, Monte sat on top of the pile, his cowboy hat silhouetted against the backdrop of the Oakland skyline, taking very dramatic drags from his cigarette. His body language was relaxed, but determined, like a lone rider headed into the sunset. More than anyone, Monte made me a believer.

Go Home

Is the idea that camps have value—to their residents and to the rest of us—a path forward, or a pipe dream? Many of the dreamers spend an unfortunate amount of time with mind-altering substances flowing through their veins, after all. I'm not naïve to the reality of addiction and mental illness. But I decided not to cling to the skeptical part of myself. Why? It felt hopeless. It felt resigned to the Amazonification of life. Whereas to cast my fate with that of my unhoused neighbors felt hopeful. To those who haven't spent time in camps, who only know the sob story version of homelessness portrayed in the media, that may sound hopelessly naïve. But to the housed people who have ventured beyond the tired narratives, beyond simplistic notions of charity, and actually spent days and weeks and months and years hanging out in camps, to the point that they've become integrated with their culture—I've met many of them over the past several years—it seems very obvious. I've found that those folks see the hope. Those folks tend to see camps as part of the solution.

At the Wood Street dinner party, Amelia, the journalist who emceed the event, shared her perspective with the crowd. "If shit goes really bad, if we have some nuclear disaster, I want to be here," she said. "This is a place where people know how to fix everything, how to pirate electricity, find food, manage conflict, and walk through the world without the resources that so many people take for granted. I think that the unhoused community could be re-billed as the survivalists of our time."

Kent from Wolfe Camp agrees. "A lot of countries got weapons pointed at us," he told me. "You got COVID, you got global warming. What's going to hit first? We don't know. But one thing for sure is that the dollar bill is going to be nothing but a piece of paper. Money is nice for stability and all that, but if you're counting on it for a source of happiness, a time is coming that might mess a lot of people up. The people who were once looked down on will be the leaders showing others how to survive."

Camps can feel like a preview of the apocalypse. Everything is tattered and broken, people straggle about, and it can feel like the only options are to either fight each other or straggle together in the name of survival. The vibe corresponds to the national mood. A poll in the worst year of our lives found that 29 percent of Americans think the apocalypse is coming. Seventeen percent said they have an "apocalypse survival plan." Nineteen percent said a pandemic will most likely do us in; 19 percent said climate change will; 17 percent said nuclear war; 2 percent said the zombies are coming; and 1 percent predicted that an alien invasion will end the world as we know it. The fear seems to be rising. A couple years later, another poll found that 39 percent of Americans believed that "we are living in the end times."

Personally, I don't believe the apocalypse is coming. I think we feel that way because we're so unhappy. The inner apocalypse is clearly here, and it doesn't appear as though the Valley has a business model that's going to disrupt it. The internet was supposed to bring us together, but it has amplified apathy and disconnection. Do the folks living in the shadow of its overlords have a remedy? They certainly have a unique ability to survive impossible circumstances, and some even seem to thrive amid the darkest sides of the human condition, all without resources. I choose to believe that here in the land of billionaires, the have-nots have something priceless to share—apocalypse or not.

For those who really engage with the unhoused, the idea of "giving back" readily morphs into a two-way relationship. Both parties have something to gain. For the housed party, there's a risk that the return devolves into a safari-like experience, to put it uncomfortably bluntly, a freak show that provides the privileged with a gritty, alive feeling that they lack in their daily lives. But it can be much more transformative. How can we grow? How can we evolve? What can we learn?

Tiny is an avid instigator and educator in this regard. Her approach is extremely radical and difficult to implement, but it resonated with me as an honest reflection of what camp communities have to offer the rest of us, if we're willing to take it to heart and give them the credibility they're due. Tiny is a rare cat who has codified those offerings into a coherent curriculum. Her school for adults, called People Skool, is not really a school so much as a series of workshops for the dissemination of poverty scholarship, the idea that poor people are better positioned to educate others about poverty than affluent folks in ivory towers. "It's not a matter of *if* you'll attend," she told me, "but when." In 2021, People Skool was held in a hybrid format—poverty scholars in personal protective equipment attended in person, while "folks with race and class privilege," like me, were invited to participate virtually.

On a Saturday morning in late August, I Zoomed into the Homefulness portal with about three dozen other students. Eventually Tiny appeared, wearing her usual tattered orange jail suit, bug-eye sunglasses, and a red bandanna covering her face, a getup she later told me was inspired by Subcomandante Marcos, the *nom de guerre* of a militant Zapatista leader, who rarely appeared in public without a ski mask. ("It's not about my face, it's about my lack of face," she told me. "It's about the invisibility of millions of unhoused, poor, disabled, broken, criminalized women, children, mothers, aunties, and daughters.") Tiny leered toward the screen like a rapper in a music video: "People Skool is not going to bore you," she said. "It's not going to be a thirty-page paper you got to write. It's theater. It's art. It's love."

She paused.

"But we're also angry!" she yelled. "Because this shit can't continue. We've been lied to about the Ameriklan dream," said Tiny. "Actually, it's an Ameriklan nightmare."

Homefulness residents introduced themselves with "slam poetry bios." Various prayers were offered, including by a leader from the Ohlone, whose people historically occupied what is now the Bay Area. Tiny and crew performed short skits and played several self-produced videos. Participants were asked to solve a math problem involving a single parent, low-wage employment, and the cost of childcare. The point was that it was impossible to solve.

Tiny gave a lengthy speech about "harm reduction hot dogs," which revolved around a story of some Homefulness volunteers-slash-wannabe-reparators who were not getting through their noggin what that actually meant. These particular volunteers were "food justice warriors" who wanted to help supply the weekly distributions, said Tiny. "The nice vegans kept giving us oatmeal," she said. "And some kind of rice dish that was like Dickensian gruel. Nobody understood that food. It's like, what the fuck is that?" After some awkward feedback, the vegans showed up with hot dogs, said Tiny, which led to more awkward feedback. "They were bringing us the Pak 'N Save twenty-five-cent hot dogs, and really proud of themselves that they did," she said. "I looked at the hot dogs and I was like, would you feed *your* kids these hot dogs? And they're like, *nooooo*. Because of course they knew they weren't a human food. I said, well, you go back and you get us those bougie fucking hot dogs from Whole Paycheck. And if you need to raise more reparations to do it, then please do. And we love you. And we'll support you and do whatever needs to be done, but don't bring that poison to our hood!" That's how, said Tiny, "we got what I call"—she lowered her voice mischievously—"harm reduction hot dogs."

We did a number of writing exercises in response to prompts that Tiny gave. "Brian looks like he's sweating bullets over these questions," she said at one point, cackling in the silence of the Zoom classroom. These included an "empathy exercise," in which both privileged folks and poverty scholars were asked to write about how they dealt with a crisis in their lives. "Everyone has had a crisis," said Tiny. "The question is, have you had a crisis you couldn't get out of? That's us poverty scholars." The privileged folks made what Tiny calls "privilege maps," which is basically a diagram, stretching as far back into one's family tree as possible, showing where your wealth, land access, social status, and so on came from. My map went all the way back to the *Mayflower*, on which one of my direct ancestors ferried across the Atlantic. "We are literally the original colonizers," I said, when it was my turn to share. I described how my ancestors settled in Western North Carolina on land that the Cherokee had been forcibly removed from, and that they'd apparently owned slaves.

After I was done, Tiny responded. "For somebody with a connection to pilgrims and chattel slavery, there's not a *question*"—she shouted the word—"that you need to be doing some reparations work." I had never before said these things in public, and it shook me up. "That means genocide was part of building you," said Tiny. "Just hold that in your heart." She seemed shook up by it too. "I'm not shaming anybody," she said. "That's not how I roll. It is only to lift up and make all of us in right relation to Mama Earth and all of our ancestors. Thank you, Brian. That was difficult. And beautiful."

MISINTERPRETATIONS

One of Tiny's headier concepts is called *trans-substantive error*. Something that is trans-substantive, I learned, is valid across multiple contexts. When Tiny talks about trans-substantive error, she's referring to situations in which a concept has been *assumed* to be true across multiple contexts, but is in fact not—such as the assumption by people of privilege that they know what people with less privilege want or need. This is one of the core philosophical prongs of poverty scholarship.

One of the "required readings" for People Skool is a Q and A with Wade Nobles, a professor emeritus in the Africana studies department at San Francisco State University. In the interview, which appeared in a turn-of-the-millennium issue of *POOR Magazine,* Nobles explains trans-substantive error by way of Daniel Patrick Moynihan, a sociologist, senator, and advisor to Richard Nixon who popularized the myth that Black poverty could be attributed largely to the prevalence of single-mother Black households (as opposed to, for example, systemic racism). The infamous "Moynihan Report," a product of his time spent peering into poor Black communities, is credited with forming the intellectual bedrock of the modern welfare system (poor people deserve handouts, but only if they behave according to standards established by privileged people) and affirmative action (people of color should be integrated into white meritocracy).

"Moynihan made a trans-substantive error because he was judging the black family based upon the value system of the European culture," said Nobles in the interview, conducted jointly by Tiny and Dee. Moynihan saw poor Black families headed by single mothers as "broken families" whose children tended to become part of the criminal underclass as a result. Nobles saw that as a misreading of what he called the "deep structure" of Black culture. "The mistake he was making was that the installation of values in the development of children is not tied to the mother-father linkage, it is tied to a system of eldership," he said. "You have older brothers, older cousins, older uncles, older aunts, older mama, grandmama, big mama, great mama, almost in this hierarchy of eldership, and all of those layers are what improve the development of children. So if you take one piece out, i.e., the father, it is not as devastating as it would be in the European family."

This is very much the way things work in the de facto families that are camps, except the children are adults and the elders are those who have been on the street longest, no matter their age, and have banked more time and space between their rock bottoms and where they're at currently. At one point Monte introduced me to Tone, his "street dad"—encampment slang for father figures who mentor the newly homeless in the arts of survival, both physical and emotional—who he credits with helping him heal. Over time, Monte found himself mentoring other residents. "Sometimes we keep people from stealing from someone, or hurting someone, or themselves," said Monte. "Helping somebody when you feel you're not worth anything yourself, it uplifts you, man. It makes you feel like you're connected again." There are very clearly defined leaders in camps—the people who are more in a position to mentor than to be mentored. They settle conflicts, enforce unspoken rules, set the tone for the community, define the group's goals, and liaise with the outer world. They might still be a mess in many respects, but they have gotten over a certain hump in their recovery, a feat readily apparent compared to those still straggling up the base of the mountain.

It's not hard to see other trans-substantive errors across the spectrum of ruling class judgment: of trans folks, Indigenous folks, sex workers, drug users, and any "other" perceived as threatening, or simply not understood. I'm reminded of an essay by the Black critic Jesse McCarthy, titled "Notes on Trap," in which he recasts trap music—a rap subgenre ostensibly concerned only with bitches and killing and wads of hundred-dollar bills—as literature. McCarthy reveals the hypermasculinity and glamorization of drug dealer culture as a covert and sophisticated critique of where power and wealth lie, and as a conscious attempt to redistribute power and wealth by subverting celebrity. Named after trap houses—Atlanta slang for drug dens—trap music, he writes, "is a form of soft power that takes the resources of the black underclass (raw talent, charisma, endurance, persistence, improvisation, dexterity, adaptability, beauty) and uses them to change the attitudes, behaviors, and preferences of others." For instance: "By making them admit they desire and admire those same things and will pay good money to share vicariously in even a collateral showering from below." In doing so, says McCarthy, trap music serves as a vehicle for young Black men growing up in poverty "to transition from an environment where raw hard power dominates and life is nasty, brutal, and short to the world of celebrity, the Valhalla of excess, lucre, influence, fame—the only transparently and sincerely valued site of belonging in our culture." Cue the affluent white teenagers partying to trap music on TikTok.

Privileged Americans' obsession with the music of the Black underclass is a modern incarnation of a timeless phenomenon, one found in Dickens's glamorization of extreme poverty and Pinkerton's love-hate relationship with tramps. We're enchanted with, and vicariously fulfilled by, the raw power of those at the bottom, while also wedded to the project of keeping them there—consciously or not—and to our place on the safe side of the poverty veil.

McCarthy's points are readily extended from drug dens to encampments. For instance, what's the deeper read on the fact that successful dealers avoid the homelessness that lurks around them, while their clients on the other side of that very thin line do not? What better options do they have than to position themselves as the winners, of a sort, in the legacy of oppression that is the street hustle? If sagging pants and the rejection of so-called proper English are not a sign of moral failing, but instead a sublimated project to engineer an alternative reality, is the stealing of catalytic converters and copper plumbing—prevalent activities within unhoused communities that supply cash for drugs—not a form of wealth redistribution?

These are complicated and uncomfortable questions, and they're closely related to the fact that Black communities have a far higher rate of homelessness per capita than white communities. Angst and criminality in poor Black communities has much to do with racism, past and present, and the interrelated trauma and poverty that flow from it. In places where hustling is a way of life, you might resort to dealing to keep a roof over your head only to find yourself hopelessly addicted to your product, and eventually unhoused. On Wood Street, I observed housed dealers who were users, unhoused users who were dealers, and people like Monte, who engaged creatively with that reality: He told me that he often paid residents with meth to clean up trash at the camp, a scheme that was not just for the sake of clearing out junk piles, but also a way for him to connect with and mentor the younger and less stable men around him.

Tiny wants to claim wealth and power for the unhoused through a subversiveness similar to trap: on the terms of the oppressed, rather than the oppressor. To think that the unhoused, or any marginalized group, seeks the inverse is, in her view, a grave trans-substantive error. In her view, top-down solutions sponsored by the government and corporations are on the terms of the oppressor—the shelters and their much-despised rules, the abyss between low-wage work and the cost of housing, the feeling that privileged people see the solution to homelessness as anything that makes homeless people disappear. Homefulness, in contrast, celebrates the unhoused as heroes and commandeers resources that allow them to be the architects of their lives. The camps do this, too, albeit in smaller ways. On Wood Street, John threw birthday parties for his campmates. At the Crash Zone, Rudy educated his neighbors about their legal rights. In Wolfe Camp, the plundering of dumpsters was a group effort. More than pulling themselves up by their bootstraps, the campers pull each other up—in their way, on their terms.

Building Homefulness was the first attack in a brick-and-mortar revolution for Tiny, who told the class that she is plotting to "Homefulness the world"— they'd just purchased a vacant lot down the street for Homefulness 2 and have plans in the works for Homefulness 3 in the Pacific Northwest. Tiny was pumped because this was the first cohort of People Skool held in housing built by poverty scholars. "I want all you beautiful Zoomers to know that this is *herrr*-story today!" She started jumping up and down. "Because poor people built *thiiiisss haawwwsse*! No government money, no bankster, no philanthropimps—no rich people throwing you a crumb. This is People Skool!" she shouted.

"Whose Skool?" shouted a sidekick from off camera, promptly followed by the Homefulness crew in unison: "People Skool!"

"De quién es la escuela?" Tiny shouted.

"Escuela de la gente!" screamed the crew.

THE POWER OF MOM

I have conflicts of interest with the cause. I'm clearly invested in maintaining status quo power structures pertaining to land and wealth, for instance, as evidenced by certain choices I've made of a speculative real estate nature. During the pandemic I purchased a home in the mountains of North Carolina—with a big financial boost from my family—and converted it into a multiunit Airbnb rental. It's in an area with loads of vacation homes, and a severe lack of non-vacation homes. I found a local family to do the cleaning—multi-generation Appalachians with Trump flags on their truck—and began raking in money while they did all the work. As I write this chapter, I keep getting distracted with real estate listings here in California—looking for my next Airbnb property, I'm ashamed to say. In my own small way, I'm a part of the machine driving up real estate prices and diverting scant housing from the locals who need it, so that affluent travelers can post pretty pictures on Instagram.

I wasn't qualified per Tiny's lived-experience standard to tell poor people's stories, but Tiny actively engages mainstream media, which means forging tenuous relationships with people like me. Media training, of a sort, is a central feature of People Skool. One participant asked Tiny how she balances the benefits of media exposure with the costs of diluting of her message. "Get every kind of corprape media you *caaaannnn*!" she replied, explaining how the issue with those $30,000 parking spaces the city insisted on at Homefulness had magically resolved after a local news story. "How do these freaking neoliberal demicans and republicrats spin the shit they do? By taking the media extremely seriously. So I say learn from those bitches, right?"

Tiny encouraged us to make People Skool very personal, to vulnerably examine our privilege, our assumptions about it, and how we might take bold, uncomfortable, norm-shattering steps to "humbly walk in a different way." At the beginning of one weeknight Zoom session, I decided to take my journalist's hat off a little further. I told the group that I was beginning to feel like my drive to accumulate wealth and status was an unconscious, and unhealthy, obsession. I'd realized that my vision of success—earning a sizable income by becoming a top-tier social impact journalist, a vision I'd thought of as humble and morally upstanding—was very much driven by the implacable gravity-defying force of upward mobility. "I feel that it is sort of an addiction," I told the group. The more I had, the more I wanted.

I also told them that while I'd gained a lot of status and resources over the years, I felt like I'd lost something essential in the process. It's something I relate to the distance I feel in relationship to my family. I recalled that as a teenager, "I wanted to go as far away as possible. And I think that was about a certain idea of becoming my own man, defining my own identity apart from my family. I've done that," I said to the Zoom room. "The question is, what has that left me with? Or what has that taken from me? I'm confused," I said.

"There is no space for sharing in the lie of success," said Tiny, after my monologue. "It's a very violent epistemology."

Then she pivoted in a way I did not expect. When she spoke of the "lie of success" and how it did not allow much "space for sharing," she meant it in a very practical sense. To illustrate, she contrasted our society with others in which multifamily living is the norm. When multiple generations live under one roof, it's easier to share resources. There are also fewer roofs needed per capita, which helps to keep real estate values under control. But in an up-by-your-bootstraps, manifest-destiny, rugged-individualist society—where there's no greater personal failure than living with your parents—we need a lot more houses and a lot more stuff because it's every person for themselves. Tiny likes to joke about how higher education keeps the fork industry alive—every time someone goes off to college, a new set of cutlery is born into the world, along with more cars, more clothes, more of most everything. College, says Tiny, sanitizes the cult of upward mobility and makes it feel inevitable, the only moral destiny, for which a teenager has spent their entire life preparing for.

Tiny believes that brainwashing people to leave home and strike out on their own is the core of the capitalist enterprise. And she says that returning home to care for your elders—"being a good son or daughter"—is the ultimate "resistance to crapitalism." In Tiny's world, The Fix for homelessness is surprisingly old-school: family life. Alongside redistribution and the correcting of trans-substantive errors, this is the third leg of Tiny's unified theory of poverty scholarship.

She spun quite a sermon about it at People Skool. The modern educational system, she believes, was crafted to divorce us from what we innately feel as babies—all I need is my loving family—and indoctrinate us into the norms of what she calls the "Away Nation."

For starters, sending one's kids off to kindergarten ensures parents have time to labor in the capitalist trenches each day: "Everybody needs those schools because otherwise they can't keep that fucking job." Tiny doesn't have an issue with the learning of reading, writing, and arithmetic. It's what she calls "the cult of angst" that she's concerned about. "A crucial element in the crapitalist machine is that something is wrong. We don't know exactly why, but you're not supposed to be happy. You're just not. There's this unspoken pressure that not only are you a failure if you actually live at home, but you're a failure if you don't have this fucking successful job, career, house—this whole crapitalist dream. It's all part of the pact that you didn't quite understand you signed onto—hit all the marks, achieve all those goals, and eventually hoard all that money and occupy all that land."

In Tiny's mind, the goal of the cult of angst is to become a word that she shouted at the Zoom screen: "CON-sumer!" By the time you get to college, you're fully brainwashed: "You're purchasing desks at Ikea and paying the lie of rent," she said. "Dorms are another product: housing for people who didn't need housing." Why? Because they should still be living with their parents.

Finally, you're delivered from college to the workforce and the real estate market, and all the things that divide us into haves and have-nots. "As Brian said: What now?" Tiny implored, leaving a dramatic pause after the question. She continued in a quiet, sober voice, the kind you use when you're brainwashing someone, or reverse brainwashing, as Tiny would have it. "The Separation Nation leads to the Isolation Nation," she said. "In this society, aloneness is seen as normal." The endgame is the ugliest part: "You die alone because you're considered unimportant and irrelevant when you can no longer produce," said Tiny.

There's pragmatic wisdom buried in her rhetoric. On an individual level, it's much harder to become homeless if you're tightly bonded with your family—you have more emotional security keeping you from self-destructive behaviors, and you can stretch resources further. On a collective level, multigenerational living is a paradigm-shattering shift in consciousness toward communalism and away from the dog-eat-dog world in which we currently live. Which is why, even if we're not at risk of homelessness, Tiny thinks we should all move back in with our parents. It may sound nuts, but as someone who relied on their very imperfect parent in a life-or-death way—and vice versa—she's dead serious about it.

At the end of one People Skool session, Tiny said our homework was to call our mom. Which I did. At another point, she told me, straight up, "Brian, there's no reason you shouldn't be home. I don't know why you're here. I think that you need to go." That made sense, per poverty scholar theory, and per the basic decency of being the son of an aging mother who needs you. Tiny also connected me with Cecilia, a UC Berkeley professor and a member of the Solidarity Family, who casually mentioned that she was about to move back across the country to care for her aging father—who happened to live one town over from my mom in the boonies of Western North Carolina. She said she'd been inspired by People Skool to do so.

I felt triply guilty. Still, I dug in my heels. I told Samira about Tiny's theory that The Fix for homelessness, the deepest structural one anyways, was to move back in with one's parents, and asked what she thought about it.

"Makes sense," she said. "Maybe your mom could come live with us?" she suggested.

I was horrified at the thought of surrendering my autonomy to the prison of living with a parent. But Samira is from Iran, where that's normal, even expected. I told her that I thought Tiny's militant attitude about multigenerational living might be a symptom of codependence resulting from her mother's seemingly pathological perspective on the parent-child relationship: that eleven-year-old Tiny should become her caretaker. Samira didn't find this so strange. In Persian culture, she explained, to not attend to your parents' needs on a daily basis, no matter how wacko they are, is considered disrespectful.

Samira's nuclear family had their own apartment in Tehran when she was growing up, yet they spent the vast majority of their time at her maternal grandmother's apartment, where several of her adult aunts and uncles, the single ones, still lived. The married ones, like Samira's mom, practically lived there, too, along with their respective families. Samira remembers spending about five nights a week on average at her grandmother's apartment—she was part of a tribe of cousins, aunts, uncles, brothers, and sisters who all slept in a puddle of mats and blankets on the living room floor, where they also sat for meals and the long, lively conversations that followed.

A crowded floor where family members eat and sleep together is an image my Western brain associates with abject poverty. But Samira comes from landed aristocracy. She and her siblings pursued doctoral degrees and found high-paying jobs overseas, a reliable ticket out of the oppressive Iranian regime. Her sister ended up in Silicon Valley, where she has worked for Apple, Amazon, and Meta—and where she now lives with their mom, along with her American husband and two children.

Samira remembers her extended family dynamic as "fun," and also, "the way that it was." She feels that growing up in a tribe-like family environment endowed her with a profound sense of physical security and emotional stability. "The downside is you don't get to experience independence," she says. "You're twenty-seven years old and you come home and your mom is cooking for you and dinner is on the table. I think that can be detrimental for developing a sense of self." She appreciates having grown up in a society in which inter-dependence is a core value, but she also sees it as a slippery slope to limiting self-expression: "Did I grow up in a traditional society or an oppressive society? It's hard to separate them. I think it's a combination of both."

Tiny's words about eldership and good sonhood worked their way deep into my intellect, my daily life, and beyond. I was absolutely not going to move in with my mom, even though I saw how that would serve as a sort of karmic offset to the broken thing she's held inside ever since her dad left. Tiny kept on me: "What are you doing here!" she yelled during a phone conversation one day. "You should be back in North Carolina!"

Devilish and Divine

When I learned that Tiny was doing a hoarded-resources tour on Morningside Drive, the hair on my neck stood up in an electrostatic salute to the mysteries of the cosmos. A second such salute occurred a few months later when I heard Tiny say the following words: "I am a daughter of Exu." Those words helped me to understand why Tiny is who she is and also why her ideas were so challenging for me to embrace, yet so inescapably resonant. To meaningfully implement the ideas of People Skool feels about as comfortable as cutting up my flesh into a bunch of pieces and sewing it back together into a different form that may or may not survive the experiment. Exu is a way to understand why it feels so painful, while also speaking to how it might be successfully accomplished.

Exu—pronounced *eh-shoo*—is a character in the Yoruba culture of West Africa, who first slipped into the Americas in the bowels of slave ships. He is one of many quasi-deities worshipped by the Yoruba, and by non-Yoruba overseas, who for centuries have mixed and melted this ancient African tradition with local cultures in places like Rio de Janeiro, Havana, Port-au-Prince, and, more recently, Oakland. To say one is the son or daughter of Exu or other characters in Yoruba cosmology means that your spiritual essence aligns with the traits of that particular figure. Exu is a trickster, a wise, mischievous character akin to coyotes, crows, and ravens in other traditions—Tiny, 100 percent. He is a source of a dark, fiery power, which practically bubbles, magma-like, from Tiny's pores. Her face is usually covered by sunglasses and red-and-black bandannas, the Satan-esque colors associated with Exu. But I will never forget the moment she lifted her shades and looked me in the eye: I have never seen such a deadly serious gaze.

Tiny invokes Exu constantly. "Bringing Exu into the room, bringing the trickster in," she said at prayer time during a People Skool session. "Fam, Exu on our side," she declared on a Signal thread that we're both on for allies and activists supporting unhoused communities in Oakland. I came to think of Exu as not only a unified theory of Tiny but of homelessness. The dark power one unearths at rock bottom? Exu. The mischief that unhoused people get into? Exu. The "trick" of finding freedom in the absence of material wealth or social status? Exu. Like the unhoused, he is profoundly misunderstood. My neck hair stood up when I heard the word because for the past twenty-plus years I have practiced a Brazilian spiritual tradition, called Umbanda, in which Exu plays a central role.

My first encounter with Yoruba spiritual practices was on an organic farm on the outskirts of Santa Cruz when I was twenty-two. An acquaintance named Norma, a sixty-ish Puerto Rican woman with a salty New York accent, had invited me to attend a ceremony that occurred there each Sunday in a whitewashed building ensconced in a grove of enormous eucalyptus trees. People dressed head to toe in white danced solemnly in a circle as several drummers beat out African rhythms. Suddenly, some of the dancers leapt and convulsed, beating their fists on their chests and making sounds like war cries. After a few minutes, they calmed down and I and the other non-initiated folks in the room were allowed to enter the circle and meet the entities—Norma said they were enlightened spiritual masters—now inhabiting the bodies of the mediums. Each of them smoked a fat cigar.

I came back every Sunday without fail and within a year had traveled to Brazil and begun my own initiation as a medium. By then I had encountered the Satan-esque side of the tradition—*esque* being an essential modifier, as I came to learn.

At a ceremony involving Exu, it would not be uncommon to find iconography of men with horns and tails holding three-pronged pitchforks. Initiates are likely to be dressed in red-and-black hooded robes. It's likely to take place in the dark of night, with nothing but red and black candles illuminating the dancing mediums as they chant and sway. It is, in other words, your mom's worst nightmare. But my experiences with Exu have nothing to do with promoting evil. If you imagine a serene house of worship bathed in white light and overflowing with all the trappings of holiness and well-being, Exu is the guy in the basement dealing with leaky pipes and cracks in the foundation—the trickster, once you get to know him, is deeply pragmatic. I think of Exu as the Yoruba equivalent of the Jungian shadow. He teaches us how to deal with our most deeply buried, unprocessed, unacknowledged shit—the archetypal skeletons in the closet— so that we may actually evolve, rather just perform hollow gesticulations of spiritual growth. He knows the tricks for unraveling the divine treats within.

Exu is an African expression of a universal spiritual principle, one that's become a tad convoluted in the Western world. When a nineteenth-century Christian missionary translated the Bible into Yoruba he translated "devil" as "Esu"—an alternative spelling of Exu—which some Yoruba spiritualists have interpreted as a deliberate attempt to demonize their faith. Two centuries later, the misinformation is beginning to be undone, with the help of the internet. Adherents post about it under the hashtag *#esuisnotsatan*, and a Nigerian linguist at Google, Kola Tubosun, tweaked the search engine's AI to set the record straight: Now when you type in "devil" or "satan" on Google Translate's Yoruba page, "esu" is no longer the result, and vice versa. "Early this morning in Mountain View California," wrote Tubosun on Facebook in 2016, "the trickster Esu was relieved of its perceived demonic duties."

Different branches of the Yoruba family tree emphasize different traits of Exu. I practice Umbanda, which blends its African roots with Indigenous and European elements, a melting pot tradition that emerged in Rio de Janeiro in the early twentieth century. Tiny is involved in Ifa, an ancient and solidly African branch that spread to the US through modern-day immigrants, rather than on slave ships. She says that for her, Exu is a guide that helps imbue her words with potency and transformative abilities. Which is why she chose 96.1 KEXU as the call name for the low-power station on which she broadcasts her radio shows. One day I called her up and asked if she would elaborate.

"It's the spirit that guides over communication, media, all of those things that all of us writers and creators do," she said. "It's the spirit of change. I pray to Exu for help in clarifying my words, but sometimes he's a trickster—sometimes the words get me somewhere that I didn't expect." Perhaps it's what got a sixth-grade dropout into Google to give a subversive talk about a radical underground housing cooperative built by homeless folks. I felt some benevolent trickery at

work when I returned to California to write this book and found that my old
Umbanda group had relocated from the farm outside Santa Cruz to a less
pastoral setting: in a warehouse near the San José airport. It's right next to the
Guadalupe River, the city's homeless superhighway, a couple miles from the
Crash Zone. It felt right.

"Whaaaatttt!" said Tiny when I told her that I, too, am close buds with Exu. I
tried my unified theory of homelessness on her. "People see camps as a horrible,
negative, dark, bad underworld," I ventured, explaining that I see that as exactly
the space in which Exu works his magic—places where the pain is more than
one can bear. That pain, I believe, is a collective one, even if it is not felt as such.

Tiny listened and agreed and said yes after every point I made. "That's a
beautiful idea," she said. And then she pivoted in a much more radical direction.
Tiny agrees that homelessness is fundamentally a spiritual issue, but for her the
salient point is not about our shadow sides *per se*, it's about decolonizing our
minds and reprogramming them with what she calls "Indigenous consciousness." For example, she is dead serious that every step taken on the path to
"homefulness" must be undertaken in concert with "the ancestors," as well as
with living representatives of the Indigenous groups affiliated with the land
in question.

One thing that means for Tiny is that every class, meeting, protest, and
performance begins and ends with prayers and rituals. The scantily clad men in
her posse, and the drumming and dancing she does with them, are an aspect
of this, one centered on Danza Azteca, an Indigenous Mexican tradition with
which Tiny is also involved. She constantly shouts "*Ometeotl!*"—an Aztec word
for the creator. She similarly employs "*ibaye!*"—a Yoruba word invoked to honor
ancestors. And she's deeply engaged with Indigenous communities across the
West, asking them for permission to pass through their lands when she travels,
or in the case of the Ohlone, who were among the Bay Area's original inhabitants, to build on them. Corrina Gould, an Ohlone leader and spokesperson
for the Confederated Villages of Lisjan, is a founding member of Homefulness's Elephant Council, a group of elders responsible for all major decisions in
the community.

During our conversation about spirituality, Tiny told me she was very upset that in a magazine article I'd written about her I hadn't mentioned that Homefulness was predicated on the permission and counsel of the relevant First Nations and ancestors. She said that she specifically asked me to mention it, which I don't remember, and that I better mention it in my book or "I'm going to ask you to take me out." Tiny refers to places by their Indigenous names, such as Huichin, the Ohlone territory comprising Oakland, Berkeley, and other parts of the East Bay. Manhattan is on Lenape land in "so-called New York." Marin County, the area north of Golden Gate Bridge where I write these words, is the land of the Miwok.

What does all that have to do with homelessness? Indigenous consciousness means different things to different people, but I came to understand that for Tiny, it's an extension of her ideas about maintaining family ties as an antidote to homelessness and the forces that spawn it—an extension into the past, and into the spiritual realm.

She doesn't see much difference, for instance, between honoring one's relationships with incarnated family members versus disincarnated ones. She views Indigenous consciousness as a natural expression of her poverty scholar theory, which elevates the hard-earned wisdom of elders above formal education systems designed to prime us for capitalist productivity. To honor Indigenous folks, for Tiny, means engaging with them and learning from them—about interdependent living, about sharing land and resources rather than treating them as commodities, and about collective, place-based wisdom. One could say that camps, in their tribal nature, embody Indigenous consciousness. They certainly inhabit a wilderness of sorts, unplugged from the mainstream economy and the security it provides, with people reliant instead on each other to survive in a brutal environment. In Tiny's view, one doesn't have to be a native person to cultivate Indigenous consciousness.

The concept is prone to romanticization, which Tiny rejects. "Ancestors and elders are not some cutesy, fetishized idea," she said at People Skool. On a practical level, she sees Indigenous consciousness as a tool for navigating the gnarliest, Exu-level shit that life, especially for homeless people, brings. Such as a mentally ill mother who's demanding that her eleven-year-old daughter care for her while they live together on the street. "My mama was not a happy person," said Tiny. "Our elders' knowledge is not cute, it's not clean, it doesn't come in a Zoom box. Sometimes it just comes because you hang out with them and you talk to them and you spend love time together. To actually decolonize and degentrifuck, you have to take away the safety container that the institution sells you, that nice clean box: this is how you learn, this is where you learn, this is what you learn."

DIFFICULT PEOPLE

Like most folks, I'm not as radical as Tiny. But I am magnetized by a simple, transformative truth that I find buried beneath the jargon of Tiny's poverty scholarship, one that I think most anyone, no matter their cultural or political persuasion, could appreciate. What I most admire in Tiny is a preternatural ability to engage with difficult people in a way that transmutes their difficulties. I, and I suspect most people, tend to be very bothered by difficult people. We disregard them. We talk about them behind their back. We say whatever nice things we need to say in order to get the hell away from them as soon as possible. I'm pretty sure all that makes difficult people more difficult.

Exu embodies a sort of blessed difficulty. During rituals he often manifests in mediums with lots of cussing, hissing, grunting, and pelvic gesticulation. Some sections of the spiritual path are all white light and strumming harps, epiphanies that haloed saints lead us to, their hand in ours. Other sections lead us to a brick wall. This is Exu's comfort zone: finding God, or at least good humor, in impossible circumstances.

Unhoused people, in my experience, are not the easiest people. They have a propensity to lie, steal, talk too much, behave irrationally, and throw their trash on the ground; they might even smell bad. Most I've known are unreliable, disorganized, and inept at follow-through. They might tell you what a hard worker they are, and then you realize that they're mainly hard at work getting high. Bobby told me once that he wanted to get a job, but when I asked him how that was going a few weeks later, he laughed and said, "I lied." One couple at Wood Street spent a staggering portion of each day screaming and cursing at each other, often in the central, communal part of the camp where people gathered to cook and hang out, so that everyone else could bathe in their drama. It's clear that their relationship is intensely traumatic for them, but it's also extremely unpleasant for those around them.

Difficult people don't tend to inspire others to be kind and giving toward them. Any compassion one might have for the unhoused on an abstract level is easily erased when someone is living on the sidewalk in front of your house, piling up trash, using your bushes as a latrine, and shooting heroin in front of your children when they come home from school. Even if it's a high-functioning, tidy, sober unhoused person, it can still feel difficult to be in their presence, though the difficulty in that case may be composed largely of feelings of guilt. Either way, we've collectively decided that the best thing to do about homelessness is to outsource dealing with the difficulty to people who are paid to do so.

I've never lived in a neighborhood with a concentration of highly visible homeless people, but I did get a taste of what that's like at the Umbanda temple in San José, where one autumn day in 2023, a guy started camping in the parking lot about twenty feet from the front door. For months he had been stumbling around on the median of a major road a few blocks away, careening dangerously close to passing cars. We'd all seen him. He seemed extremely unwell and now he had positioned himself so that we could not ignore his presence. There was much whispering among the small group that runs the temple: Should we ignore him? Should we talk to him? Should we tell the landlord? Should we call the police?

He'd made a sort of nest with scraps of carpet padding, around which were scattered items that appeared to be trash—there was no structure to sleep under, or even recognizable belongings. This was the entrance to our sacred space. His presence also reduced our parking, which was already in short supply. It was hard to tune out those thoughts and put them in their proper perspective against his far greater needs. No one in the group was comfortable approaching him, so Samira and I volunteered. He appeared to be in such a deep state of psychosis that I was unsure whether he would speak or acknowledge us when we walked over to him with a plate of homemade food and a bag of snacks and drinks.

"Hi, how's it going?" I said.

He jumped up faster than I was expecting and grabbed the food with an energy that conveyed a belly that had not recently been full.

"Thanks," he mumbled, retreating quickly back to his nest with a bashful look.

"I'm Brian," I said. "What's your name?"

"Bruce," he said.

"Nice to meet you," I said.

He didn't seem comfortable talking further, so we walked away. I thought about offering to help him to move to one of the nearby camps, where he might benefit from being part of the community, but I didn't want to impose the idea on him for the sake of getting our parking space back. Maybe he preferred to be alone. After much debate, an idea emerged: to ask if we could help him to move his camp about fifteen feet to a spot next to the sidewalk. In the parking space, he was on private property, and the police would certainly remove him if the landlord called. Next to the sidewalk he would be a few feet inside the public right-of-way—I checked the property boundaries online— where he would have the legal right to camp per *Martin v. Boise*. This seemed like a reasonable compromise.

We live ninety minutes from the temple and are only there once a week, but I vowed to return with a tent, sleeping bag, and sleeping pad as a gift when I approached him about moving. Driving home that night, the first rains of fall came pouring down. I felt horrible imagining Bruce lying there in his open-air nest, soaked to the bone, but I could not muster the energy to pull a U-turn and do something about it. When I came back a week later with an armful of camping gear from Walmart, his camp was gone.

Nobody *likes* dealing with difficult people, though we all do it—parent, child, sibling, spouse, coworker, overworked DMV employee. But when the difficulty supersedes a threshold determined by our degree of investment in, or attachment to, the relationship, most of us split. The easiest way to deal with difficulty is to abandon it, and unhoused strangers are very easy to abandon—high difficulty, zero attachment to the relationship.

But there are exceptions to the rule. It can be easier to deal with difficult people you're not as close to—a lack of attachment and intimacy can provide the space for greater tolerance. It's much easier for me to remain equanimous with a very unpleasant unhoused person, for instance, while behavior from my mother that might be considered at worst mildly off-putting, from an objective perspective, sparks a meltdown. I could not have imagined that the gestalt of People Skool would be to examine and heal one's familial relationships. But then again, if homelessness is a product of broken relationships, it makes sense. If interdependence means not abandoning difficult relationships—holding them together even if they are broken—then I can understand how Tiny's concept of Indigenous consciousness applies on a practical level to homelessness, and to me.

One interpretation of Indigenous consciousness is to behave as though other people's problems are also collective problems. This holistic perspective is abundant in camps—people drive each other crazy, but they stick together anyways. In my observation, unhoused people have off-the-charts tolerance for difficulty, even if it's only because they can't readily get away from it. Tiny is now housed, and her mother is in the spirit realm, but she continues to put herself in the way of difficulty. She constantly talks about how overwhelmingly difficult it is, for instance, to live communally with a bunch of other highly traumatized folks, while also running a poverty alleviation project, a media empire, a housing development, and multiple educational programs with them on a volunteer basis. *Difficult* is an apt adjective for Tiny's lifestyle.

One of the posse's most astounding endeavors is something they call "revolutionary love cleans." This entails going to the homes of people who are living in filth, which is not uncommon among the precariously housed population, and doing a deep cleaning—gratis. One of their clients is Bruce, a different Bruce, who is a member of the extended Homefulness family for whom Tiny once asked me to go to Walmart to buy slippers and sweatpants. Tiny said Bruce was homeless for two decades before he got into subsidized housing and that his place was pretty rough—"I'm talking about hardcore," she said, "like fecal matter on the wall."

One of the many reasons they do this is because cleanliness and hoarding issues are a top justification given by supportive housing organizations for evicting their residents, putting them back on the street. For families, filth can be cause for a call to Child Protective Services. "It's one of the ways in which we move interdependently to take care of each other," said Tiny. "Uncle Bruce was a fuckin' Vietnam War veteran who saw absolute horrible shit as a very young man. He will never be OK in a normalized society way. You can't help Bruce by showing up for him once. You have to be a part of Bruce's life-slash-support team. You have to be part of Bruce for life."

BRINGING IT HOME

The cabin on Solitude Lane I moved to when I got divorced was not a random place I picked on the North Carolina map. It was a five-minute walk from a notable neighbor: my mom. It was the worst year of my mother's life as well—around the time I announced my divorce, she developed a serious health issue. She was in no position to offer emotional support, and with both of us in a bad space we developed an antagonistic dynamic with each other, which further amplified our misery. My mother and I had a fairly charged relationship to begin with, which is why I moved to a place down the street from her, rather than into her spare bedroom. Yet there we were in quarantine, alone together.

If I were to become homeless, my family would open their homes to me in a heartbeat. I could muddle through the discomfort for a while, if I had absolutely no other choice, especially if I was living with my dad or brother. But if my dad and brother weren't an option, and I had to move in with my mom, I think the expiration date on the arrangement would arrive pretty quick. Why was it so difficult to share space with her? Something between us was broken, but I didn't really understand what had gone wrong.

This is the fertile ground in which homelessness grows: There is no unhoused person I've gotten to know for whom a family schism was not a turning point in their journey toward living on the street. Monte, Kent, Rudy, Tiny—it's a central theme in all their stories. When you can't pay your rent, what's the fallback plan? It generally involves staying with family, whether biological or chosen. For some, the schism happens at birth. For others, it's a divorce.

Some unhoused people don't have family they can turn to in the first place, because they're dead, on drugs, or abusive. For others it's just a slow erosion of relationships: They live with family for a while, but when the bonds are weak or overstretched, they eventually break.

I'm reminded, for instance, of my uncle Alex, one of my dad's brothers, who grew up a scrawny gay boy in the sixties. He was picked on by his peers, abused at home, and, perhaps unsurprisingly, tried to burn down his high school. This landed him in prison, where I once visited him with my family when I was a child. I remember him as a bitter, whiny guy—very difficult—who my dad briefly employed as a janitor at the condo complex where he was the maintenance supervisor. But Alex was a terrible employee, and my dad had to fire him. During this time, when I was in my early teens, Alex lived in a nearby SRO. He also crashed for a while in our living room, while his partner, Jay, slept in his car in a cul-de-sac a block from our house. Alex did mention this; we discovered the arrangement one night when the family awoke to Jay being chased across our yard by the police, who a neighbor had called.

Chris later lived with his mom, and after she died he managed to get into subsidized housing. He claims to have a litany of physical infirmities, which he ministers to with frightening doses of prescription opioids. My dad didn't use the word *addiction* when he told me this—it was just Chris being the trouble-maker that he's always been. My dad says that Chris has become increasingly paranoid over the years, going on and on about the people out to get him, though my dad didn't use *mental illness* to describe the situation. No one in the family talks to him much, or seems to worry much about him. Maybe they would if he was physically homeless, which he easily could be. As it is, he's still just Chris, the relative nobody wants to deal with.

In San Francisco there's a nonprofit organization, called Miracle Messages, dedicated to the idea of "relational poverty" as an overlooked cause of home-lessness, which acts as a private detective agency helping to reconnect people on the streets with loved ones. Its founder, Kevin F. Adler, co-wrote a book on the topic, called *When We Walk By*, which declares relational poverty—"a profound lack of nurturing relationships combined with stigma (and often shame) that makes fostering social ties incredibly difficult"—as perhaps "the most universal characteristic of people experiencing homelessness," other than the lack of permanent housing. It points out the many ways that "social capital can be converted into financial capital" and delves deep into the literature on loneliness, which basically says that most everything is worse (health, self-esteem, job prospects) when we're not part of a tribe.

One large-scale study found that "individuals with strong ties to relatives, friends, and religious community" were about two-thirds less likely to find themselves unhoused at some point in their lives compared to those who identified as having "weak·ties." Adler's book cites San Francisco statistics showing twice as many people exiting the city shelter system as a result of being reunited with family or friends compared to those exiting into housing provided by the government. It also references data showing that approximately one-third of the homeless population has lost their "social support" systems, a number I found very curious. I'm pretty sure if the question was whether people had lost the social support systems they'd had *before* becoming homeless, the number would be far higher. The fact that it's only a third may reflect a reality that is often lost on those seeking to help the homeless: the support networks people develop on the street after becoming homeless. It's the quality of the support that matters, not the source.

Broken relationships, rock bottom, Exu's shadow: These are the brew of homelessness, in my mind, and also the map to The Fix. Tiny's way of expressing these ideas was too doomsdayish for me to embrace directly, but I was moved to find my own way of acting on the theories of poverty scholarship—particularly the idea of interdependence. There are many forces in the world at large that encourage independence over interdependence—capitalism being Exhibit A. But there are also interior forces that shut us off from the softness of heart and receptivity to others that interdependence requires.

As I fished for a path forward, I felt like I needed an access point where I could anchor, a place of departure for taking my life narrative in my hands and soberly contemplating it—then maybe I could cut it up and sew it back together to remake myself as a more whole person. I felt like my maternal grandfather might be the way in.

My grandmother was the fifth of my grandfather's six wives; or sixth of seven, depending on which relative you ask. Sometimes marriages don't work out—but a half dozen? That's a sign of something else. My grandfather died when my mother was thirteen. His obituary in the *New York World-Telegram*, where he worked as a copyreader in the business section at the time of his death, described him as "a quiet man who usually remained deeply engrossed in his work no matter what distractions were offered." He spent his leisure time studying stock tables and finance charts—"the subject he loved," said the obituary. He lived with his final wife at the other end of Manhattan, a half hour from Harlem, but never once came to visit his daughter. "In accordance with his wishes, no funeral services are planned," said the obituary. I get the feeling he was a lonely, broken, walled-off man.

I can see that in the broken branches of my family tree, we've all had our walls: my grandfather, my grandmother, my mom, my ex, me. My grandmother's walls were illustrated by the walls of her apartment—a collage of words and images that left no question about who she was, or at least how she wanted to be perceived: indomitable. One wall hanging that sticks out in my mind was a cartoon drawing of a gray-haired woman banging at the steel-plated doors of the prison-industrial complex, while several burly guards cower, terrified, on the other side, refusing to let her in. But I sense that this larger-than-life identity also boxed her in. My mother inherited her mother's rage, which she channeled into her poetry and performance art, à la Tiny, producing a cathartic body of work that probes the personal within the political. The pain of abandonment by her father has been a running theme in her work, along with emotional abandonment by her mother, who excelled at hosting parties and forging bonds with strangers on the street, but struggled to connect with her own daughter.

I've spent a lifetime psychoanalyzing these walls, which has not made them disappear. But I think Tiny is right—we have to accept the difficult parts of people as they are, and not let the difficultness keep us apart. In sifting through my family history, I land on the feeling that self-acceptance is the barometer by which my ability to accept others is defined. To accept my mother in all her challenging complexities is to accept myself. To accept myself is to allow my armor to dissolve—and to allow my armor to dissolve is to foster a relationship that supports the dissolution of hers. To fix homelessness—the inner variety, if not the literal one—is to welcome the unacceptable into the womb of our heart. This is what I learned from camps.

* * *

There is no greater forgiveness than that afforded by death. My grandmother slowed down in her late nineties, but she maintained her underlying angst until she passed away a year and a half before the worst year of my life. My mother and I were at her bedside when she exhaled her last breath at 1:40 A.M. on an October morning. I never felt so close to my mom as I did at that moment. All the walls were gone, all the veils lifted. I would like to get back to that homeful place, where ancestrality is alive and we are all relatives in the family of humanity.

Now that my grandmother's public life has reached its tidy posthumous conclusion, the socially acceptable thing is to bask in memories of her achievements, her force of personality—to inflate her persona even larger in death than it was in life, and solidify it, like a statue. But doing so would permanently eclipse the story of her own vulnerability, and the more complicated truths it illuminates. I do not remember her in the simplicity of heroic symbols. I remember her in the emotional complexity of her favorite song, a haunting folk ballad called "Goodnight, Irene." The tender, slow refrain suggests a lullaby, but the verses invoke domestic bliss come undone, and the bowels of despair.

My grandmother loved to sing—"If I Had a Hammer" and "We Shall Overcome" were standbys—but "Goodnight, Irene" was not just another folk song. It was a guiding star. As dementia dissolved the boundaries of her mind, she sang it on repeat. This lasted several years, during which the lyrics were slowly reduced to just the chorus, then to *Goodnight, Irene*, and eventually it was just *Irene, Irene, Irene*, all day long, not sung so much as croaked. *Irene* became the verbalization of her every move—*Irene* when she struggled to her feet; *Irene* when she groaned her way into a chair; *Irene* when she was fed a spoon of food.

At Christmas when she was 102, my brother, trying to make conversation, asked her who Irene was. "Irene?" my grandmother replied, as though surprised he didn't know. Then she became serious. "Irene is the manager of heaven," she said.

On her deathbed, Irene became *I-ree, I-ree, I-ree*. In her final moments, she mouthed, *I, I, I*. I remember my grandmother struggling to take her last breaths. I remember the shape of her mouth, its roundness, as she finally let go and her spirit sailed out. At her memorial service, at the very end, we all sang "Goodnight, Irene" in the church basement. Everyone cried.

Acts of Erasure

During the two years I spent hanging out on Wood Street, the crew became known around Oakland and beyond as the vanguard of the local homeless empowerment movement. Several residents spoke at a Martin Luther King Day rally put on by the Anti Police-Terror Project, a reincarnation of sorts of the Black Panthers, groups that both sprang from the Lower Bottoms. Kev Choice, a local MC who serves on Oakland's Cultural Affairs Commission, invited Monte and John to speak at another event. Samira and I joined them in the offices of state lawmakers to discuss policy. They became a local news staple, resulting in some of the most street-informed reporting on homelessness that I've come across in mainstream media. They even developed a brand for their movement: "Homeless Helping the Homeless."

I followed Monte as he zigged and zagged from public spaces to bedside intimacy, from the highs of his limitless lust for life to the crashing waves of tears that choke him on days when his mind isn't right. We developed an epic bromance, predicated only in part on our shared desire to change the homeless narrative. The other parts were no different than any other friendship—we have similar interests and enjoy talking about life together. We connected through our mutual affection for trees and had long conversations about nature being both a definition of our deepest selves and a code for unlocking human potential, like DNA that provides a blueprint for spiritual evolution.

As an outdoorsman and gardener, I tend to see that code in what I think of as fairly pure environments. Monte helped me to find it in places I normally see as the antithesis of nature. He is an avowed tree hugger and counted the few specimens at the camp as intimate relations. I hadn't really believed his story about sleeping in the arms of the pine tree in front of his future homestead until one day when I watched him do an hourlong "yoga" session in the tree, which involved swinging gracefully from branch to branch as he transitioned from one pose to another, chanting and talking softly to the pine as he did. It was like watching a hybrid gymnast and yogi. Then I believed him.

One night we explored Wood Street's deepest recesses, an unpopulated area beneath the overpasses at the back of the camp, a spot known as a place dismembered bodies are dumped after being murdered. After walking in the dark for a bit, Monte pried open a narrow door under an on-ramp. Inside was a cavernous room, roughly the size of an Olympic pool, its original purpose seemingly lost to time; it was easily the sketchiest place I have ever been. The ground was a thick, pasty mud that clung to our shoes. The walls were covered in elaborate graffiti, which we studied in the pitch-black space by the light of our phones. "Hell can't be worse than this" was spray-painted on one wall. A flock of pigeons, their slumber having been disturbed, dive-bombed us. Monte said some of the crew had lived in this concrete cave during the early days of the camp, improvising boardwalks with scrap lumber to stay out of the mud.

Back outside, the body-dumping zone felt less ominous. There's an ephemeral stream there, which spring rains had swollen into a shallow lake. The lamps from the highway above reflected like moonlight on the water. Baby frogs chirped in competition with the whoosh of traffic. Monte led me to a tiny palm tree, no more than four feet tall, that he was particularly fond of. He commenced a praying-chanting thing that he does with trees. After a few minutes, a pair of headlights, the stern eyes of a Caltrans truck with a security guard at the wheel, approached. Monte told me to hide behind the tree with him. We crouched as low as possible behind the miniature palm, which of course did not fool the security guards, who told us that we better split or they would call the police.

"This is private property," said the guard.

"OK," said Monte. "I just pray at this plant," he continued, with a combination of BS and sincerity. "Often," he improvised. "When I'm in town."

"That sounds good," said the guard. "But—"

Monte interjected. "I heard you," he said, getting irritated.

He eventually acquiesced, and we began walking very slowly toward the camp as the security guard's headlights trailed us from about 150 feet back. All this time, because Monte is preposterous in the most random and wonderful ways, he'd brought a bullhorn on our adventure to the body-dumping area. Now, strolling in the artificial moonlight among the chirping frogs, he turned it on and chanted in Hindi at the guards, and to the cosmos beyond: "Shri raam jai raam jai jai raam. Shri raam jai raam jai jai raam. Shri raam jai raam jai jai raammmmmmmmmm."

We came to a small acacia tree, standing alone in a field of barren earth beneath an overpass. It was covered in puffy white honey-scented flowers that glowed in the moonlight. Monte put down the bullhorn and again commenced his ritual of arboreal communion. Eventually, the headlights arrived again.

"I asked y'all nicely," said the guard.

"I'm leaving," said Monte.

"You said that back there," said the guard.

"I *am* leaving," said Monte. "I'm doing my last ritual." The guard again threatened to call the police. "That's fine, call them," said Monte.

"I'm going to do that right now," said the guard, who instead continued to harp.

"That's enough," said Monte. "You said you're going to call them—go do your job and call them." He was enjoying schooling the guard. "Nobody can get in between spirituality—they'll tell you that. It's my right and it's against the law for you to tell me not to. Nobody owns the earth." His words didn't quite make sense. But they kind of did.

MONTE AND GOLIATH

After the Caltrans sweep, the city made it clear that the remainder of the camp, which was on city-owned land, would soon be swept, though no one knew exactly when. In the meantime, their movement grew. They got more and more media attention. They threw even more parties. I threw one for them, inviting musicians and aerial dancers, who performed suspended from the overpass at the back of the camp. Monte got a job—three, actually, all of them occasional. He washed dishes in a nearby soul food joint, assembled port-a-potties, and worked at an auto body shop. He bought a decent car to replace the one that needed endless repairs. He was thriving.

After the first eviction on Caltrans land, the camp had expanded its legal team and tried to build a more robust case to prevent the city-owned portion of the camp from being swept. That winter was one of the rainiest in California history. A "bomb cyclone" and "atmospheric river" combined to drop eighteen inches of rain on Oakland in a three-week period, the wettest three weeks on record in the city. One night, winds reached up to one hundred miles per hour. Structures were destroyed, parts of the camp were underwater, and the rest became a mud pit; everyone was wet and cold. In the middle of that three-week period, the city posted notices that they would soon begin the sweep. The lawyers pounced and Judge Orrick again granted a temporary restraining order, citing the same reasons as before and scolding the city for initiating the sweep in the midst of a record-breaking rainy season. But again, it was only temporary. By spring, the city had opened a tiny-home facility at the other end of Wood Street, and Orrick lifted the order.

As the eviction date drew near, three years after I set out on my quest to find The Fix, John and Monte's upward trajectory plateaued, then declined. They fought often with each other. Monte started using more heavily again. In the weeks leading up to the eviction, I could hardly talk to him. He would zoom in and out of the camp in a rage, yelling at people and accusing them of things they hadn't done. He started sleeping in his car, getting just one or two hours of rest each night because he thought people were after him. "I'm back in the pit of my despair," he told me one night, his eyes in a wayward gaze. "On that ledge again." He seemed to be having a psychotic break. Early in the morning on the first day of the eviction I was walking through the neighborhood to the camp when he sped past me in his car and yelled, "Fuck you! You wanted this to happen!"

The final battle had come. Monte told me that when the police came to remove him from the shack, he intended to take his life—making his point through martyrdom. It was hard to know how much credence to give to that, but I took it seriously.

That morning the police and workers established a fence line across Wood Street at one end of the remaining block-long section of the camp. They began amassing machinery on their side of the fence. On the other side, the residents and their supporters held a press conference. A local priest spoke, along with John, LeaJay, Tiny, and others. Xochitl walked around with a goblet of smoldering herbs and wafted the smoke with a feather. Monte, a master of dramatic entrances, screeched up in his car in the middle of the press conference like a stunt driver. He got out and walked rapidly toward the crowd with a palpable spray of anger emanating from his pores.

"We ain't going nowhere!" he screamed. "We live here. This is our house!"

He approached the fence where a half-dozen cops stood guard and screamed at them through the wire mesh. "This has been my home for a very long time. I have blood here. Sweat. Tears." He made an orator's pause after each statement. "Friends. Family. A new lease on life." He told the cops that "what we need is for you guys to get behind us and funnel resources to us. I'm not leaving!" he screamed. "Not standing, anyways."

Monte continued yelling at the cops like this for at least half an hour without stopping. I was amazed that his vocal cords could maintain that volume for so long. "You guys need to get on board with us!" he screamed. "Put some empathy back into your hearts. We're trying, we're doing the best we can. We have goals. Aspirations. We're just like you. We're normal people."

The cops had remained stone-faced amid Monte's histrionics, but eventually the one closest to him piped up. "I'm just doing my job," he said, in a slightly apologetic tone.

Monte looked ready to kill the guy. He grabbed the chain-link fence in front of the officer's face and leaned in close. "Your system is failing!" Monte screamed. "I'm trying to do the best I can and you're perpetuating the problem!"

"I'm sorry," said the officer, a man with dark shades, dark beard, and dark cropped hair.

"You're sorry?" said Monte, incredulously. He told the officer that the OPD had told him and many other residents that Wood Street was the one place in the city where they could live without being kicked out. "You guys sent us down here. You guys told me I'd be alright here."

"The city asked us to be out here today," said the officer, who sounded like he would rather not be. "What can I do? I can't just get up and walk away."

"So you're going to harm me?" asked Monte in a taunting tone.

A couple dozen residents and activists stood with Monte at the fence line, listening tensely. Monte was sweating heavily in the sun. "When are we gonna get some protection? We po' folk. Does that mean we can't have no protection? It's David and Goliath," he said, except Goliath got garbled in Monte's lisp. "I can't say it because I don't have no teeth!" he screamed. "But you know what I'm saying!" It was both funny and not.

The workers behind the police had started loading junk from the street into garbage trucks and cranking vehicles onto tow trucks. There was much clanging and grinding and beeping from the trucks and machinery. The row of cops continued to stand there stone-faced, looking into the distance from behind their shades. "All you guys can do is stare into blank space," said Monte, who offered a suggestion. "You guys can turn around right now and do the same pose that you're doing toward us toward them and tell them to stop. They're trying to come in here and build an apartment building that will not house any one of us. Affordable housing is not affordable for us."

He told the cops about the tiny-home facilities that the city had been building for them. One of the sites nearby used Tuff brand garden sheds, which can be purchased at Home Depot, to house the homeless. "The new thing is these Tuff sheds," said Monte. "I can't go into a Tuff shed. I have mental problems. I have three dogs. Ten years' worth of stuff. My tools. What do I do? I tell you what I do. I lose my job and I go back to jail. Then I get out and I create hell. Because I'm angry now. I have nothing, nowhere to go." He was still yelling. "The system they are providing for us is a failed system. It does not work. And they're spending millions of dollars. Where is it going? I'll tell you. It's going towards your smile sir. And your beautifully kept beard. It's going toward your cologne that you have on and your Ray-Ban glasses."

Monte told them that he had observed what happens in the city's rule-based shelter facilities. "I know a person who OD'd that you pushed into one of those sites. They died. Because they couldn't handle it. There was way too many restrictions. They couldn't even have a visit from the one person that kept them cool. So he chose to OD. Purposely. Suicide. He's not the only one. I'm not just talking. These things are actually happening. These people are actually dying. Our numbers out here are getting smaller. And it's not because you guys are housing us. We're dying!"

The workers started loading a minivan onto a tow truck nearby. "That's that man's house," Monte yelled, pointing at it. "Now where's he going to sleep?" He pointed to one of the workers who appeared to be in a good mood—"And people like him have this big-ass smile on his face? You, my friend—fuck you!" he screamed. The comrades at his side echoed in unison: "Fuck you!"

He turned his attention back to the cops. "Not one person understands what I'm saying. Not one person feels me," he said. "That means if they asked you to kill me, you would. If someone asked you to pull your sidearm, you would pull it. If they asked you to fire, you would fire. No questions asked. We're right back where Martin was. We're right back where Malcolm was. Where Harriet Tubman was. Only now it's a class thing. When we going to stop this shit? And lend a hand to one another? Assist one another?"

Monte told them a real-life fable to illustrate. "I saw a lady today—she was in her panties at the bus stop. Trying to cover up with some fucking newspaper. I stopped and gave her my pants. I didn't know that lady from Adam. But it's my duty to assist where I can. I'm not telling you that story to pat myself on the back. I'm telling you the story because"—he began banging his fists on the fence for emphasis at each word—"So. Too. Should. You."

After a solid half hour of screaming, Monte lowered his voice for the first time. He pressed his face to the fence and studied the officer in front of him.

"What can I do?" Monte asked, almost in a whisper. "What would you do? If this was your home? And now they want you out. With no alternatives. What would you do?"

"I can't tell you what to do, sir," said the officer.

"No, I didn't ask you that," said Monte. "I said what would you do?"

"I'm not in your position," said the officer. "I haven't been in your position."

"And that's the reason why we're having this problem," said Monte, his voice beginning to rise again. "Because you're not even willing to put yourself in my shoes. That means you have no empathy whatsoever for me. I came out here to die. To commit suicide. And I found a community that you guys are trying to destroy. Where is that going to put me? I don't know. I might become suicidal again."

He then began lecturing the cops about the difference between government solutions and the camp's solution. "Environments like this need to exist," he said, describing the huge number of young men who end up on Wood Street after getting out of jail. "You guys just write them off. We service those individuals. We help them. They come here for various reasons. Some of them just need to talk. You guys don't have a system to envelope them." He implored the cops to consider their alternative. "Nobody is willing to step out. To take a chance. Sometimes you have to. This city would become a much better place. Because systems like this would multiply. And I don't mean the filth. I mean the camaraderie that I found here. The heart. The empathy. The love."

Finally, Monte relinquished his soapbox. He turned and walked away, his body deflated.

"I wish you well," said the officer.

The evictions were brutal, and they went on for a month. People were arrested; last-minute restraining orders were filed against the city by lawyers allied with the camp. A group of the camp's supporters set up a tiny camp of their own at the site and stood guard as each resident's area was cleared, contesting the process at every turn in an effort to wear down the evictors. Monte mostly stayed away from the camp during the sweep but would occasionally screech up in his car and scream at the police.

At first the sweepers concentrated on clearing the people living directly on Wood Street. One day, while no one was on guard, they knocked down a portion of the chain-link fence that separated the bulk of the camp from the street. That night the campers re-erected it, after which the block-long fence line became a line in the sand, with people posted throughout each day at equally spaced points along it. I volunteered to stand watch whenever I could. The plan was to scream for help if it looked as if the city was gearing up to enter again and put as many bodies in the way as possible.

One day while standing at the fence, I heard the woman one post up from me scream. I came running over, along with a dozen or so residents and volunteers who were in the vicinity, as the police attempted to breach it from the other side. People jabbed metal bars at the cops through the wire mesh. They put their fingers between the blades of the bolt cutters that the police were using to cut through. Monte happened to be there that day and ran to fetch a five-gallon bucket of feces that apparently he'd been saving for a moment such as this. He climbed up on a pile of junk next to the fence and threatened to dump it on the heads of the policemen. "Don't do it!" people screamed, knowing he would surely be arrested. He heeded their advice, and for a while we all pushed against the fence and yelled in the cops' faces. At some point, a scream erupted from my chest: "Baaaackkkkk oooofffffffffff!" I roared.

The police eventually gave up their offensive for the day. After the altercation subsided, Monte climbed onto the roof of an RV that was parked along the fence line and faced the police, who were still standing nearby; he sat down cross-legged, closed his eyes, and meditated.

Because of Monte's martyrdom comments, the camp's volunteers had been plotting about how to keep him away when the sweepers came to bulldoze his shack. They ended up taking him out to lunch at just the right moment. He later told me that he had poured gasoline throughout his shack and was hunting for a lighter when they showed up. But he decided to go get some food instead.

TAZ ME

What if we let camps be? What if, instead of pushing homeless people around from place to place, we focused on the root causes and allowed that effort to take its course, investing the money saved on sweeps into permanent housing and supporting people to live better while on the street?

There has been much debate in government circles about "sanctioned camps," which seems to be a reflection of exasperation among the bureaucrats tasked with fixing the homelessness crisis, who clearly recognize the impossibility of the task (whether they say so publicly is another question). Wood Street Commons was tacitly sanctioned for years, but here and there cities have officially sanctioned camps. These are typically conceived of as a temporary measure until additional tiny homes, safe parking lots, and other interventions can be established in the area. And they generally do not happen at the site of an existing camp; rather, the city designates a location and establishes rules designed to keep the camp as clean and lifeless as possible. Which means they're not much different than tiny-home facilities, safe parking lots, and so on—it's a tightly controlled environment, only they give you a tent instead of a shed, bed, or parking space. Some sanctioned camps tout that they are co-managed by their residents in collaboration with city officials and the contractors who run the facilities. I was intrigued by the idea but after some investigation determined that most co-governed camps are not what they sound like—it's typically residents who are not rule-breakers sitting on a committee and giving input that does not demand that the rule enforcers cede their near-total authority.

The only example of a fully self-governed, city-sanctioned camp I found was in Sacramento, a place known as Camp Resolution, which was closely connected with Wood Street Commons. The camp hosted the Wood Street crew when they biked to Sacramento to speak with state lawmakers, which has become an annual event, and spearheaded a statewide network of homeless unions, which includes an active chapter in West Oakland. In 2023, after furiously resisting eviction for several years, Camp Resolution negotiated a rent-free lease with the city to remain in place. It was the cleanest, most organized camp I'd ever visited, which I'm sure helped make the case to the city that they could manage their own affairs. The city provided the residents with port-a-potties, a hand-washing station, regular trash service, and a number of trailer homes, but otherwise left them alone. There were no rules, except that people had to live in trailers, rather than on the ground in tents, because the soil was contaminated. News spread through the homeless empowerment movement of a shining model of its ideals being not only put into practice but embraced by local officials. Government-run sanctioned camps are typically managed by homeless services agencies with six- and seven-figure contracts, but Camp Resolution was virtually cost-free for the city (the trailers came from FEMA). The experiment, however, lasted only eighteen months. In 2024, the county district attorney threatened to sue the city unless the camp was removed, citing the public health risks associated with the contaminated soil. After one final standoff, the community was dismantled.

Sanctioned camps could be a reasonable compromise between cities and their unhoused residents, but it depends on how—and by whom—they're operated. My perspective—my observation—is that a sizable chunk of the unhoused population will not willingly accept residence in a rule-based environment.

Some will definitely accept it; for those folks, such facilities are a stepping stone back to society. But many in the unhoused community are not headed in that direction, whether because they are too low-functioning, or because they are simply not constitutionally disposed to it. The latter are in the lineage of the hobohemian, the wandering minstrel, the dervish. They aren't built for the status quo, but they have what it takes to survive in the anarchy of camps, if not thrive. And they perform an essential service: acting as patient companions for the hyper-traumatized low-functioning folks, with whom they have much in common.

All cities have underutilized space where camps could conceivably be allowed to exist. And I imagine that if some of the resources that are invested in sweeps were put into waste management and basic infrastructure, many of the less desirable attributes of camps, from a housed person's perspective, could be mitigated. Bathhouses, lockable storage, and even tiny homes could be provided—yes, these will tend to get busted up without security guards lording over them, but if random corporate security guards are replaced by safety patrols composed of people trusted in the community, I think the facilities could be reasonably maintained.

It goes against the anarchic grain of camps for a city to say where, and under what rules, they could be "sanctioned," but I think if unhoused folks knew there were places in cities where their presence was generally welcomed, they would be less resistant to the idea that other areas were off-limits. Figuring that out would be a dance between housed and unhoused, with one gently nudging the other in the directions that feel comfortable for each. It doesn't work to come in and make a grand declaration about where they can be and where they can't, any more than it works in a marriage to storm into the living room and tell your spouse that they better move that fucking pile of clothes off the armchair, or else!

I know that's a lot to ask of cities and their constituents, but I believe it is ultimately the most pragmatic approach. Because I don't think one can reasonably expect unhoused communities to take the role of the more yielding and accommodating spouse. That would be forcing a proverbial round peg into a square hole. It's the housed folks who have to give up something in the relationship, because for pretty much ever we've been the angry, intolerant half of the marriage. We're actually the ones who need counseling.

When I was a sophomore in college, during my Tarp Period, I took a class on anarchy for which we were assigned to read *T.A.Z.: The Temporary Autonomous Zone, Ontological Anarchy, Poetic Terrorism*. It was published in 1991 by Hakim Bey, the pen name of a prolific anarchist author named Peter Lamborn Wilson, an epically weird dude whose interest in anarchy seemed to be influenced as much by obscure mystical sects as by an interest in overthrowing the state. The common denominator for him was a quest for existential freedom, an ideal he chased in the prose of someone on acid (he was apparently part of William S. Burroughs's scene and very much into psychedelics). Wilson's writings remind me of some of the street-side philosophers I've encountered in camps, who probably do have something very profound to say, though it can easily come off as nonsense if you don't take the time to disengage from your linear brain and tap into their circular thinking. A typical Wilson sentence reads like this: "Chaos comes before all principles of order & entropy, it's neither a god nor a maggot, its idiotic desires encompass & define every possible choreography, all meaningless aethers & phlogistons: its masks are crystallizations of its own facelessness, like clouds."

Wilson is famous in anarchist circles for coining the term *temporary autonomous zones*—defined as simply a space that is, in a given moment of time, free of state rules and status quo norms, where the binding agent of social order is accountability to the relationships you have with the people around you. A party is basically a TAZ. People's Park in Berkeley was a quintessentially TAZ project. Early internet chat rooms were virtual TAZs. The encampments of the Occupy movement are one of the most famous examples of the idea. Burning Man is a TAZ, though I'm guessing most anarchists would probably see its current incarnation as having been co-opted by capitalism, a place for techies and hipsters to temporarily *perform* anarchy. A homeless camp is unquestionably a TAZ, however.

Wilson acknowledged that no anarchist revolution had yet succeeded in overthrowing the state and implementing its ideals for any length of time, so he suggested that maybe they should just have some fun and try out those ideals in small doses for brief periods wherever possible. "Absolutely nothing but a futile martyrdom could possibly result now from a head-on collision with the terminal State," he wrote. "Its guns are all pointed at us, while our meager weaponry finds nothing to aim at but a hysteresis, a rigid vacuity, a Spook capable of smothering every spark in an ectoplasm of information, a society of capitulation ruled by the image of the Cop and the absorbent eye of the TV screen." His hyper-indulgent prose had a simple and sober point, which is that a TAZ is a very practical thing, a way to satisfy the anarchist impulse in the present, rather than staying grumpy and ranting about capitalism until you die.

Not everyone wants to live by anarchist ideals, but history suggests that there is always a small percentage of people who insist on it. I would suggest that those communities, while outliers, supply a critical source of new ideas and a necessary questioning of assumptions that keeps the mainstream fresh and on its toes. I think that's an essential resource camps provide to the rest of us. But most importantly, they are places for people to exist who—for a multitude of reasons—have no other comfortable place to exist. These autonomous zones don't have to be there forever, only as long as they are needed. But if you force those folks into situations that they are guaranteed to rebel against, the chaos and dysfunction grows. I see camps as pressure relief valves for a world that is boiling over.

The current approach to the issue is to punish people in camps for behaviors defined by those in power as antisocial, immoral, unsafe, undesirable, or uncomfortable. It is clear that this approach does not cause the behaviors to cease. It is more likely to entrench them—as evidence, there are endless studies about the relationship between incarceration and recidivism. Why not allow a little anarchy in the street? Anarchy in small doses is clearly medicinal, not just for anarchists but for the rest of us. The overwhelming popularity of Burning Man—a TAZ relief valve for housed people—is a case in point.

Obviously, there are ways in which the ideals of anarchy are unrealistic and incompatible with our current world. The planet is plastered in hierarchical systems of governance, which are trending increasingly authoritarian. Maybe instead of seeing anarchy and capitalism as incompatible opposites, it's about embracing them as a complementary duality. Maybe anarchy would work better with a bit of top-down organization; maybe capitalism would taste better if marbled with a million little TAZs. Maybe it's more reasonable to say that anarchy, rather than being the natural state of humanity, has an important role to play at certain times, in certain situations, for certain people. The more hierarchical and capitalistic we become, the greater its importance. The more intolerance there is toward the unhoused, the more important it is for the housed to taste the bittersweet reality of camps.

The Spark

Samira and I live on a steep hillside overlooking San Francisco Bay. My office window looks out onto the upper reaches of an oak tree's canopy. Beyond its leaves I can see Angel Island, where Japanese Americans were rounded up and held before being sent to internment camps during World War II. And in the distance, holding up the sky above downtown San Francisco, is Salesforce Tower, the shape of which seems to have been inspired by an uncircumcised penis. I've spent many days gazing at this view and contemplating The Fix. Crows, for reasons I don't understand, love our yard; sometimes they land on the branches of the oak tree, within a few feet of my window, and gaze back. I'd turned over every little rock I could find in the world of Bay Area homelessness, and as I sat here trying to fit those pieces together into a story, all arrows pointed to the black mirror of the crows' eyes. The Fix is an illusion. There is no grand solution, only the dark nights of our souls and the tiny fixes they spark between one human and another.

I don't mean that as a hopeless statement—quite the contrary. There is no silver bullet, but there is so much that can be done. Stopping the sweeps. Getting to know our unhoused neighbors and supporting them on their journey. Redistributing wealth and privilege. Sanctioning camps and helping them function even better. Shoring up our own frayed connections with friends and family.

The temporary autonomous zone is a useful framework, as it allows The Fix to shape-shift, to be what it needs to be in different contexts, meeting people where they are at, rather than where we wish them to be. In the camp as TAZ, individuals arrive based on need, are transformed by their experience, and hopefully leave in a better condition, moving on to the next place that best suits them, whether another TAZ, a government-sponsored tiny-home community, or an apartment and a nine-to-five job. The unhoused are anything but a monolith—The Fix is a million tiny fixes.

America's unhoused are as diverse as America, their traumas unique as novels. In Richardson Bay, a small body of water near our apartment, a community of poor folks lives on boats anchored just offshore, rent-free. There are artists, hippies, and substance users, some more functional, in the status quo sense, than others. One hesitates to call them homeless, though when they lose their boats, they tend to turn up in tents onshore. The community has existed for decades. And for decades, local officials, urged by their constituents, have attempted to evict them. Because they inhabit federal waters, this has proven difficult, jurisdictionally speaking. But since we moved here, there's been a significant increase in evictions—which in this case means having your boat towed to shore and literally smashed to bits at an Army Corps of Engineers dock in nearby Sausalito.

The situation of the Richardson Bay "anchor-outs," as they're known, is different from, say, a Latinx encampment under a bridge in Los Angeles, or a Black family living in a New York shelter. The uniting factor, in my opinion, is not just their need for housing; it is their shared experience in the shadow of the American Dream. Most would benefit from better shelter—when people are bleeding, apply the necessary first aid. Then look at the source of trauma, so as not to replicate it. Most importantly, let the traumatized tell you what would be helpful for their healing. Give them the resources and let them decide. Recently, a group of anchor-outs sued their evictors, resulting in thirty of them receiving $18,000 apiece, with the stipulation that they receive the funds directly and choose how they are spent—a small, rare redistribution of both wealth and agency.

A growing number of studies have shown that Tiny is right—handing over cash to homeless people has an overwhelmingly positive impact. In a Vancouver study, a group of unhoused folks were given a lump sum of 7,500 Canadian dollars. Over the course of the following year, the recipients were housed ninety-nine days more on average compared to a control group. If the government had paid to house the recipients in temporary shelters for ninety-nine days—which most homeless folks resist—it would have cost taxpayers $777 more per person than the lump sum amount, which also produced a slew of other benefits for the recipients. A basic income program in San Francisco that provided $500 per month had even more astonishing results: Two-thirds of recipients were housed within six months. Virtually all basic income programs for the unhoused have shown positive results, prompting bigger investments in the idea, including from Google, which has put up the funds to pay 225 unhoused families in the Bay Area $1,000 per month for a year.

A USC report on the topic noted that cash transfers generally result in far more housing per dollar spent than government-funded housing, which entails enormous bureaucratic inefficiencies and a million rules dictating how it must be built, plus huge overhead costs for staff, consultants, and all that barbed wire. However, a homeless guy might very well know a dude who will let them crash in their spare room for $400 per month until he can get back on his feet—no bureaucracy, no lease application, no credit check, no security deposit, just cash.

"There is every indication from multiple pilot projects that a very significant number of unhoused people can accomplish more for less," said the USC report. The authors described a range of advantages. "These subsidies can be provided to people excluded from other government funded voucher programs, including immigrants and formerly incarcerated people," they wrote. They also "afford more choice and dignity by allowing unhoused or housing insecure people to be treated like any other prospective tenant or lodger." Basic income is a quick fix with a fantastic cost-benefit analysis, whereas building both temporary and permanent housing for the homeless is exorbitantly expensive and takes practically forever—and nobody seems to want it in their backyard.

And for those who may be wondering: People receiving basic income don't buy more drugs. The San Francisco program found that recipients spent 2 percent of their financial resources on addictive substances, the same percentage as in the control group. A Stanford meta-analysis of nineteen studies of cash subsidy programs found that on average, spending on "temptation goods" actually decreased among recipients.

Basic income produces tangible results in the short term and has the potential to restructure broken relationships between labor, land use, and social norms in the long term. David Graeber, the late anarchist anthropologist and Occupy architect, wrote in his book *Bullshit Jobs* that basic income is "a stepping-stone toward the most profound transformation of all: to unlatch work from livelihood entirely." Also notable: It's a trendy concept among the Valley's libertarian billionaires. They have their own reasons for promoting it, but it is nonetheless a rare place of overlap with anti-capitalists like Tiny.

Giving money directly to homeless people is a relatively simple fix. There are more difficult ways to support the unhoused that are also important. For instance, it's hard for people struggling to survive on the street to get their pitchforks in order and storm city hall. But those of us with access to pitchforks can distribute them; we can give rides to city hall. Don't take the easy way out and show up at city hall acting as though your pitchfork speaks for theirs. Mingle. Be patient. Don't expect people who have been raped, beaten, evicted, and addicted to behave in ways you deem rational. Quietly fill in the gaps where they fall short.

I was initially very skeptical of the hipsters banging drums on Wood Street, but over the course of several years I saw a solid cohort of volunteers who did what Tiny calls "Love Work"—reminding residents of appointments, cleaning up their trash, copy editing their proposals to the city, basically any little thing that needed doing. They were not paid, recognized by those in power, or affiliated with an organization. It was friends helping friends.

They've made a profound difference in the lives of their unhoused neighbors, but for the most part their vibe is too radical, too angry, too grungy to be taken seriously by the powers that be in Oakland—which is a feat given that Oakland is one of the most left-leaning cities in the country. Even Tiny, who has conjured rent-free townhomes out of thin air and should have won the Nobel Peace Prize by now, seems to elicit eye-rolling from Oakland's city councillors and bureaucrats. What can you do? Talk to your unhoused neighbors. Talk to people in power. Talk to people who trust you. Talk to people who will not listen to the unhoused and their grungy activist friends, but will listen to you.

Do not speak for them—translate for them. Mediate. When the pitchforks come out, stay calm and committed to constructive conversation. This is difficult. People don't change their minds easily.

One of my goals is to get the billionaires onboard. Self-determination is at the core of libertarianism, after all. People like Tiny who help themselves without taxpayer assistance should appeal to anyone with an up-by-the-bootstraps sensibility. I thought maybe Wombat would be down, but he was too busy being angry at Facebook. The media handlers for Benioff, the Salesforce CEO, blew me off. But Samira, who hangs out with Davos types, is on the case. The sort of folks who quickly sniff out the grungy activist hiding in my closet see her as one of them.

A while back she was summoned to a meeting in a conference room on the tenth floor of the Twitter building in San Francisco, not long before the company became X. She was there to meet with Gaymon Bennett, an anthropologist who studied the tech industry, and Barry Brown, a Valley leadership consultant with a master's in divinity studies. Samira was a subject in a book Bennett was writing about the intersections of science, tech, and spirituality. Brown has had his feet as deep in homeless camps as in Valley boardrooms. When he moved to San Francisco in the eighties, he was part of a grassroots group that lived in a communal house together with unhoused neighbors that they invited to stay. His decades-long relationships with the unhoused inform his work with tech executives, which is largely about getting them to take a very hard look in the mirror—which may or may not make them more successful in business, but might make them more successful at leading a fulfilling and self-aware life.

I have a very sensitive BS meter when it comes to techno-optimists and leadership consultants, but Brown passes the sniff test. This is in part because he's as much at home in a homeless camp as in a boardroom, and also because he doesn't use his optimism as a shield to hide from the dark sides of the soul. My impression, after some very deep conversations with him, is that his optimism, which is notably bountiful, has emerged through embracing darkness. His consulting practice is a Trojan horse for getting into boardrooms and minds that might otherwise be shut to such beliefs. Samira, Brown, and Bennett were at Twitter that day to discuss how they might band together to bring the Valley's shadow side into the light, one techie at a time.

One of the "hallmark features" of Valley culture, said Bennett in a podcast series Samira later hosted about the dark sides of tech, "is it doesn't really have a theory of evil attached to it. Like there isn't a downside, there isn't a darkness." Bennett, who was fighting stage-four lung cancer and has since passed away, said, "I think if you operate long enough with that kind of half-truth—this idea that there can be light without shadow—the lights grow brighter and brighter and brighter. Lots of things can be achieved. But the shadows grow deeper and deeper and deeper, to the point where they become wounds on the social body."

When one is in denial of their dark side, said Brown, "those who are homeless, or those who are part of the marginalized, remain in the shadow." It's an "ethos of people we don't need to see," he continued. "We will fix their problem further down the road. Of course they're homeless now, but what we're going to come up with is going to make it all worthwhile," he said, facetiously. "We just need brighter tools, faster devices," because "somewhere in the direction we've been moving lies the answer." Brown likes to implicate himself, which helps me to trust him. "I've always thought, personally, in the corner of my shadow are my wounds," he said.

One of the teachings of Exu is that all transformation requires loss. Which I think is why transformation, in the spiritual sense, is so rare—giving up things of value goes against human nature. In my observation, spiritual transformation occurs primarily in response to loss that is experienced unwillingly, unintentionally. But in our rock bottoms—"the pit of my despair," as Monte describes it—is something of priceless value. We have a name for it in the tradition: Luzbel, which translates as "beautiful light." Luzbel is a synonym for Lucifer in some Latin countries, but in the esoteric sense it refers to the tiny, pure, invincible speck of light at the center of the black holes of consciousness. "In the darkest place, there is a last ray of light—the light that we find only when we've lost everything else," Beremi, a priestess in the tradition, once told me. "This is Luzbel."

In Latin, *lucifer* means "bringer of light," and was used in ancient times as the word for "morning star"—a guiding light that emerges after the night has passed. At some point in the early evolution of Christianity, Lucifer was transmogrified into an angel who fell from grace—he sinned!—and was permanently demonized. No second chances for Satan! Demonization requires ongoing maintenance—much has been invented to prevent us from seeing the light in that place, in those angels. We have to keep them totally in the dark. It's an easy stance to go along with, unless you get to know some.

MEET ME AT THE CROSSROADS

Kent has a thing for scary masks, but he's a softy underneath. When he spoke alongside the mayor at the grand opening of the Leigh Avenue Senior Apartments, he told a story about a lady in Cupertino, one of Wolfe Camp's most vocal haters, who yelled at them from her car on a daily basis—until one day when she was at a stoplight and saw Kent helping a disoriented blind person, who'd gotten stuck in the median at rush hour, to cross the street. "As she's walking away with her cane, that very lady who hated us pulled up. *That's pretty nice what you did*, she said. It blew her mind, because she thought we were scum." It's a quaint story, perfect for the cameras, but for Kent it was a truly transformational experience—like an alchemist, he'd opened a closed mind and heart. I wasn't at the grand opening, but he cried when he relayed the story to me later.

Housing has been good for Kent. He gets to tell his story to more housed people, and he has an abundance of time and space to contemplate what's important. He seems to now reside in the philosophical mood that is his natural home.

"I've had a lot of great adventures," he told me on a recent visit. "There's shameful ones too—I'm trying to stay away from those. I'm accountable for everything I do," he continued. "I can't blame my wife because she left me. That's not a valid excuse in the court of God. But the funny thing is, the closer you get to God, the harder the devil comes at you. It's like the devil wants those he doesn't have—he doesn't want those he's already got."

Kent has been feeling very cozy with God, which is helping him to let go of regret. "I keep coming back to, *man, it's OK*. Because I know in the end—boy, *whooo!* What a ride. It seems like forever here, but when you go back home to eternity, it was only a five-minute roller coaster. It's all kinds of ups and downs, left and right, but when it's all said and done, in hindsight, you have a different view." Kent told me about a pessimistic friend of his whom he's trying to win over with his optimism. "I keep telling him, *when it's all over you'll be begging to do this shit again."* He wasn't referring to homelessness per se, but to life in all its cruelty. "This is something we argue about—he insists he's not going to want to do it again. And I say, *Well, we'll see. You're going to be in front of me, jumping up and down, going me, me, me, me, me—can we do it again, Dad? You're gonna be in line begging dad to do it again."*

Rudy, however, has not been doing well. About a week after his standoff with the police, the sweep crew came back to the Crash Zone and told him again that he had to go. This time he agreed. There was no crowd of supporters—I was out of town—and he didn't want to risk being arrested again, after what had happened the last time. The sweepers had him sign a document stating that any items he left behind could be discarded—an apparent tactic to avoid legal accountability. Late that night, Rudy loaded his belongings onto a metal cart and pushed them—many loads of them—a couple hundred yards to the far side of the camp, where he set up a new spot next to Scott and Mr. Fujio.

Rudy never felt comfortable in the new spot. It was close to a noisy road and crowded—many of those evicted from the main part of the Crash Zone had resettled on this side of the park—and there was no elderberry tree for shade and birds. A year later, the sweepers came again. Again, he refused to leave. He'd obtained a small camper to live in, but it was not in towable condition and he lacked a vehicle with which to move it anyways. With the help of an advocate, Rudy filed suit in federal court to prevent his eviction. The judge granted a series of hearings and told the city to let him stay put while his case was heard. The once-crowded fields around him became barren as the bulldozers swept through. Many of the RV dwellers escaped to a much smaller adjacent field, which became a densely packed parking lot, until that, too, was cleared.

Rudy represented himself in court. "They've been destroying all my property, and based on *Garcia v. Los Angeles* and *Martin v. Boise*, it's not right," he told the judge. The judge expressed sympathy for his situation, but it quickly became clear that without a lawyer and a mountain of documentation to support his claims, the case would ultimately be dismissed. However, the judge instructed the city to repair Rudy's RV and move it to a location where he would not be immediately swept again. He said the city had to ensure that any possessions that could not fit in the RV were safely stowed in a self-storage facility nearby. None of Rudy's fellow residents received such accommodations.

He saw it as a small victory but was disappointed that his larger goal—a class-action lawsuit to prevent the city from displacing unhoused residents and destroying their belongings—was not realized. And the effort to achieve even that small victory took an enormous toll on him. In court, Rudy seemed much older than when I'd first met him, his body slouched, his normally astute demeanor slack. "I'm a human being," he told the judge, beginning to cry. "I've been so stressed out lately. I can't eat. I'm losing my hair. You don't know how hard it is. You don't. I'm afraid I'm going to die because of all of this. I'm really deathly afraid."

Rudy's experience of being swept is fairly universal, though most homeless folks never have the opportunity to describe it to a federal judge. The case got a fair bit of local media attention, as well. I hounded the main reporter covering it to make sure she understood that Rudy was no crackpot, but was actually on solid legal ground. She'd never heard of *Martin v. Boise* and seemed surprised to learn that cities don't have the right to evict unhoused people and destroy their belongings.

I found that these small, one-on-one conversations can have a big effect. I've had hundreds of them—when people in the Bay Area learn you're writing a book about homelessness, they have questions, *lots* of questions. I try not to come off too heavy-handed when I answer, giving them a quieter, more user-friendly translation of Tiny's angsty rhetoric. And, as Tiny teaches, I look for opportunities to support the unhoused in speaking for themselves. When I was invited to speak about homelessness to the Kiwanis Club of Palo Alto, of all places, I said I'd do it on one condition: that Tiny would be the speaker, and I would interview her onstage. They agreed.

Tiny seemed to be slowly inching her way into the mainstream. A children's book she wrote was made into a short animated film that won awards at film festivals all over the country, significantly expanding her platform. Despite her distaste for higher education, and despite having not graduated middle school, she applied, successfully, to an MFA program at Goddard, a small liberal arts college in Vermont. She wrote a play as part of her coursework that she is working to adapt to film, with unhoused friends as actors. Her intention, of course, was to subvert the educational system from within. She was later selected as an activist-in-residence at UCLA.

I wouldn't consider myself an anti-capitalist. I'm not looking to burn Babylon down. But I understand the sentiment. There are valid reasons to feel that way, and I support those who do, such as my mom. She asked me recently about the conclusion I'd reached through my research in camps. When I told her that healing broken relationships was the closest thing I'd found to a fix, she seemed disappointed. "What about economics?" she asked.

I told her I believed economics had much to do with the raw numbers of people on the streets—there are fewer, on average, where the rent is lower—but not as much as one might expect. Inexpensive markets like Tallahassee, Savannah, and Amarillo have roughly as many unhoused residents per capita as San Francisco. Obviously, poverty, in whatever form, whether it's poor people living indoors or out, is an issue of economic justice. But that's usually the extent of the conversation, which often escalates into an unproductive shouting match. I think a relational perspective—What is the nature of this person's fragility? What can I offer them? What can I learn from them? How can I connect with them?—is a decent way to sneak around the polarization.

I hadn't yet told my mom about Tiny's theories on not abandoning one's family. I hadn't told her because doing so would be admitting that she was right all along: I made too much out of our differences, and wielded them as a shield to avoid having to deal with, much less be close to, the person who gave me life. Finally, I caved; my mom cried. "I think our relationship has been getting better," she said. I had been working on it—forgiving, getting over it, letting down my guard, being a grown-ass man. I don't get agitated with her like I used to.

I am still overwhelmed with grief about the person I was when I got on that plane to California after my divorce. That person still exists inside me. When I look back at my time at rock bottom, an image sometimes enters my mind: me, sitting crumpled and alone on the sidewalk, my aura emanating addiction and houselessness to passersby, who keep on passing me by. I once had a dream set in such a scene, where I was trying to find a place to bed down for the night against the brick wall of an apartment building. Tiny appeared out of nowhere, sat down at my side, and put her arm around me; I felt profoundly comforted by her care. We're not that close in waking reality, but she has somehow worked her way deep into my subconscious self. I wasn't going to be moving back in with my mom as Tiny insisted, but I have taken down some of the walls holding me back and am trying instead to persuade her to move to California. I felt Luzbel hiding inside those walls—that blue-colored feeling of loving through pain.

Speaking of the blues, it's worth noting that Exu lurks in the foundations of American music. The minor chord vibe of the blues, which both haunts and heals, is Luzbel. The title of Jimi Hendrix's blues-rock anthem "Voodoo Child" refers to the followers of Vodun, the Haitian incarnation of Yoruba spirituality. Hendrix was inspired by Robert Johnson, the great granddaddy of American blues, who is said to have obtained his musical powers by making a deal with the devil late one night at a crossroads, part of the mythology of the Southern Black culture of the day. Crossroads are Exu's mythological home, the place where West African culture meets the Faustian bargain. These are popular legends. But the esoteric reading of the crossroads is that it's a place where suffering can be converted to raw power. Perhaps this is simply because it is a place where one must make a choice about which direction to go. Choice is agency. Choice is power. Choice is complicated.

People I've gotten to know on the street sometimes refer to homelessness as "the lifestyle." And it's not uncommon to hear the expression of being "ready" to leave it behind. There is often a connotation of recovering from substance use in the sentiment. But in general, being ready means arriving to a point at which one is prepared to do things like get a job and jump through the hoops of social service programs to obtain things like a driver's license and an address. Bobby sometimes told me that he was "almost ready." This makes it sound like homelessness is a matter of "choice." Choice is a factor, just not in the archconservative sense of people choosing to be addicted, unemployed, and dependent on the government. More in the sense of me choosing to hold onto grudges with my mom—it's not rational, it just *is*. At some point, you get to the end of the homelessness rope, and you are ready. Many die before they get there. And getting there does not mean you magically have a job and an apartment—that can take years.

The leaders of camps, who are generally the highest-functioning residents, are often ready, or nearly so. My observation is that they help rehabilitate lower-functioning residents, so that they might someday be ready too. In other words, the messy-looking social services provided by camps reach the folks that institutional forms of aid do not and prime them to one day be in a place where they might be more receptive to the lanyard-and-clipboard crowd. In this way, stopping sweeps and helping camps to grow and flourish is actually complementary to top-down approaches to The Fix.

John from Wood Street became ready during the time that I knew him. He quit drugs, mostly, and began the long slog of returning to society. He told me he'd gotten very tired of not having a bathroom, and of living in chaos. His cost-benefit analysis had shifted. The TAZ had served him well, but he was ready to move on from anarchy. Monte, his brother-in-arms, was not far behind. Part of the equation was their impending eviction. They'd lived at Wood Street for years, poured blood, sweat, and tears into the place. They had both breached fifty years of age, and it was hard to imagine starting over with a new camp—they felt it was time to focus more on themselves, as Monte's mom had been urging.

Monte started sleeping again after the sweep. In the days before his shack was crushed to bits by a bulldozer, I helped buy him a run-down RV, thanks to a check my wealthy neighbor, whose mentally ill mother had recently become homeless, wrote for the cause. Monte moved the RV about a mile away to a parking lot for Google commuters. I'd given him a potted redwood tree on his fiftieth birthday, which was nearly dead at that point, but he planted it next to his new spot anyways. I brought him a bucket of water in hopes of reviving it.

John, like many others from the camp, moved into the tiny homes that the city had placed on a lot at the other end of Wood Street. They were given three months to stay there—no visitors allowed. Monte, however, would not be caught dead in one of those places. There was only one other person living at his new spot in the parking lot, but he went back to Wood Street regularly to visit. The campers had moved their giant white canopy to the curb out-side the tiny-home lot, which the city let be. A new camp quickly sprung up around it.

Monte and I have stayed in touch. He continues to work on himself; he contin-ues to inspire me to do the same. One night he explained his chanting to me.

"I close my eyes and take some deep breaths, in my nose and out of my mouth, and think of something positive," he said. "And I, *Shri raam jai raam jai jai raam. Shri raam jai raam jai jai raam. Shri raam jai raam jai jai raam-mmmmmmmmm.*" He did this a few times and then was silent. After a while, his eyes still closed, he opened his mouth: "*Ommmmmmmmmmmmmmmmmmm mmmmmmmmmmmmmm.*"

Monte continued, his voice trancelike. "I do that to center myself now, when my emotions are getting out of control. It's not a bad thing, because I'm a human—we're supposed to get out of control sometimes. But it allows me to slow down and actually observe my emotions. To sit with them. They are valid—if to no one else, to me. It's OK to feel how anyone is feeling at the time that they're feeling it. Fear? I'm OK with that. Yes, I'm afraid of a lot of things. I embrace that. Anger? Yeah, of course. Hurt? Any emotion, it's OK for you to feel it. Sit with it," he said, his eyes suddenly snapping open, "and let it pass."

Monte told me that he was resolved to walk out of his darkness. He'd made a firm choice. "I'm not staying out here to kill myself," he said. "I do see a light at the end of the tunnel." He continues to waver on his sobriety and is still in a struggle for daily survival, both materially and spiritually. But on Wood Street, he'd found something that couldn't be taken away—it nearly was during the eviction, but he's managed to hold on to a sliver of inner stability. "Spirits, energy," he waxed, "can't be destroyed, can't be consumed." He was beaming. "It's our spark. That spark still exists after the flesh is gone. It's what's given me a new lease on life."

I love this man. He's helped give me a new lease on life as well, which I tell him often. We haven't seen each other as much since the eviction, but when we do, it always feels like family. One night I took him and Mona, another Wood

Street resident, out to dinner at a chicken-and-waffles place not far from the camp. We spent the evening giggling. When I dropped them off at the end of the night, Monte turned to me and said something I will never forget: "I feel like we're making memories together." He looked me in the eye. "Healthy ones," he said.

Epilogue

Not long after typing the final words of this manuscript, the story of homelessness in America took an abrupt turn. *Martin v. Boise*, a case that deemed sweeps unlawful, at least in some contexts, was effectively overturned by the Supreme Court. At question was whether arresting a homeless person for sleeping on public land violates the Eighth Amendment, which protects against "cruel and unusual punishment." As of June 28, 2024, it no longer does. This period of legal protection, a golden era for homeless communities, lasted four and a half years.

Martin v. Boise spawned a cascading series of lawsuits on behalf of unhoused residents. One advocate I got to know, who was not a lawyer, figured out how to file restraining orders in federal court and would do so whenever a camp he was connected with received a removal notice. These were generally successful in delaying eviction, and sometimes actual lawyers would take up the case and attempt to block the sweep indefinitely. Most of those cases were not ultimately successful, however, if only because the unhoused plaintiffs were out-lawyered by the government defendants. The legal protection of *Martin v. Boise* was not particularly robust—cities found lots of loopholes and gray areas to slip through in their mission to make homeless people disappear. But it definitely slowed down the process and made cities more selective about which camps they targeted.

The case was symbolically meaningful, however. Unhoused residents felt that a powerful American institution, miraculously, had their back. It made them bolder—they felt a measure of security to pitch their tents on "Front Street," in full public view—and provided ammunition for their efforts to resist. I don't think it's a coincidence that homelessness became more visible in the years following *Martin v. Boise*. Likewise, I don't think it's a coincidence that the homeless empowerment movement gained steam.

The movement hasn't lost steam as a result of the case being overturned; if anything, it's raised the stakes of the battle, as cities are newly emboldened to crack down on camps. The overturning of *Martin v. Boise* was pushed forward by an extensive bipartisan coalition of local governments from across the western US—anti-homeless sentiment has become a rare cause uniting politicians on both sides of the aisle. After the Supreme Court handed down its decision, Governor Newsom, the most high-profile and outspoken member of the group advocating for it, exclaimed relief that the state could finally get on with the task of eliminating camps, a sentiment echoed by countless local leaders across the state.

The Eighth Amendment is no longer a bulwark against sweeps, but other legal remedies remain. A landmark case in San Francisco, for instance, is pushing forward; four of its thirteen claims were dismissed after the Supreme Court decision, but the rest, including Fourth Amendment claims concerning the confiscation of unhoused residents' property, were not. And the ballot box remains a weapon. During the pandemic, voters began favoring candidates with hard-line positions toward camps, but I think if the media can do a better job at helping the public understand that sweeps make homelessness worse, their views will change. The mission to pierce the veils of misunderstanding between housed and unhoused neighbors could not be more urgent.

Notes

Prologue

60 to 120 percent of Oakland's median income Oakland City Council resolution, "Wood Street—Affordable Housing ENA," December 11, 2018, oakland.legistar.com/LegislationDetail .aspx?ID=3759867&GUID=ECC644E3-BC09-4E5E-A98E-A04FCE3B7F11&Options =ID%7CText%7C&Search=1707+wood. See page 25 of resolution report PDF: oakland.legistar .com/View.ashx?M=F&ID=6791161&GUID=0B6B3BF9-A7AC-4A06-A976-C2BCED444F73.

roughly $75,000 to $150,000 These figures change annually, but in 2024, 60 percent AMI for a two-person household in Oakland was $72,487; 120 percent AMI for a two-person household was $149,500. See "2024 Income Limits," City of Oakland Housing and Community Development Department, effective date June 6, 2024, cao-94612.s3.us-west-2.amazonaws.com/documents /2024-City-of-Oakland-Income-Limits-effective-June-1-2024_2024-06-07-231543_nnpy.pdf.

more than a million dollars per unit "How Much Does It Cost to Construct One Unit of Below Market Housing in the Bay Area?," Bay Area Council Economic Institute, bayareaeconomy.org /how-much-does-it-cost-to-produce-one-unit-of-below-market-housing-in-the-bay-area/.

affordable housing in California Liam Dillon and Ben Poston, "Affordable Housing in California Now Routinely Tops $1 Million per Apartment to Build," *Los Angeles Times*, June 20, 2022, latimes.com/homeless-housing/story/2022-06-20/california-affordable-housing -cost-1-million-apartment.

Chapter 1: Wolves

Zuccotti Park and Tahrir Square "The Symbolism of Guy Fawkes," London Museum, london-museum.org.uk/collections/london-stories/symbolism-of-guy-fawkes/.

third of the nation's homeless population Margot Kushel and Tiana Moore, *Toward a New Understanding: The California Statewide Study of People Experiencing Homelessness* (University of California San Francisco: 2023), p. 11, bcsh.ca.gov/calich/meetings/materials/20230907 _study_homelessness.pdf.

1.6 camps per business day They swept 403 camps in the financial year 2018–2019; there are 260 business days per year, equivalent to 1.55 sweeps per day.

sufficiently affordable price points Manuela Tobias, "California Homeless Population Grew by 22,000 over Pandemic," *CalMatters*, October 6, 2022, calmatters.org/housing/2022/10/california -homeless-crisis-latinos/; Ben Christopher, *CalMatters*, "Homelessness: Where Are California's Billions Going? Here's the New, Best Answer," *Desert Sun*, February 16, 2023, hdesertsun.com /story/story-series/california-homeless/2023/02/16/homelessness-where-are-californias-billions -going-heres-the-new-answer/69911396007/.

$5 billion campus Abigail Johnson Hess, "Here's How Much Every Inch of Apple's New $5 Billion Campus Cost to Build," *CNBC*, October 9, 2017, cnbc.com/2017/10/09/how-much-every -inch-of-apples-new-5-billion-campus-cost-to-build.html.

$85 million landscaping job Adam Brinklow, "Here's How Much Apple Park Cost," *Curbed SF*, October 5, 2017, sf.curbed.com/2017/10/5/16425952/apple-park-permits-headquarters.

plums, apricots, . . . apples Steven Levy, "Apple Park's Tree Whisperer," *Wired*, June 1, 2017, wired.com/story/apple-parks-tree-whisperer/.

gleaming edifice . . . subterranean ones Steven Levy, "Inside Apple's Insanely Great (or Just Insane) New Mothership," *Wired*, May 16, 2017, wired.com/2017/05/apple-park-new-silicon -valley-campus/.

"custom-made . . . Louis Vuitton" Kif Leswing, "Photos from Inside Apple's New $5 Billion Headquarters," *Business Insider*, February 4, 2018, businessinsider.com/instagram-photos-from -inside-apple-park-2018-2.

"ecologically rich oak savanna" Kyle Vanhemert, *Wired*, "New Glimpses of Apple's 'Spaceship' Campus," *CNN*, November 19, 2013, cnn.com/2013/11/19/tech/innovation/apple-spaceship -campus/index.html.

worth around $20,000 The median South Bay home price in 1963 was $18,000. See Herbert G. Ruffin, *Uninvited Neighbors: African Americans in Silicon Valley, 1769–1990* (University of Oklahoma Press, 2014), p. 262, endnote 13.

$3 million Zestimates only go back ten years, so you can no longer see back to 2012, but you can see the trends here: zillow.com/homedetails/807-Parnell-Pl-Sunnyvale-CA-94087/19618342 _zpid/.

California's minimum wage The minimum wage in California in 2020 was $12 to $13 per hour, depending on employer size. Using a baseline of 160 hours per month, pay is about $2,000 per month; thus $3,000 per month is 50 percent higher. See "Minimum Wage Frequently Asked Questions," State of California Department of Industrial Relations, updated December 2024, dir .ca.gov/dlse/faq_minimumwage.htm.

average rent in Cupertino I got this average rent from Zillow, and it's actually gone up to $3,831 (I can no longer find the Zillow data for 2020, when I first interviewed Kent). See zillow.com /rental-manager/market-trends/cupertino-ca/.

afford a two-bedroom apartment The figure comes from Santa Clara County, which says that their $110,000 figure equates to $54 per hour, which is 4.1 times more than $13 per hour. See "County of Santa Clara and City of San José Release Preliminary Results of 2022 Point-in-Time Homeless Census," County of Santa Clara, press release, May 16, 2022, sccgov.org/news-release /county-santa-clara-and-city-san-José-release-preliminary-results-2022-point-time.

smog-belching factories See Louis Hyman, *Temp: The Real Story of What Happened to Your Salary, Benefits, & Job Security* (Viking, 2018), chap. 10.

"Proteomic . . . Disease" Federico Martinelli, Russell L. Reagan, David Dolan, Veronica Fileccia, and Abhaya M. Dandekar, "Proteomic Analysis Highlights the Role of Detoxification Pathways in Increased Tolerance of Huanglongbing Disease," *BMC Plant Biology*, vol. 16, no. 1, July 2016, p. 167, pubmed.ncbi.nlm.nih.gov/27465111/.

original garage Luke Dormehl, "Today in Apple History: Apple Moves Into Bandley 1, Its First Custom HQ," Cult of Mac, January 28, 2025, cultofmac.com/525273/apple-history -bandley-1/.

"stay here and pay taxes" Jay Yarow, "Cupertino Councilwoman: Here's Why I Asked Steve Jobs for Free Wifi," *Business Insider*, June 10, 2011, businessinsider.com/apple-spaceship-cupertino -councilwoman-2011-6.

Chapter 2: Hobo Sapiens

Persian dervishes Hamid Algar and Mansour Shaki, "Darvīš," Encyclopaedia Iranica, December 15, 1994, iranicaonline.org/articles/darvis.

copious cannabis use Vincent Burgess, "Indian Influences on Rastafarianism" (Ohio State University, senior thesis, 2007), kb.osu.edu/items/923e4735-c308-5050-b909-3e89a9a0cd9e.

in search of God Kalyan Das, "Let Our Monks Defecate in the Open: Jain Group to MP Govt," *Hindustani Times*, May 1, 2016, hindustantimes.com/bhopal/let-our-monks-defecate-in-open -jain-group-to-mp-govt/story-QdtOIySL9Zhk3hGX6MAiPJ.html.

traveling performers in India K. S. Jayamaran, "European Romanis Came from Northwest India," *Nature India*, December 1, 2012, nature.com/articles/nindia.2012.179.

higher pay and better conditions "Old Poor Laws: 1349 Through 1781," English Legal History and Its Materials, course wiki, Columbia University, updated December 3, 2014, moglen.law .columbia.edu/twiki/bin/view/EngLegalHist/StatuteofLabourers.

"theft and other abominations" "Ordinance of Laborers, 1349," Internet History Sourcebooks Project, Fordham University, sourcebooks.fordham.edu/seth/ordinance-labourers.asp.

"vagabond acts" "Old Poor Laws: 1349 Through 1781."

"masterless men" "Vagabond Act," UK Parliament, parliament.uk/vagabondact/.

"executed as a Felon" "1535: 27 Henry 8 c.25: Punishing Sturdy Vagabonds and Beggars," Statutes Project, statutes.org.uk/site/the-statutes/sixteenth-century/1535-27-henry-8-c-25 -punishing-sturdy-vagabonds-and-beggars/.

forehead for the latter William F. Maher and William E. Williams, "Vagrancy—a Study in Constitutional Obsolescence," *Florida Law Review*, vol. 22, no. 3 (1970), floridalawreview.com /article/79069-vagrancy-a-study-in-constitutional-obsolescence/attachment/165023.pdf.

decent portion of gruel Peter Higginbotham, "Work," Workhouse: The Story of an Institution, workhouses.org.uk/life/work.shtml.

escaped slaves and former indentured servants Kristin O'Brassill-Kulfan, "Vagabonds and Paupers: Race and Illicit Mobility in the Early Republic," *Pennsylvania History: A Journal of Mid-Atlantic Studies*, vol. 83, no. 4 (2016), journals.psu.edu/phj/article/download/63314 /62212/72326; Kenneth L. Kusmer, *Down and Out, on the Road* (Oxford University Press, 2002), p. 15.

our tongues around this time *Permanent Supportive Housing: Evaluating the Evidence for Improving Health Outcomes Among People Experiencing Chronic Homelessness* (National Academies Press, 2018), app. B, ncbi.nlm.nih.gov/books/NBK519584/.

about ninety thousand in 1893 Ellen Bassuk and Deborah Franklin, "Homelessness Past and Present: The Case of the United States, 1890–1925," *New England Journal of Public Policy*, vol. 8, no. 1 (1992), p. 71, scholarworks.umb.edu/cgi/viewcontent.cgi?article=1538&context =nejpp.

around sixty-three million "Population of the United States by States and Territories: 1890," US Census Office, October 30, 1890, census.gov/library/publications/decennial/1890/bulletins /demographics/12-population-of-the-us-by-states-and-territories-1890.pdf.

on par with modern-day rates Today the population is around 340 million, or about 5.4 times higher; the federal government's homeless population estimate in recent years has been around 550,000, or about 6.1 times higher.

fraction of what it is now Bassuk and Franklin, "Homelessness Past and Present," p. 71.

five hundred thousand homeless people Nels Anderson, *The Hobo: The Sociology of the Homeless Man* (University of Chicago Press, 1923), p. 105.

rates far higher than today Anderson, *The Hobo*, p. vi.

Hoovervilles spread across the country "Hoovervilles and Homelessness," Great Depression in Washington State, 2009, depts.washington.edu/depress/hooverville.shtml.

oft-cited estimate . . . is two million "Transient Division Newsletter from Macon, Georgia: Introduction," Great Depression and the New Deal, University of Illinois Library, iopn.library .illinois.edu/scalar/the-great-depression-and-the-new-deal-transient-divisn-newsletter-from -macon-georgia/introduction.

"homeless were far more visible" and **"back doors or on street corners"** Kusmer, *Down and Out*, p. 7.

"these tramps . . . steal something" "Our Vagrant Population," *New York Times*, December 28, 1873, newspapers.com/article/the-new-york-times-nyt-28-dec-1873cost/36017834/.

"is at war . . . upon it" Kusmer, *Down and Out*, p. 8.

"tramp menace" "On the Road Again: Pinkerton on the Tramp," History Matters, George Mason University, historymatters.gmu.edu/d/5309/.

primary characters, if not stars Pamela Robertson Wojcik, "Is the Home Ever Not Precarious? The Long Arc of Genres of Precarity," *Mediapolis*, November 12, 2021, mediapolisjournal.com /2021/11/is-the-home-ever-not-precarious/.

descendant of the Roma Ian Hancock, "Charlie Chaplin's Romani Roots," *Travellers' Times*, August, 15, 2023, travellerstimes.org.uk/features/charlie-chaplins-romani-roots-ian-hancock.

childhood in London workhouses "Charlie Chaplin," Workhouse: The Story of an Institution, workhouses.org.uk/Chaplin/.

his father's alcoholism "Charlie's Father: Charles Chaplin Sr.," Charlie Chaplin, charliechaplin .com/en/articles/217-Charlie-s-Father-Charles-Chaplin-Sr.

his mother's mental health struggles Brigit Katz, "The Cinema Museum, Housed in the Workhouse Where Charlie Chaplin Spent His Formative Years, Is Under Threat," *Smithsonian*, December 15, 2017, smithsonianmag.com/smart-news/campaign-hopes-save-workhouse-where -charlie-chaplin-spent-unhappy-childhood-180967548/.

leftist sympathies for the lower class Christopher Schmidt, "Was Charlie Chaplin's Tramp Un-American?," *JSTOR Daily*, October 16, 2014, daily.jstor.org/charlie-chaplins-tramp-un-american/.

"critique of the necessity for home" Wojcik, "Is the Home Ever Not Precarious?"

"What miles . . . are covered" and **"dallyings by . . . bridges"** and **"drinking of . . . springs"** Allan Pinkerton, *Strikers, Communists, Tramps and Detectives* (G. W. Carleton, 1878), pp. 28–29.

"Jesus Christ . . . a tramp" Pinkerton, *Strikers*, p. 33.

"Exalt . . . in all countries" Pinkerton, *Strikers*, p. 27.

"Journeymen" were the tradesmen Melissa Eddy, "Cleaving to the Medieval, Journeymen Ply Their Trades in Europe," *New York Times*, August 7, 2017, nytimes.com/2017/08/07/world/europe/europe-journeymen.html.

pejorative . . . in the British Isles David Donaldson, "Is It Time Scottish Society Re-Thought Its Language Use?," *Travellers' Times*, January 31, 2018, travellerstimes.org.uk/features/it-time-scottish-society-re-thought-its-language-use-0.

broadly known as Travellers *The Traveller Community and Homelessness* (Pavee Point Traveller and Roma Centre, 2021), paveepoint.ie/wp-content/uploads/2015/04/Pavee-Point-Traveller-Homelessness-Advocacy-Paper-Oct2021.pdf.

Woonwagenbewoners in the Netherlands "Honderd Jaar Woonwagenbeleid in Nederland," [Dutch] Woonwagen Wijzer, web.archive.org/web/20160327190957/. woonwagenwijzer.nl/woon wagenbeleid/.

Skøyere in Scandinavia "Farende Fanter," [Norwegian] Skiensatlas, skiensatlas.org/content/download/3835/25611/file/FANT+og+TATERE+-leksikalske+opplysninger.pdf.

Camminanti in Sicily Arianna Todisco, "The 'Walkers' of Sicily Survive on the Tradition of Selling Balloons," *Washington Post*, April 26, 2021, washingtonpost.com/photography/2021/04/26/walkers-sicily-survive-tradition-selling-balloons/.

Pavee in Ireland "Romani (Gypsy), Roma and Irish Traveller History and Culture," Traveller Movement, travellermovement.org.uk/gypsy-roma-and-traveller-history-and-culture.

"Their wandering . . . tramps" and **"Suddenly . . . filled with them"** Pinkerton, *Strikers*, pp. 33–34.

precursor of the Secret Service "Pinkerton, Lincoln, and McClernand at the Secret Service Headquarters," Pinkerton, October 8, 2024, pinkerton.com/our-insights/blog/pinkerton-lincoln-and-mcclernand-at-the-secret-service-headquarters.

"manufactured tramps . . . in herds" and **"highway pirate"** and **"there is no doubt . . . from choice"** Pinkerton, *Strikers*, pp. 39, 44.

first nationwide strike in American history Steven Mintz and Sara McNeil, "The Great Railroad Strike," Digital History, digitalhistory.uh.edu/disp_textbook.cfm?smtID=2&psid=3189.

it was violently squashed Ryan Zickgraf, "The 1877 Class War That America Forgot," *Jacobin*, July 23, 2022, jacobin.com/2022/07/great-upheaval-railroad-strike-1877.

"seemed to suddenly spring . . . of the night" and **"The slums . . . common purpose"** Pinkerton, *Strikers*, pp. 229–230.

even spend the night Todd DePastino, *Citizen Hobo: How a Century of Homelessness Shaped America* (University of Chicago Press, 2003), pp. 95–105, press.uchicago.edu/Misc/Chicago/143783.html.

campfires and skinny-dipping Anderson, *The Hobo,* p. 17.

"anarchist streak in the American character" and **"By adopting extralegal forms . . . mentality"** Kusmer, *Down and Out,* pp. 9–10.

sheriffs Anderson, *The Hobo.*

twenty thousand at its peak Lisa Hix, "Don't Call Them Bums: The Unsung History of America's Hard-Working Hoboes," *Collectors Weekly,* April 16, 2015, collectorsweekly.com/articles/dont-call-them-bums-the-unsung-history-of-americas-hard-working-hoboes/.

inspired by life on the road "Hobo News," St. Louis Public Library Digital Collections, cdm17210.contentdm.oclc.org/digital/collection/hobonews.

"religious talk will get you a free meal" "Sample of Some Hobo Signs," National Security Agency, nsa.gov/portals/75/documents/about/cryptologic-heritage/museum/hobo-signs-definitions.pdf.

Industrial Workers of the World Matthew S. May, *Soapbox Rebellion: The Hobo Orator Union and the Free Speech Fights of the Industrial Workers of the World, 1909–1916* (University of Alabama Press, 2013), p. 1.

"we are forming the structure" "Preamble to the Constitution of the Industrial Workers of the World," Industrial Workers of the World, iww.org/preamble/.

could be a member "Joining the IWW," Industrial Workers of the World, iww.org/membership/.

agriculture, logging, and construction knowledge.uchicago.edu/record/3462/files/Suits_uchicago_0330D_15926.pdf.

"The hobo . . . drinks and wanders" Anderson, *The Hobo,* p. 87.

"delivered a floating subculture to . . . activism" and **"by virtue of . . . workers"** DePastino, *Citizen Hobo,* p. 97.

his socialist leanings Jack London, *How I Became a Socialist* (Athol Books, 1977).

everything from the mental and **physical health traits** and **homosexuality** and **"continued in . . . name of the IBWA"** Anderson, *The Hobo,* pp. 70, 66, 144, 247.

"In pointing out . . . criminality" Anderson, *The Hobo,* p. 249.

"With no status . . . abolished" Anderson, *The Hobo,* p. 167.

homelessness receded from the American imagination DePastino, *Citizen Hobo.*

more of a street-based phenomenon Kusmer, *Down and Out.*

loss of . . . one million SRO units Edward Pinto and Hannah Florence, "The Decline of SROs and Its Consequences for Housing Affordability," American Enterprise Institute Housing Center, May 28, 2024, aei.org/wp-content/uploads/2024/05/The-history-of-SROs-FINAL-v2.pdf.

people committed . . . one-fourth that of 1960 *Permanent Supportive Housing.*

"making rude toilets . . . towels" and **"when they get . . . songs and laughter"** and **"They have a cabin . . . ambition may suggest"** Pinkerton, *Strikers*, pp. 60–61.

"All that is requisite" and **"Sequestered in the dark"** and **"joking and chatting . . . brought for the day"** Pinkerton, *Strikers*, pp. 61–62, 64.

"The name given . . . civilized being" Brian Morris, "Basic Kropotkin: Kropotkin and the History of Anarchism," Anarchist Library, October 2008, theanarchistlibrary.org/library/brian -morris-basic-kropotkin.

"at their very simplest . . . power corrupts" David Graeber, "Are You an Anarchist? The Answer May Surprise You!," David Graeber archive, davidgraeber.org/wp-content/uploads/2009 -Are-you-an-anarchist-The-answer-may-surprise-you.pdf.

"even if you don't realize it" Graeber, "Are You an Anarchist?"

Graeber . . . member of the IWW Matt Apuzzo, Associated Press, "IWW Professor Kicked Out of Yale," International Workers of the World, October 23, 2005, archive.iww.org/node /1535/.

"hell is . . . not especially good at" David Graeber, *Bullshit Jobs* (Simon & Schuster, 2018), p. 19.

"The men scatter" Anderson, *The Hobo*, pp. 23–24.

large numbers of Black Americans Ricky Rodas, "'Retired from the Waterfront, but Not from the Struggle': Clarence Thomas' New Book on Port Labor Activism," *The Oaklandside*, July 9, 2021, oak-landside.org/2021/07/09/retired-from-the-waterfront-but-not-from-the-struggle-clarence-thomas -new-book-on-port-labor-activism/.

Brotherhood of Sleeping Car Porters "16th Street Station," Oakland Heritage Alliance, oak-landheritage.org/16th-street-station.

Harlem of the West, emerged nearby Justin Phillips, "A Bygone Jazz Club Is the Forgotten Story of Oakland's 'Harlem of the West' Era," *San Francisco Chronicle*, October 31, 2019, sfchronicle .com/food/article/A-bygone-jazz-club-is-the-forgotten-story-of-14583167.php.

poor have lived in Oakland for generations Sidd Joag, "Curse of Geography: Lower Bottoms," ArtsEverywhere, June 2, 2022, artseverywhere.ca/curse-of-geography-the-lower-bottoms/.

white households . . . higher than Black households For white households, median income is $110,000; for Black households, it's $38,000. See "Financial Health," City of Oakland, data .oaklandca.gov/stories/s/Financial-Health/2z9b-x57f/.

half . . . Black in 1980 In the 1980 census, the number was 47 percent. See "City of Oakland," Bay Area Census, bayareacensus.ca.gov/cities/Oakland70.htm.

less than a quarter today The Black population is now 22 percent. See "QuickFacts: Oakland City, California," US Census Bureau, census.gov/quickfacts/oaklandcitycalifornia.

Burning Man parties and other events "Distrikt Revel Station," Do the Bay, dothebay.com /events/2014/6/7/distrikt-revel-station.

fifty-dollar organic bouquet "Prom, Senior Prom, Winter Ball!," Boxcar Flower Farm, boxcar-flowerfarm.com/prom.

$700,000 condos on the other "1309 Wood St," Redfin, last sold on April 28, 2022, redfin.com /CA/Oakland/1309-Wood-St-94607/home/22651942.

Chapter 3: New Friends

biannual "point-in-time" count Tanya de Sousa, Alyssa Andrichik, Marissa Cuellar, Jhenelle Marson, Ed Prestera, and Katherine Rush, *The 2022 Annual Homelessness Assessment Report (AHAR) to Congress* (US Department of Housing and Urban Development, 2022), part 1, huduser .gov/portal/sites/default/files/pdf/2022-AHAR-Part-1.pdf.

HUD's extraordinarily obtuse definition De Sousa et al., *2022 Homelessness Report.*

national point-in-time count . . . 550,000 to 650,000 De Sousa et al., *2022 Homelessness Report*, p. 10. The 2024 numbers showed a big jump, but this is attributed largely to newly arrived immigrants in a handful of cities. This is certainly relevant, but it is a distinct issue in many respects.

30 and 50 percent since 2007 De Sousa et al., *2022 Homelessness Report*, p. 29.

"hell is . . . not especially good at" Margot Kushel et al., *Toward a New Understanding: The California Statewide Study of People Experiencing Homelessness* (University of California San Francisco, 2023), p. 2, homelessness.ucsf.edu/sites/default/files/2023-06/CASPEH_Executive _Summary_62023.pdf.

highest . . . rate of homelessness and **nine times . . . next-closest state** De Sousa et al., *2022 Homelessness Report*, p. 16.

stadium in Anaheim and **Silicon Valley . . . 83 percent** De Sousa et al., *2022 Homelessness Report*, p. 33.

first comprehensive census Kushel et al., *Toward a New Understanding.*

Roughly half Kushel et al., *Toward a New Understanding.*

unhoused population . . . of six million Kevin F. Adler, Donald W. Burnes, Amanda Banh, and Andrijana Bilbija, *When We Walk By: Forgotten Humanity, Broken Systems, and the Role We Can Each Play in Ending Homelessness in America* (North Atlantic Books, 2023), p. 2.

with a garden hose Jonathan Franklin, "A San Francisco Business Owner Is Arrested After Spraying Homeless Woman with a Hose," *NPR*, January 19, 2023, npr.org/2023/01/19/1150051995 /san-francisco-gallery-owner-arrested-homeless-woman.

fought back after being sprayed Jesse Barron, "Jurors Find San Francisco Homeless Man Not Guilty in Pipe Beating," *New York Times*, December 23, 2023, nytimes.com/2023/12/23/us/san -francisco-homeless-man-not-guilty.html.

sleeping bag on fire with him in it Lauren Hepler, "SF Police Offer $25,000 Reward for Information About Slaying of Man Whose Sleeping Bag Was Set on Fire," *San Francisco Chronicle*, September 1, 2022, sfchronicle.com/bayarea/article/S-F-police-offer-25-000-reward-for -information-17414219.php.

shot and killed three homeless men James Queally, Noah Goldberg, Richard Winton, and Ruben Vives, "Suspect in 'Bone-Chilling' Homeless Killings Charged with 4 Counts of Murder," *Los Angeles Times*, December 4, 2023, latimes.com/california/story/2023-12-04/suspect-in -homeless-killings-charged-with-4-counts-of-murder.

"I shouldn't have to worry . . . every day" Justin Keller, "Open Letter to SF Mayor Ed Lee and Greg Suhr (Police Chief)," Svtble, February 14, 2016, justink.svbtle.com/open-letter-to-mayor-ed -lee-and-greg-suhr-police-chief.

"hyenas . . . in a while" Will Oremus, "San Francisco Techie Says 'Lower Part of Society' Should Be Segregated," *Slate*, December 11, 2013, slate.com/technology/2013/12/greg-gopman -facebook-post-homeless-ruining-san-francisco-should-be-segregated-from-rich-techies .html.

HIV rates . . . range from two Kinna Thakarar, Jake R. Morgan, Jessie M. Gaeta, Carole Hohl, and Mari-Lynn Drainoni, "Homelessness, HIV, and Incomplete Viral Suppression," *Journal of Health Care for the Poor and Underserved*, vol. 27, no. 1 (2016), pp. 145–156, pmc.ncbi.nlm.nih .gov/articles/PMC4982659/.

sixteen times higher "The Connection Between Housing and Improved Outcomes Along the HIV Care Continuum," US Department of Housing and Urban Development, files.hudexchange .info/resources/documents/The-Connection-Between-Housing-and-Improved-Outcomes -Along-the-HIV-Care-Continuum.pdf.

By the early eighties, 630 homes "History," Guadalupe River Park Conservancy, grpg.org /History.shtml.

time in foster care "Housing & Homelessness," National Foster Youth Institute, nfyi.org/issues /homelessness/.

stealing cat food Tiny [Lisa Gray-Garcia], *Criminal of Poverty: Growing up Homeless in America* (City Lights Books, 2006), pp. 19, 22.

"embodiment of all that was other" and **"brief period of very rich times"** Tiny, *Criminal of Poverty*, pp. 29, 34.

her mom's caregiver Tiny, *Criminal of Poverty*, chap. 1.

money in the bank Tiny, *Criminal of Poverty*, p. 76.

"It was a testimony" and **"11 going on 40"** and **"I could kill myself"** and **"relief it would give me"** Tiny, *Criminal of Poverty*, pp. 84, 53, 70, 116.

Chapter 4: The Ecosystem

another area along the river Jessica York, *Santa Cruz Sentinel*, "Santa Cruz Sets End Date for Largest Homeless Camp," *Mercury News*, April 19, 2022, mercurynews.com/2022/04/19/santa -cruz-sets-end-date-for-largest-homeless-camp/.

Ram Dass, Hare Krishnas and **fruitarianism** and **apple cider business** Walter Isaacson, *Steve Jobs* (Simon & Schuster Paperbacks, 2013), pp. 33–34, 63, 39.

labor and environmental abuses Asad Ismi, "'Toxic Bob' Wastes Burma," Canadian Centre for Policy Alternatives, March 1, 2001, policyalternatives.ca/news-research/march -2001-toxic-bob-wastes-burma/.

Fred Turner . . . book Fred Turner, From Counterculture to Cyberculture: Stewart Brand, the Whole Earth Network, and the Rise of Digital Utopianism (University of Chicago Press, 2006), p. 118.

Whole Earth Truck Store Bo Crane, "Remembering Menlo Park's Hippie Past—and the Whole Earth Truck Store," *InMenlo*, January 22, 2019, inmenlo.com/2019/01/22/remembering-menlo -parks-hippie-past-and-the-whole-earth-truck-store/.

Whole Earth Software Catalog Anna Wiener, "The Complicated Legacy of Stewart Brand's 'Whole Earth Catalog,'" *New Yorker*, November 16, 2018, newyorker.com/news/letter-from -silicon-valley/the-complicated-legacy-of-stewart-brands-whole-earth-catalog.

begat *Wired* magazine Kyle Vanhemert, "How a Band of Rebels and Pioneers Launched WIRED's First Website 20 Years Ago Today," *Wired*, October 27, 2014, wired.com/2014/10/wired -hotwired-anniversary/.

Brand . . . "brokered a long-running encounter" See book jacket of Turner, *From Countercul- ture to Cyberculture.*

cuckoo . . . each millennium Wiener, "Complicated Legacy."

punch cards in San José "IBM in San José," 825mph, May 4, 2019, 825mph.com/ibm-in-san -José.

orchards carpeted much of the region and **Valley of Heart's Delight** "Historic Orchard," Guadalupe River Park Conservancy, grpg.org/HistoricOrchard/.

poem by a local writer Clara Louise Lawrence, *Poems Along the Way* (Tucker, 1927).

Cupertino did not exist "History," City of Cupertino, cupertino.gov/Your-City/About-Cupertino /History.

Glendenning family Mary Lou Lyon, Early Cupertino (Arcadia, 2006).

farm was on Pruneridge Avenue Barbara Krause, "Top Secret Fruit Orchard at Apple Computer HQ," *Edible Silicon Valley*, May 30, 2018, ediblesiliconvalley.ediblecommunities.com/think/top -secret-fruit-orchard-Apple-Computer-Headquarters.

prune capital of the world "Prune Capital of the World," Historical Marker Database, August 27, 2020, hmdb.org/m.asp?m=155315.

30 percent of the global market Jonathan Vankin, "Silicon Valley Boom and Bust: Where California's Tech Mecca Came from, and Why It Always Survives," *California Local*, Febru- ary 17, 2023, californialocal.com/localnews/statewide/ca/article/show/27217-silicon-valley -technology-layoffs-boom-bust/.

next to the mothership On Google Maps, you can see that the old right-of-way passes near the new theater.

$23,814,257 for a half mile "City Council Staff Report," City of Cupertino, October 15, 2013, cupertino.granicus.com/MetaViewer.php?view_id=18&clip_id=1560&meta_id=86030.

storage for landscaping equipment Kristi Myllenbeck, "Barn at Apple Park Represents 'Hard Work' of Generations of 'Visionaries,'" *Mercury News*, July 14, 2017, mercurynews.com/2017/07 /14/barn-at-apple-park-represents-hard-work-of-generations-of-visionaries/.

"dedicated to . . . odor issues" South Bay Odor Stakeholders Group, sbosg.info/.

South Bay Fucking Smell "South Bay Fucking Smell," Reddit, reddit.com/r/SouthBayFuck ingSmell.

DARPA . . . IT revolution sprang Stephen Mihm, "How the Department of Defense Bankrolled Silicon Valley," review of *The Code: Silicon Valley and the Remaking of America*, by Marga- ret O'Mara, *New York Times*, July 9, 2019, nytimes.com/2019/07/09/books/review/the-code -margaret-omara.html.

military-industrial complex . . . mud flats Sharon Weinberger, *The Imagineers of War: The Untold History of DARPA, the Pentagon Agency That Changed the World* (Knopf, 2017).

dirigible hangar "The Largest Aircraft Hangars in the World," Poente Technical, August 25, 2022, poentetechnical.com/news/the-largest-aircraft-hangars-in-the-world/.

blossomed between DOD installations Margaret O'Mara, *The Code: Silicon Valley and the Remaking of America* (Penguin, 2019).

Lockheed . . . biggest employer Alexis C. Madrigal, "Silicon Valley Abandons the Culture That Made It the Envy of the World," *The Atlantic*, January 15, 2020, theatlantic.com/technology /archive/2020/01/why-silicon-valley-and-big-tech-dont-innovate-anymore/604969/.

"some defense-industry DNA" Margaret O'Mara, "Silicon Valley Can't Escape the Business of War," Opinion, *New York Times*, October 26, 2018, nytimes.com/2018/10/26/opinion/amazon -bezos-pentagon-hq2.html.

precursor to DARPA O'Mara, "Silicon Valley"; Fred Kaplan, "How an Agency of Oddballs Transformed Modern War and Modern Life," review of *The Imagineers of War: The Untold History of DARPA, the Pentagon Agency That Changed the World*, by Sharon Weinberger, New York Times, June 30, 2017, nytimes.com/2017/06/30/books/review/imagineers-of-war-untold -history-of-darpa-sharon-weinberger.html.

engineer at Lockheed Dave Blanchard, "2014 Hall of Fame Inductee: Steve Wozniak," *Industry-Week*, November 3, 2014, industryweek.com/iw-manufacturing-hall-of-fame/article/21963994 /2014-hall-of-fame-inductee-steve-wozniak.

parking of private jets "A Fighter Jet and Friends in Congress: How Google Got Access to a NASA Airfield," *Tech Transparency Project*, September 8, 2020, techtransparencyproject.org /articles/fighter-jet-and-friends-congress-how-google-got-access-nasa-airfield.

around the central Googleplex "The Rise of the Corporate Campus," Instant Group, October 31, 2017, theinstantgroup.com/en-us/breakthrough-insights/research-articles/the-rise-of -the-corporate-campus/.

school district were homeless Anna Medina, "Ravenswood School District Superintendent Tackles Growing Housing Crisis," *Palo Alto Online*, March 10, 2017, paloaltoonline.com/news /2017/03/10/ravenswood-school-district-superintendent-tackles-growing-housing-crisis.

"The welfare of wildlife" Sue Dremann, "Fires Point to Risky Conditions in Ravenswood Triangle," *Palo Alto Online*, July 10, 2020, paloaltoonline.com/news/2020/07/10/fires-point-to -risky-conditions-in-ravenswood-triangle/.

"Build a wall" Alistair Barr, "In Google's Mountain View Backyard, RV Living Becomes a Desperate Act," *Los Angeles Times*, May 22, 2019, latimes.com/business/la-fi-google-mountain -view-rv-living-20190522-story.html.

"several million dollars" "Crews Clear North San José Homeless Encampment on Apple Property," *CBS San Francisco*, September 2, 2021, sanfrancisco.cbslocal.com/2021/09/02/crews -clear-north-San-José-homeless-encampment-on-apple-property/.

only four thousand units of housing "San José City Leaders Approve Google's Downtown West Project," *NBC Bay Area*, May 25, 2021, nbcbayarea.com/news/local/making-it-in-the-bay/san -José-city-leaders-to-consider-approval-of-googles-downtown-west-project/2553682/.

$765-per-month increase and **"I don't think that is realistic"** Kyle Martin, "New Report: Google Campus Will Lead to $235M More in Rent Spikes," *San José Spotlight*, June 12, 2019, san-Joséspotlight.com/new-report-google-campus-will-lead-to-235m-more-in-rent-spikes/.

gone up by exactly $763 "San José California Residential Rent and Rental Statistics," Department of Numbers, deptofnumbers.com/rent/california/san-José/.

"nation's largest homeless camp" Lisa Fernandez and Nanette Miranda, "Nation's Largest Homeless Encampment, 'The Jungle,' Dismantled," *NBC Bay Area*, December 5, 2014,nbcbayarea .com/news/local/game-of-whack-a-mole-homeless-upset-to-be-evicted-by-police-from-the -jungle-in-san-José/1983791/.

"Living in The Jungle means . . . fear"Alexia Fernández Campbell and Reena Flores, "How Silicon Valley Created America's Largest Homeless Camp," *The Atlantic*, November 25, 2014, the-atlantic.com/politics/archive/2014/11/how-silicon-valley-created-americas-largest-homeless-camp /431739/.

"Dilapidated, muddy and squalid" Khaleda Rahman, "'Where Are They Going to Go? We Can't Magic up Homes for Them,'" *Daily Mail*, December 4, 2014, dailymail.co.uk/news/article-2860695 /Inside-squalor-Silicon-Valley-homeless-camp-ruled-gangs-300-people-homes-bulldozed.html.

"wheel his belongings" Barbara Grady, "Few Options for Homeless as San José Clears Camp," *New York Times*, December 4, 2014, nytimes.com/2014/12/05/us/driven-from-silicon-valleys -jungle-homeless-face-limited-options.html.

"New Jungle" a half mile away "Finding a New 'Jungle,' Homeless Plan to Create Second Camp in San José," *CBS San Francisco*, December 5, 2014, sanfrancisco.cbslocal.com/2014/12/05 /former-jungle-homeless-residents-planning-to-create-new-camp-in-san-José/.

between the lines of the posts San José Heritage Rose Garden, Facebook page, facebook.com /SJHRG/.

$6 million playscape "Rotary PlayGarden," Guadalupe River Park Conservancy, grpg.org/visit /guadalupe-gardens/rotary-playgarden/.

"homeless problem is becoming a PR problem" Brian Hackney, "Silicon Valley Visitors See Growing Homeless Camp Along Guadalupe River upon Arrival," newscast clip, posted on November 24, 2019, by KPIX | CBS News Bay Area, YouTube, youtube.com/watch?v=vyA1kEY3lyQ.

reviews of Guadalupe River Park "Guadalupe River Park," Tripadvisor, tripadvisor.com/Attraction _Review-g33020-d524657-Reviews-or10-Guadalupe_River_Park-San_José_California.html.

"welcome and safe" Grace Stetson and Katie Lauer, "What's Next for Guadalupe River Park and SJ's Homeless Crisis?," *San José Inside*, March 26, 2021, sanJoséinside.com/news/whats-next-for -guadalupe-river-park-and-sjs-homeless-crisis/.

"It's something that I've never seen" Marisa Kendall, "San José May House Homeless Residents Along Guadalupe River," *Mercury News*, February 16, 2021, mercurynews.com/2021/02/16/san -José-may-house-homeless-residents-along-guadalupe-river/.

Chapter 5: Fronting

hit-and-run by the 280 overpass "Bicyclist Joseph Clifford Camarda III Dies in Hit-and-Run on Interstate 280 (Cupertino, CA)," Sweet Lawyers, August 21, 2020, sweetlaw.com/bicyclist-Joseph -clifford-camarda-iii-dies-hit-and-run-crash-interstate-280-cupertino-ca/.

killed while sleeping "Car Runs Over Man Sleeping in Santa Clara Parking Lot," *CBS San Francisco*, October 21, 2020, cbsnews.com/sanfrancisco/news/car-runs-over-man-sleeping-in-santa-clara-parking-lot/.

retroactive payments California normally ends unemployment benefits after twenty-six weeks, but the CARES Act created the PEUC and PUA programs, which extended the benefits. See bea.gov/help/faq/1415 and cbpp.org/research/economy/how-many-weeks-of-unemployment-compensation-are-available.

"Human happiness . . . elegant simplicity" Satish Kumar, "Top 60 Satish Kumar Quotes," Quotefancy, quotefancy.com/satish-kumar-quotes.

city of sixty thousand "About Cupertino," City of Cupertino, cupertino.gov/Your-City/About-Cupertino.

142 units of subsidized apartments "City of Cupertino: Request for Qualifications; Below Market Rate Housing Program Administration," Association of Bay Area Governments, p. 1, abag.ca.gov/sites/default/files/documents/2024-05/Cupertino-BMR-Housing-Program.docx.

up to $55,300 annually "Below Market Rate (BMR) Informational Workshop," Hello Housing, presentation slides, September 24, 2020, p. 7, hellohousing.org/wp-content/uploads/2020/09/Cupertino-BMR-Presentation-8.28.20.pdf.

complex that opened in 2019 and **both senior citizens and disabled** Marisa Kendall, "Google v. Apple: While One Takes on the Housing Crisis, the Other Stands Back," *Reveal*, October 28, 2019, revealnews.org/article/google-v-apple-while-one-takes-on-the-housing-crisis-the-other-stands-back/.

102 unhoused . . . last HUD-mandated count *Point-in-Time Report on Homelessness: Census and Survey Results* (County of Santa Clara, 2022), p. 11, cadresv.org/wp-content/uploads/2022-PIT-Report-Santa-Clara-County.pdf.

rooftop park . . . world's largest Roland Li, "Cupertino Megaproject Will Include World's Largest Green Roof. Here's What It Will Look Like," *San Francisco Chronicle*, March 24, 2022, sfchronicle.com/bayarea/article/Cupertino-Vallco-green-roof-17024842.php.

dominated by NIMBYs Richard Mehlinger, "Cupertino Mayor: 'Build the Wall,'" Medium, February 7, 2019, medium.com/@rmehlinger/cupertino-mayor-build-the-wall-cb34fb3cc9fa.

"key design wins" Steven Scharf, LinkedIn profile, linkedin.com/in/stevenscharf/.

State of the City address in 2019 Emily Deruy, "Cupertino Mayor: City Will Build Wall and San José Will Pay for It," *Mercury News*, February 6, 2019, mercurynews.com/2019/02/05/cupertino-mayor-city-will-build-wall-and-san-josé-will-pay-for-it/.

$4 billion plan Adam Brinklow, "Housing-Starved Cupertino Wonders What to Do with Vacant Mall," *Curbed SF*, November 28, 2017,sf.curbed.com/2017/11/28/16706244/vallco-cupertino-redevelopment-2017.

calls for 2,400 units Thy Vo, "Vallco Project: Cupertino Accused of Trying to Sink Housing Plan," *Mercury News*, June 18, 2019, mercurynews.com/2019/06/17/state-senator-accuses-cupertino-of-trying-to-sink-vallco-project/.

two and a half times as many jobs The city's report says the development will employ 3,800 more office workers than the 2,400 proposed residential units, meaning a total of 6,200 office workers. 6,200 divided by 2,400 gives a 2.58 jobs-to-housing ratio. See "Detailed Status Report on the Vallco SB 35 Development Project," City of Cupertino, September 7, 2021, cupertino.gov/files /assets/city/v/1/departments/documents/community-development/planning/major-projects /the-rise/vallco-historical-project-information/correspondence/attachment.pdf

YIMBY Action . . . below-market rates "Better Cupertino Community Forum Faced Pushback from YIMBY's," *Cupertino Today*, March 13, 2018, cupertinotoday.com/2018/03/13/better -cupertino-community-forum-faced-pushback-from-yimbys/.

Better Cupertino . . . stop construction in 2018 "Friends of Better Cupertino vs. City of Cupertino: Vallco SB 35 Is Not Compliant," blog, Better Cupertino, August 30, 2018, bettercupertino.blogspot.com/2018/08/FBC-vs-city-sb35-not-compliant.html.

fired its city attorney Marisa Kendall, "Explosive New Vallco Allegations: Cupertino Official Plans to Sue City," *Mercury News*, October 24, 2018, mercurynews.com/2018/10/22/explosive -new-vallco-allegations-cupertino-official-plans-to-sue-city/.

"YIMBY neoliberal fascists" "Cupertino Planning Official Faces Backlash for Calling Pro-Growth Activists 'Neoliberal Fascists,'" *San José Inside*, July 3, 2019, sanJoséinside.com/2019 /07/03/cupertino-planning-official-faces-backlash-for-calling-pro-growth-activists-neoliberal -fascists/.

Completed in 2016 Chetana Ramaiyer, "Main Street Cupertino Celebrates Grand Opening on Sept. 17," *El Estoque*, September 20, 2016, elestoque.org/2016/09/20/news/main-street-cupertino -celebrates-grand-opening-on-sept-17/.

Chapter 6: Raining Solutions

2020 State of the State Gavin Newsom, "Governor Newsom Delivers State of the State Address on Homelessness," State of California, February 19, 2020, gov.ca.gov/2020/02/19/governor -newsom-delivers-state-of-the-state-address-on-homelessness/.

when Newsom was elected in 2018 Phil Matier and Andy Ross, "Gavin Newsom's Top Issues for California: Affordability and Homelessness," *San Francisco Chronicle*, June 6, 2018, sfchronicle .com/bayarea/matier-ross/article/Gavin-Newsom-s-top-two-issues-for-CA-12971065.php.

perceptions that he was soft Gideon Rubin, "Crime, Homelessness Tank Newsom's Poll Numbers: UC Berkeley Poll," *Patch*, February 18, 2022, patch.com/california/berkeley/crime -homelessness-tank-newsoms-poll-numbers-uc-berkeley-poll.

elected in 2019 with a mandate Phil Matier, "What's the Answer to Quality-of-Life Crimes in SF. DA Candidates Give Answers," *San Francisco Chronicle*, October 27, 2019, sfchronicle.com /local-politics/article/What-s-the-answer-to-quality-of-life-crimes-in-14563426.php.

recalled from office Megan Cassidy, "Boudin Recall Margins Narrow, with Voters Split 55% to 45% in Support," *San Francisco Chronicle*, June 13, 2022, sfchronicle.com/bayarea/article /Boudin-recall-margins-narrow-with-voters-split-17238684.php.

"The future happens here first" Gavin Newsom, "'The Future Happens Here First': Gavin Newsom Touts California's Diversity at APEC Reception," remarks at Asia-Pacific Economic Cooperation welcome, posted on November 13, 2023, by Forbes Breaking News, YouTube, youtube.com/watch?v=8feqzrPTCiQ.

Shellenberger Michael Shellenberger, *San Fransicko: Why Progressives Ruin Cities* (HarperCollins, 2021).

20,933 complaints about feces and **pee corroding their metal bases** George F. Will, "Progressives Ruined San Francisco, but at Least 'Advocacy' Is Thriving," Opinion, *Washington Post*, November 12, 2021, washingtonpost.com/opinions/2021/11/12/progressives-ruined-san -francisco-least-advocacy-is-thriving/.

150,000 canines in the city Adam Brinklow, "The Problem with San Francisco Poop Maps," *Curbed SF*, April 23, 2019, sf.curbed.com/2019/4/23/18511865/sf-poop-human-waste-map-forbes-dpw-dog.

ten times . . . unhoused residents Yoohyun Jung and Mallory Moench, "How Many People Are Homeless in San Francisco? Here's What the Data Shows," *San Francisco Chronicle*, May 16, 2022, sfchronicle.com/sf/article/How-many-people-are-homeless-in-San-Francisco-17155544.php.

"wraparound services" "Housing First," National Alliance to End Homelessness, March 20, 2022, endhomelessness.org/resource/housing-first/.

"pathological altruism" "The Heroism of Recovery: Selected Quotes from *San Fransicko* by Michael Shellenberger," Julian Conor Reid, julianconorreid.com/2022/02/24/the-heroism-of -recovery-selected-quotes-from-san-fransicko-by-michael-shellenberger/.

"More police, more psychiatry, and more probation" Michael Shellenberger, "Michael Shellenberger's Solution for the Homeless Problem in California," interview by Joe Rogan, posted on March 30, 2022, by PowerfulJRE, YouTube, youtube.com/watch?v=TsTDA2DT72k.

"problem with housing first" Olga Khazan, "The Revolt Against Homelessness," *The Atlantic*, June 2, 2022, theatlantic.com/politics/archive/2022/06/california-governor-race-shellenberger -homelessness-san-francisco/661164/.

landmark eviction moratorium https://www.gov.ca.gov/2021/01/29/governor-newsom-signs -legislation-to-extend-eviction-moratorium-and-assist-tenants-and-small-property-owners -impacted-by-covid-19/.

bigger and better than . . . other states "Governor Newsom Signs Legislation to Extend Eviction Moratorium and Assist Tenants and Small Property Owners," State of California, January 29, 2021, gov.ca.gov/2021/01/29/governor-newsom-signs-legislation-to-extend-eviction -moratorium-and-assist-tenants-and-small-property-owners-impacted-by-covid-19/.

"unacceptable" Manuela Tobias, "Newsom on Homelessness: 'We've Gotta Clean up Those Encampments,'" *CalMatters*, January 11, 2022, calmatters.org/housing/homelessness/2022/01 /california-homelessness-camps-newsom/.

force them into conservatorship "Governor Newsom Launches New Plan to Help Californians Struggling with Mental Health Challenges, Homelessness," State of California, March 3, 2022, gov .ca.gov/2022/03/03/governor-newsom-launches-new-plan-to-help-californians-struggling-with -mental-health-challenges-homelessness/.

"We are leaning into conservatorships" Liz Kreutz, "Here's Everything to Know About Gov. Newsom's Proposed 2022 Budget Plan," *ABC7 News*, January 10, 2022, abc30.com/newsom-2022 -budget-ca-california-surplus/11451458/.

"wished them luck" Benjamin Oreskes, "Newsom, in Recall Fight, Says It's 'Not Acceptable' for Homeless to Camp on Streets," *Los Angeles Times*, August 5, 2021, latimes.com/homeless

-housing/story/2021-08-05/newsom-in-recall-fight-says-its-not-acceptable-for-homeless-to
-camp-on-streets.

people entering homelessness exceeds . . . construction Joe Colletti, "The Persistence of Chronic Homelessness in California," Homeless and Housing Strategies in California, January 27, 2020, homelessstrategy.com/the-persistence-of-chronic-homelessness-in-california/.

reopening of the wait-list . . . thirteen years "Section 8 Housing Choice Voucher Waiting List Lottery to Open on Monday," Housing Authority of the City of Los Angeles, hacla.org/en/news /section-8-housing-choice-voucher-waiting-list-lottery-open-monday.

closed again for fifteen years Johnny Khamis, "Section 8—Open for Business," *San José Spotlight*, July 28, 2021, sanJoséspotlight.com/khamis-section-8-open-for-business/.

ten thousand affordable units Sam Liccardo, "How San José Can Build Housing Our Children Can Afford," Opinion, *Mercury News*, January 22, 2018, mercurynews.com/2018/01/21/how-san -José-can-build-housing-our-children-can-afford/.

Only 901 were built "Affordable Housing," City of San José, sanJoséca.gov/your-government /departments-offices/housing/resource-library/affordable-housing-dashboard.

only one in five . . . willing to accept Nichole Fiore, Will Yetvin, Kimberley Burnett, Lauren Dunton, and Jill Khadduri, *San José, California: Community Encampment Report* (US Department of Housing and Urban Development, 2020), p. 8, huduser.gov/portal/sites/default/files/pdf/SanJosé -Encampment-Report.pdf.

vacant hotel rooms . . . converted "Governor Newsom Visits Project Roomkey Site in Bay Area to Approve 'Homekey,' the Next Phase in State's COVID-19 Response to Protect Homeless Cal- ifornians," State of California, June 30, 2020, gov.ca.gov/2020/06/30/governor-newsom-visits -project-roomkey-site-in-bay-area-to-announce-homekey-the-next-phase-in-states-covid-19 -response-to-protect-homeless-californians/.

ten times greater "Governor Newsom Signs Historic Legislation to Boost California's Housing Supply," State of California, September 16, 2021, gov.ca.gov/2021/09/16/governor-newsom-signs -historic-legislation-to-boost-californias-housing-supply-and-fight-the-housing-crisis/.

"extremely low income" "Governor Newsom Signs Historic Housing and Homelessness Fund- ing Package as Part of $100 Billion California Comeback Plan," State of California, July 19, 2021, gov.ca.gov/2021/07/19/governor-newsom-signs-historic-housing-and-homelessness-funding -package-as-part-of-100-billion-california-comeback-plan/.

972,083 more ELI households "The GAP: California," National Low Income Housing Coalition, nlihc .org/gap/state/ca.

only 7 percent "California Affordable Housing Needs Report 2023," California Housing Partnership, March 2023, chpc.net/wp-content/uploads/2023/03/HNR_CA_CHPC-Master2023-FINAL.pdf.

roughly two thousand units Some 42,000 affordable units were built between 2000 and 2018, or about 2,210 per year. See Egon Terplan, "How Much Housing Should the Bay Area Have Built to Avoid the Current Housing Crisis?," San Francisco Bay Area Planning and Urban Research Association, February 21, 2019, spur.org/news/2019-02-21/how-much-housing-should-bay-area -have-built-avoid-current-housing-crisis.

households earning up to $266,880 "Area Median Income & Eligibility for Affordable Housing," SV@Home, siliconvalleyathome.org/resource-map/finding-affordable-housing/.

I met a housing activist Amy Ridout.

Another housing activist Jessica Clark.

This limits resources that can funnel down Ed Gramlich, "Overview of Key AFFH Definitions," National Low Income Housing Coalition, March 3, 2028, nlihc.org/sites/default/files /OVERVIEW_OF_KEY_AFFH_DEFINITIONS.pdf.

ELI units . . . one in ten I determined this by adding up the number of units for different affordability levels and dividing by the number of ELI units. See "Housing Needs by State: California," National Low Income Housing Coalition, nlihc.org/housing-needs-by-state/california.

community for seniors Alyssa Bereznak, "The Neighborhood That Google Swallowed," The Ringer, August 18, 2016, theringer.com/2016/08/18/tech/google-santiago-villa-housing -4ac4b1ca49fe.

Advanced Technology and Projects group Michael del Castillo, "Modern Day Renaissance Man Aims to Give Google Project Tango a 3D Sense of Self," *Business Journals*, June 6, 2014, bizjournals.com/bizjournals/news/2014/06/06/modern-day-renaissance-man-aims-to -give-google-s.html.

joined the bandwagon and published Roger McNamee, *Zucked: Waking up to the Facebook Catastrophe* (Penguin, 2019).

I'd profiled him Brian Barth, "Big Tech's Big Defector," *New Yorker*, November 25, 2019, newyorker .com/magazine/2019/12/02/big-techs-big-defector.

band played for the Occupiers "Interview: Roger McNamee. Musician, Investor, Occupier," HeadCount, headcount.org/headcount-updates/interview-roger-mcnamee-musician-investor -occupier/.

invested $210 million in Facebook Alexei Oreskovic, "Elevation Partners Buys $120 Million in Facebook Shares," Reuters, June 29, 2010, reuters.com/article/idUSTRE65S0CZ20100629/.

"Silicon Valley's . . . poster boy" *Gawker*, gawker.com/5859890/job-killing-plutocrat-loves -occupy-wall-street.

Benioff had supported a ballot proposition Kate Larsen, "Salesforce's Marc Benioff Pushes for Proposition C in San Francisco," *ABC7 News*, October 31, 2018, \gawker.com/5859890/job -killing-plutocrat-loves-occupy-wall-street.

"Marc: you're distracting" Gabrielle Canon, "Twitter and Salesforce CEOs Bicker over Who Is Helping the Homeless More," *The Guardian*, October 12, 2018, theguardian.com/us-news/2018 /oct/12/jack-dorsey-marc-benioff-homelessness-twitter-san-francisco.

to get every . . . off these streets Caitlin Reilly, "A Big Gift for Homelessness from the Tech Billionaire Begging His Industry to Do More," *Inside Philanthropy*, December 11, 2018, inside-philanthropy.com/home/2018-12-10-a-big-gift-for-homelessness-from-the-tech-billionaire -begging-his-industry-to-do-more.

"root causes of homelessness and identify" Laura Kurtzman, "UCSF Launches New Benioff Homelessness and Housing Initiative with $30M Gift," University of California San Francisco,

May 1, 2019, universityofcalifornia.edu/news/ucsf-launches-new-benioff-homelessness-and -housing-initiative-30m-gift.

launched research programs on topics "Our Impact," Benioff Homelessness and Housing Initiative, University of California San Francisco, homelessness.ucsf.edu/our-impact/studies.

Salesforce Park "Salesforce Park," Transbay Joint Powers Authority, tjpa.org/salesforce-transit -center/salesforce-park.

she wrote an open letter Tiny [Lisa Gray-Garcia], "An Open Letter to Marc Benioff About Homelessness," *48 Hills*, September 24, 2019, 48hills.org/2019/09/an-open-letter-to-the-marc -benioff-about-homelessness/.

$1 billion to the cause Conor Dougherty, "Facebook Pledges $1 Billion to Ease Housing Crisis Inflamed by Big Tech," *New York Times*, November 4, 2019, nytimes.com/2019/10/22/technology /facebook-1-billion-california-housing.html.

Apple upped the ante Marie C. Baca, "Apple Says It Will Spend $2.5 Billion on Housing Crunch," *Washington Post*, November 4, 2019, washingtonpost.com/technology/2019/11/04/apple-says-it -will-spend-billion-housing-crunch/.

TECH Fund "Google Invests $50 Million in Housing Trust's TECH Fund," Housing Trust, press release, July 24, 2019, housingtrustsv.org/google-invests-50-million-in-housing-trusts-tech-fund/.

garners up to 2 percent interest "$25,000,000: Housing Trust Silicon Valley," offering memorandum, August 8, 2019, housingtrustd1.wpengine.com/wp-content/uploads/2020/04/HT -Offering-Memorandum-190808.pdf.

first TECH Fund development and **other local dignitaries** "Leigh Avenue Becomes First TECH Fund–Backed Affordable Housing to Open Its Doors," Housing Trust, November 17, 2021, housingtrustsv.org/leigh-avenue-becomes-first-tech-fund-backed-affordable-housing-to -open-its-doors/.

Chapter 7: World Building

slice of hippie heaven "History," People's Park, peoplespark.org/wp/history/.

university backed off . . . plans "History," People's Park.

police shot her to death Philip Hager and Michael S. Arnold, "Armed Woman Killed in UC Chancellor's Home: Berkeley," *Los Angeles Times*, August 26, 1992, latimes.com/archives/la-xpm -1992-08-26-mn-5920-story.html.

"cute little brown bears" Tiny [Lisa Gray-Garcia], *Criminal of Poverty: Growing up Homeless in America* (City Lights Books, 2006), p. 83.

"post-modern Zoot suit" Tiny, *Criminal of Poverty*, p. 89.

"We are depressed" Tiny, *Criminal of Poverty*, chap. 12.

"docent tours" Tiny, *Criminal of Poverty*, p. 160

"process of extracting one's own skin" Tiny, *Criminal of Poverty*, p. 162.

Tiny and Dee rubbed elbows Tiny, *Criminal of Poverty*, p. 154.

book-writing workshops for poverty scholars "About," *POOR Magazine*, poormagazine.org /about.

trenches of POOR Magazine "About Us," POOR Press, poorpress.net/about.

San Francisco State Tiny, *Criminal of Poverty*, p. 195.

Tiny's review . . . Nomadland Tiny, "Performing Poverty in 'Nomadland' and 'White Tiger,'" review of *Nomadland*, dir. Chloe Zhao, *48 Hills*, March 7, 2021, 48hills.org/2021/03/performing -poverty-in-nomadland-and-white-tiger/.

overdoses rose 30 percent Benjamin Linas and Joshua Barocas, "What Our Simulation Models Project Will Happen After Boston Dismantles Mass. and Cass Encampments," Opinion, *Boston Globe*, November 8, 2021, bostonglobe.com/2021/11/08/opinion/what-our-simulation-models -show-will-probably-happen-after-boston-dismantles-mass-cass-encampments/.

"claim your power" Lloyd Alaban, "'We're Losing Everything': The Fight to Keep San José Homeless Camp," *San José Spotlight*, July 20, 2021, sanJoséspotlight.com/were-losing-everything -the-fight-to-keep-san-José-homeless-camp/.

clean up 1,262 camps "California Clears More Than 1,250 Homeless Encampments in 12 Months," State of California, gov.ca.gov/2022/08/26/california-clears-more-than-1250-homeless -encampments-in-12-months/.

displaced residents . . . follow-up study Ananya Roy et al., (Dis)placement: The Fight for Housing and Community After Echo Park Lake (University of California Los Angeles, 2022), escholarship.org/uc/item/70r0p7q4.

According to a 2019 audit Nichole Fiore, Will Yetvin, Kimberley Burnett, Lauren Dunton, and Jill Khadduri, *San José, California: Community Encampment Report* (US Department of Housing and Urban Development, 2020), huduser.gov/portal/sites/default/files/pdf/SanJosé-Encampment -Report.pdf

264 unsheltered residents "PIT Report," County of Santa Clara, 2022, cadresv.org/wp-content /uploads/2022-PIT-Report-Santa-Clara-County.pdf.

Public Works Department and Ocean Blue "Ocean Blue," County of Los Angeles.

three hundred encampments per year "Homeless Encampments," Ocean Blue, ocean-blue.com /homeless-encampment.

A page in the Ocean Blue files Tiny, *Criminal of Poverty*, p. 138.

worth $1.425 million Tucker Construction purchase order, City of San José.

$105,000 in restitution *Hernandez et al. v. Mark Tucker et al.*, civil case, Superior Court of California, County of Santa Clara. See case number 19CV360241 at public portal: traffic.scscourt.org/search.

yearlong citywide injunction Bay City News, "Federal Judge Refuses to Suspend Injunction Against SF Encampment Sweeps," *KRON 4 News*, April 4, 2023, kron4.com/news/bay-area /federal-judge-refuses-to-suspend-injunction-against-sf-encampment-sweeps/.

behest of local business Jack Healy, "Phoenix Dismantles a Homeless Encampment, One Block at a Time," *New York Times*, May 10, 2023, nytimes.com/2023/05/10/us/phoenix-homeless-camp -the-zone.html.

"engaged" with . . . HomeFirst Email communication with Steven Aponte, San José Police Department, September 29, 2021.

Louis Hyman Louis Hyman, *Temp: The Real Story of What Happened to Your Salary, Benefits, & Job Security* (Viking, 2018).

"components onto the circuit boards" Louis Hyman, "The Undocumented Workers Who Built Silicon Valley," *Washington Post*, August 30, 2018, washingtonpost.com/outlook/2018/08/31/undocumented-workers-who-built-silicon-valley/.

afoul of the Fourth Amendment "Homeless Sweeps—Important Case Law and Frequently Asked Questions," American Civil Liberties Union Washington, April 17, 2017, aclu-wa.org/docs/homeless-sweeps-%E2%80%93-important-case-law-and-frequently-asked-questions.

awarded $5.5 million Marisa Kendall, "Caltrans Settles Claims of Unconstitutional Homeless 'Sweeps' for $5.5 Million," *Mercury News*, February 20, 2020, mercurynews.com/2020/02/19/caltrans-settles-claims-of-unconstitutional-homeless-sweeps-for-5-5-million/.

weighing less than fifty pounds *Kimberlee Sanchez et al. v. California Department of Transportation et al.*, Superior Court of California, County of Alameda, p. 47, aclunc.org/sites/default/files/2020.07.14%20%20FINAL%20JUDGMENT.pdf.

Garcia v. City of Los Angeles "Court Prohibits Los Angeles City from Summarily Destroying Homeless Individuals' 'Bulky' Items."

notices to vacate From my photo: Personal property* collected will be stored at a City facility for 90 days unless it is perishable, dirty or soiled, contaminated, hazardous or explosive, disassembled or broken items (including electronic parts stripped for copper, bike parts, pallets, or wood or other metal parts), weapons, obvious trash, or items that present an immediate health or safety hazard.

*Personal property includes tax/medical records, ID/Social Security cards, medications, jewelry, eyeglasses, books, tools, radios/electronics, durable medical equipment, stoves/generators, photos, purses/backpack/briefcases, tents (unless soiled, contaminated), pots/pans, bicycles (with all parts attached).

Mobile Crisis Assessment Team Mark Sayre, "San José Mayor Asks for New Officers for Specialized Mental Health Response Unit," *KTVU Fox 2*, June 13, 2022, ktvu.com/news/san-José-mayor-asks-for-new-officers-for-specialized-mental-health-response-unit.

Chapter 8: Infiltration

spreading across the country I know of unions in Oakland, Sacramento, Atlanta, and New York. A national union, which had petered away in the nineties, has been revived.

2.4 million subscribers Talks at Google, YouTube channel, youtube.com/talksatgoogle.

"I'm from LA" and "otherwise you're just talking about us without us" Tiny [Lisa Gray-Garcia], "AuthorTalks—Criminal Poverty—Growing Up Homeless in America," talk at Google, posted on February 11, 2018, by Stare Back, YouTube, youtube.com/watch?v=5tVRBUfeb0Q.

Worker Agency The Worker Agency, theworkeragency.com/.

Tiny posted her own video "Stolen Land Tour thru Sillycon Valley (Muwekma Territory)," talk at Google, posted on February 10, 2018, by Stare Back, YouTube, youtube.com/watch?v=UxHj4zzCmWk.

"kindly young grandmother . . . lion with an ulcer" *The Lady Is a Fighting Lion*, documentary on Marie Runyon, dir. Laura Collins, posted on May 8, 2021, YouTube, youtube.com/watch?v =4xiesZaWwf4.

"burn this motherfucker down" "A Message from the Greatest Generation (NSFW)," political video, posted on October 25, 2012, by MoveOn, YouTube, youtube.com/watch?v =f17fWth3YgA.

hilarious court appearance Associated Press, "Grannies Cleared of Disorderly Conduct Charge," *NBC News*, April 27, 2006, nbcnews.com/id/wbna12516376.

basis for . . . "Radical Chic" Personal communication from Michael McKee.

"Yeah, but this guy is" *The Lady Is a Fighting Lion*.

"If Malcolm X came along" Linda Greenhouse, "Mrs. Runyon Faces Six Challengers in 70th Assembly District Primary," *New York Times*, August 27, 1976, nytimes.com/1976/08/27 /archives/mrs-runyon-faces-six-challengers-in-70th-assembly-district-primary.html.

One time she helped organize Laura Molik, "Martin Sostre—Enemy of the State," *Minnesota Journal of Law & Inequality*, vol. 42, no. 1 (2024), p. 179, scholarship.law.umn.edu/cgi /viewcontent.cgi?article=1704&context=lawineq.

The governor acquiesced Sam Roberts, "Marie Runyon, a Liberal Firebrand into Her 90s, Dies at 103," Obituaries, *New York Times*, October 10, 2018, nytimes.com/2018/10/10/obituaries/marie -runyon-dead.html.

she swiftly hired the man Alexandria Symonds, "Overlooked No More: Martin Sostre, Who Reformed America's Prisons from His Cell," Obituaries, *New York Times*, April 24, 2019, nytimes .com/2019/04/24/obituaries/martin-sostre-overlooked.html; Joseph Shapiro, "How One Inmate Changed the Prison System from the Inside," *Code Switch*, NPR, April 14, 2017, npr.org/sections /codeswitch/2017/04/14/507297469/how-one-inmate-changed-the-prison-system-from-the -inside.

"He has no heart" *The Lady Is a Fighting Lion*, documentary on Marie Runyon, dir. Laura Collins, posted on May 8, 2021, YouTube, youtube.com/watch?v=4xiesZaWwf4.

"early radical" style Clyde Haberman, "NYC; A Biography, Abridgement by the FBI," *New York Times*, February 7, 2001, nytimes.com/2001/02/07/nyregion/nyc-a-biography-abridgment-by-the -fbi.html.

"Forty Years' War" with Columbia Clyde Haberman, "NYC; Tenant Rebel Accepts Peace and an Honor," *New York Times*, December 6, 2002, nytimes.com/2002/12/06/nyregion/nyc-tenant -rebel-accepts-peace-and-an-honor.html.

displaced during her first decade Stefan M. Bradley, "1968 Protests at Columbia University Called Attention to 'Gym Crow' and Got Worldwide Attention," *The Conversation*, August 27, 2018, theconversation.com/1968-protests-at-columbia-university-called-attention-to-gym-crow -and-got-worldwide-attention-102093; Stefan M. Bradley, *Harlem vs. Columbia University: Black Student Power in the Late 1960s* (University of Illinois Press, 2012).

Tiny had been . . . People's Park Soumya Karlamangla, "What to Know About Plans to Build Housing in People's Park in Berkeley," *New York Times*, March 13, 2023, nytimes.com/2023/03 /13/us/peoples-park-berkeley.html.

residence of Dwight D. Eisenhower Christopher Gray, "Streetscapes: The Columbia President's House; An Elegant 1912 Home with a Vacancy Sign Out," *New York Times*, May 12, 1991, nytimes .com/1991/05/12/realestate/streetscapes-columbia-president-s-house-elegant-1912-home-with -vacancy-sign.html.

$11.7 million apartment Vince Dimiceli, "Columbia University President Lee Bollinger Lands Central Park West Apartment for $11.7M," Real Deal, February 5, 2022, therealdeal.com /new-york/2022/02/05/columbia-university-president-lee-bollinger-lands-central-park-west -apartment-for-11-7m/.

Grant Houses "To Break Ground for Housing," *New York Times*, July 14, 1954, timesmachine .nytimes.com/timesmachine/1954/07/14/84126187.html.

"greatly feared invasion" Themis Chronopoulos, *Spatial Regulation in New York City: From Urban Renewal to Zero Tolerance* (Taylor & Francis, 2012), pp. 10–20.

halt the . . . "slums" Wayne Phillips, "Slums Engulfing Columbia Section; The Cancer of Slum Housing Mars the Face of Morningside Heights," *New York Times*, June 9, 1958, timesmachine .nytimes.com/timesmachine/1958/06/09/81863380.html?pageNumber=25.

$6.3 billion expansion project Nathan Kensinger, "The Demolition of Manhattanville," Abandoned & Industrial Edges of New York City, August 31, 2011, kensinger.blogspot.com/2011/08 /demolition-of-manhattanville.html.

"blighted" Charles V. Bagli, "Court Upholds Columbia Campus Expansion Plan," *New York Times*, June 24, 2010, nytimes.com/2010/06/25/nyregion/25columbia.html.

Chapter 9: Piercing the Veil

"mystical dinner party" Amelia Rayno (@ameliarayno), "We are manifesting it: this will be the grandest, weirdest, most mystical dinner party ever held in the heart of an unhoused encampment," Instagram, August 26, 2021, instagram.com/p/CTBvAOgLgqO/.

elected to city council "Janani Ramachandran," Ballotpedia, ballotpedia.org/Janani _Ramachandran.

$25,000 university grant "Kyla Whitmore (2021): Advancing Food Security in West Oakland's Wood Street Encampment," Undergraduate Research and Scholarships, UC Berkeley, research .berkeley.edu/stronach-winners/kyla-whitmore-2021-2/.

"Moose and I walked" Amelia Rayno (@ameliarayno), "Wood St. in 5 days We cleared out space in front of Moose's for a patio!," Instagram, September 8, 2021, instagram.com/p/CTk -dE3pmE6/.

mounting a GoFundMe campaign "Cob on Wood: Community Support Stuctrues," GoFundMe campaign, Essential Food and Medicine, gofundme.com/f/cob-on-wood-community-support -stuctrues.

artist known as Supafray Supafray (@supafray), Instagram profile, instagram.com/supafray/.

musician AshEl "About AshEl," AshEl "Seasunz" Eldridge, ashelseasunz.com/ashel/.

Soulestial Church Band "Soulestial Church," AshEl "Seasunz" Eldridge, ashelseasunz.com /soulestial-church/.

"mutual aid" "Mutual Aid 101: History, Politics, and Organizational Structures of Community Care," CUNY Urban Food Policy Institute, August 22, 2023, cunyurbanfoodpolicy.org/news /2023/08/22/mutual-aid-101-history-politics-and-organizational-structures-of-community -care/.

"Solidarity, not charity" Emily Kestel, "Solidarity, Not Charity: A Look at Mutual Aid in Iowa," *Fearless*, July 2, 2021, fearlessbr.com/solidarity-not-charity-a-look-at-mutual-aid-in-iowa/.

"colonialism all over again" "Theo Cedar Jones at the Wood Street Commons," posted on June 13, 2021, by Theo Cedar Jones, YouTube, youtube.com/watch?v=XbJ-lK7qgNw.

extended interview with Monte "The Oakland, California Homeless Problem Is Beyond Belief," posted on November 7, 2021, by Nick Johnson, YouTube, youtube.com/watch?v=yRWmKh13b50.

Nicoletti had thrown . . . into the filing *Jackson Blain et al. v. California Department of Transportation et al.*, US District Court, Northern District of California, filed July 22, 2022, court-housenews.com/wp-content/uploads/2022/08/Wood-St-temp-order.pdf.

litany of peril See defendant arguments in case, gov.ca.gov/wp-content/uploads/2022/07 /Caltrans-Opposition-to-TRO-Blain-v.-Newsom.pdf.

Chapter 10: Go Home

national mood Jamie Ballard, "How Americans Believe the World Will End," *YouGov*, March 18, 2020, today.yougov.com/topics/society/articles-reports/2020/03/18/apocalypse-climate-change -pandemic-coronavirus.

"living in the end times" Becka A. Alper, "How Religion Intersects with Americans' Views on the Environment," Pew Research Center, November 17, 2022, pewresearch.org/religion/2022/11 /17/how-religion-intersects-with-americans-views-on-the-environment/.

ski mask Burhan Wazir, "Why Did Marcos Keep His Mask On?," review of *Our Word Is Our Weapon: Selected Writings of Subcomandante Insurgente Marcos*, edited by Juana Ponce de León, *The Guardian*, March 4, 2001, theguardian.com/books/2001/mar/04/politics.

Wade Nobles . . . interview Reprinted in Lisa "Tiny" Gray-Garcia, Dee Garcia, and the *POOR Magazine Family, Poverty Scholarship: Poor People–Led Theory, Art, Words, & Tears Across Mama Earth* (POOR Press, ebook, 2019), pp. 219–221.

"Moynihan Report" Margery Austin Turner, "The Moynihan Report Revisited," Open Society Foundations, June 2013, opensocietyfoundations.org/publications/moynihan-report-revisited.

essay by . . . McCarthy Jesse McCarthy, "Notes on Trap," *n+1* magazine, Fall 2018, nplusonemag .com/issue-32/essays/notes-on-trap/.

Chapter 11: Devilish and Divine

under the hashtag "#esuisnotsatan," Google search, google.com/search?q=hashtag+%23esuisn otsatan.

"trickster Esu was relieved" "'Esu' Isn't 'the Devil'; but You Knew That Already," Yoruba Name, blog.yorubaname.com/2016/12/16/e%e1%b9%a3u-isnt-the-devil-but-you-knew-that -already/.

Aztec word for the creator "Ometeotl," Nahuatl Dictionary, nahuatl.wired-humanities.org /content/ometeotl.

word invoked to honor ancestors Akissi M. Britton, "Lucumi and the Children of Cotton: Gender, Race, and Ethnicity in the Mapping of a Black Atlantic Politics of Religion" (City University of New York, PhD thesis, 2016), academicworks.cuny.edu/cgi/viewcontent.cgi?article =1735&context=gc_etds.

Bay Area's original inhabitants "Historical Overview," Muwekma Ohlone Tribe, muwekma .org/historical-overview.html.

Confederated Villages of Lisjan "Tribal History," Confederated Villages of Lisjan, villagesoflisjan .org/home/tribal-history/.

Huichin, the Ohlone territory "Lisjan (Ohlone) History & Territory," Sogorea Te' Land Trust, sogoreate-landtrust.org/lisjan-history-and-territory/.

Manhattan is on Lenape land Betsy McCully, "Lenape Native: The History and Culture of New York's First People," New York Native, November 12, 2018, newyorknature.us/lenapes/.

land of the Miwok Marin Miwok, marinmiwok.com/.

Miracle Messages "About Us," Miracle Messages, miraclemessages.org/about.

most universal characteristic of . . . homelessness and **social capital . . . financial capital** Kevin F. Adler, Donald W. Burnes, Amanda Banh, and Andrijana Bilbija, *When We Walk By: Forgotten Humanity, Broken Systems, and the Role We Can Each Play in Ending Homelessness in America* (North Atlantic Books, 2023), pp. 22, 25.

"weak ties" Kevin Corinth and Claire Rossi-de-Vries, "The Impact of Social Ties on Homelessness," American Enterprise Institute working paper, July 2017, aei.org/wp-content/uploads/2017 /05/The-Impact-of-Social-Ties-on-Homelessness-updated.pdf.

twice as many people . . . being reunited and **social "support" systems** Adler et al., *When We Walk By*, p. 23.

"a quiet man" See Marie Runyon Papers, 1955–2008, Columbia University Archives, findingaids .library.columbia.edu/archives/cul-6606156.

Chapter 12: Acts of Erasure

one hundred miles per hour "A Parade of Storms Impact Bay Area," National Weather Service, from December 26, 2022, to January 17, 2023, weather.gov/mtr/AtmosphericRivers_12_2022-01_2023.

Orrick again granted . . . order Order Maintaining Temporary Restraining Order, *Janosko et al. v. City of Oakland*, filed February 10, 2023, courthousenews.com/wp-content/uploads/2023 /02/orrick-wood-street-tro.pdf.

Orrick lifted the order Bay City News Service, "Court Allows City to Close Homeless Encampment at 1707 Wood Street," *SFGate*, March 1, 2023, sfgate.com/news/bayarea/article/court -allows-city-to-close-homeless-encampment-at-17814946.php.

Tuff brand garden sheds "From Sidewalks to Services: Oakland Opens 5th Community Cabin Site (Mandela Community Cabins)," City of Oakland, July 3, 2019, oaklandca.gov/news/from -sidewalks-to-services-oakland-opens-5th-community-cabin-site.

a place known as Camp Resolution and **community was dismantled** Marisa Kendall, "Sacramento Gave a Homeless Camp a Lease as an Experiment. Here's What Happened," *CalMatters*, March 11, 2024, calmatters.org/housing/homelessness/2024/03/california-homelessness/.

we were assigned to read Hakim Bey [Peter Lamborn Wilson], *T.A.Z.: The Temporary Autonomous Zone, Ontological Anarchy, Poetic Terrorism* (Autonomedia, 2003).

Peter Lamborn Wilson Penelope Green, "Peter Lamborn Wilson, Advocate of 'Poetic Terrorism,' Dies at 76," Obituaries, *New York Times*, June 11, 2022, nytimes.com/2022/06/11/us/peter-lamborn-wilson-dead.html.

into psychedelics Richard Marcus, Blogcritics, review of *William S. Burroughs vs. the Qur'an*, by Michael Muhammad Knight, *Seattle Post-Intelligencer*, May 2, 2012, seattlepi.com/lifestyle/blogcritics/article/Book-Review-William-S-Burroughs-vs-The-Qur-an-3530181.php.

"Chaos comes . . . clouds" Bey, *T.A.Z.*, p. 3.

"Its guns . . . TV screen" Bey, *T.A.Z.*, p. 99.

relationship between incarceration and recidivism Francis T. Cullen, Cheryl Lero Jonson, and Daniel S. Nagin, "Prisons Do Not Reduce Recidivism: The High Cost of Ignoring Science," *Prison Journal*, vol. 91, no. 3 suppl. (2011), journals.sagepub.com/doi/abs/10.1177/0032885511415224?journalCode=tpjd.

Chapter 13: The Spark

Angel Island "History of Angel Island Immigration Station," Angel Island Immigration Station Foundation, aiisf.org/history.

smashed to bits Nikki Silverstein, "Anchor-Outs Living on Richardson Bay Fear More than Foul Weather," *Pacific Sun*, January 11, 2023, pacificsun.com/anchor-outs-living-on-richardson-bay/.

anchor-outs sued Nikki Silverstein, "Sausalito Agrees to Pay $540,000 to Homeless Encampment Residents," *Pacific Sun*, August 5, 2022, pacificsun.com/sausalito-settles-with-homeless-union/.

7,500 Canadian dollars Ryan Dwyer, Anita Palepu, Claire Williams, and Jiaying Zhao, "Unconditional Cash Transfers Reduce Homelessness," *Proceedings of the National Academy of Sciences USA*, vol. 120, no. 36 (2023), pnas.org/doi/10.1073/pnas.2222103120.

Two-thirds . . . housed within six months "Miracle Money," Miracle Messages, miraclemessages.org/money.

basic income . . . positive results Gary Blasi, Benjamin F. Henwood, Sam Tsemberis, and Dan Flaming, "Basic Income Grants to Reduce Homelessness in Los Angeles," Homelessness Policy Research Institute, University of Southern California, 2024, hpri.usc.edu/wp-content/uploads/2024/04/Basic-Income-Grants-to-Reduce-Homelessness-in-Los-Angeles_draft.pdf.

pay 225 unhoused families "About the Pilot," It All Adds Up, italladdsupsf.org/the-pilot.

USC report Blasi et al., "Basic Income Grants."

"accomplish more for less" and **"afford more choice and dignity"** Blasi et al., "Basic Income Grants," pp. 6, 8.

spending on "temptation goods" Blasi et al., "Basic Income Grants."

"unlatch work from livelihood entirely" David Graeber, *Bullshit Jobs* (Simon & Schuster, 2018), p. 281.

podcast . . . dark sides of tech "Valley of Shadow," *Make People Better Podcast*, April 12, 2023, podcasts.apple.com/us/podcast/valley-of-shadow/id1675161861?i=1000608650808.

Rudy filed suit Jana Kadah, "San José Sidesteps Lawsuit from Homeless Resident," *San José Spotlight*, September 20, 2022, sanJoséspotlight.com/san-José-sidesteps-lawsuit-from-homeless-resident/.

activist-in-residence at UCLA "UCLA Activist-in-Residence," Luskin Institute on Inequality and Democracy, challengeinequality.luskin.ucla.edu/activist-in-residence/.

as many unhoused . . . as San Francisco "Homelessness in US Cities: California Is Facing a Crisis," City Mayors Society, citymayors.com/society/usa-cities-homelessness.html.

Acknowledgments

I am eternally grateful for the unhoused friends who opened their lives to me, shared their stories, and made this book what it is. Kent, Dave, Bobby, Troy, Walter, Yesenia, Jen, Rudy, Scott, Monte, John, Leajay, Tone, Moose, Mahnaz, Kellie, Lydia, Mona, Theo, Jared, Freeway, Joel, Mavin, Henry, Jaz, Aaron, Tamara: I hope my gratitude is felt on every page. You are the experts and I pray that I've represented your views faithfully. Thank you for taking me on this journey. And to Tiny Gray-Garcia and the entire Homefulness crew: thank you for what you do. You steered me in the right direction from day one and taught me that the answers to the questions posed by the homelessness crisis are not found in the places policymakers and journalists typically look. They are found at places like poorpress.net, the local street corner, and deep in our hearts.

For reasons I hope I've made clear in the preceding pages, I steered clear of big-budget nonprofits, social service agencies, academics studying homelessness from their ivory towers, and most everyone involved in the "professional" work associated with controlling the lives of our unhoused neighbors. In their place, I liaised with many housed advocates, volunteers, and street-based shoestring-budget organizations who pour their blood, sweat, and tears into unhoused communities, all in an effort to support their empowerment. They receive almost zero recognition from those in the industry of managing homelessness, who are often outright hostile to their efforts. Love and Justice in the Streets, an Oakland-based group, is at the vanguard of this approach. Artists Building Communities and Emergency Food and Medicine, a pair of collectives that emerged from Oakland's housed community, made a profound and lasting impact on the lives of Wood Street residents during the time I spent there. In particular, I would like to thank Talya "Boots" Husbands-Hankin, Xochitl

Bernadette Moreno, Annmarie Bustamante, Robbie Powelson, Brigitte Nico-letti, Nick Goyhenetche, Zelda Hazel, Leah Van Winkle, Veronica Ramirez, Amelia Rayno, Armando Solorzano, Nori, Fade, Cee, Delphine, Banasidhe, Skyfire, Gail Osmer, and Cynthia Ford.

On the other side of the coin is the cadre behind the scenes who has enabled these stories to get out in the world—writing a book takes a village. I am foremost indebted to Melissa Flashman, my agent at Janklow & Nesbit, the first person to see the potential of the book and the great need for it to be out in the world, who then became its champion in the big scary universe of publishing. Alessandra Bastagli and Ben Schrank shared her enthusiasm, ushering the project to its rightful home at Astra House, whose mission to publish books that make us question our assumptions made for a flawless fit. Maya Raiford Cohen and Emily Bell, the most dynamic editing duo I could have wished for, took it from there and knocked it out of the park.

There are so many others. Rodrigo Corral intuitively grasped the concept and magically transformed it into the art that graces the cover. I am much obliged to the sharp insights of Joseph Gunther, whose copy editing and fact-checking chops made the manuscript significantly tighter. I am deeply grateful to Type Investigations and the Economic Hardship Reporting Project for their generous funding that allowed me to dig deeper into my reporting than would have otherwise been possible, and to my colleagues at *The Guardian*, *Mother Jones* and *OneZero*, esteemed publications where some of the material above originally appeared.

This book project has already become a multimedia project, with a documentary film, tentatively titled *The Spark*, following on its heels. There has been a tremendous synergy between the two: The countless days and nights I spent filming on the streets of Oakland effectively doubled my reporting, deepening my understanding of the unhoused experience in ways that became essential to the book. That would not have been possible without the dogged efforts of my partners in crime, Emrys Mayell and Gabriel Studer-Randall, two of the most talented young cinematographers to come out of the Bay Area. I am also indebted to my friend Suitcase Joe, the legendary Los Angeles street photographer, who gleefully agreed to a request that most people would run from—spending a few nights with me camping in a homeless community, a pivotal experience that shaped the book and inspired me to make a film.

When I first began this journey I could not have imagined how personal it would become. I am profoundly grateful for the inspiration my mother and grandmother seeded in me over the course of decades, unwittingly leading me to write this book by way of the lives they've lived and the values they ascribe to, and unexpectedly appearing as key characters. I met my wife, Samira, the week that I landed in Silicon Valley to start work on the book—not coincidentally, as it would turn out. She too became an unexpected character. She also became my primary sounding board, listening and nodding and helping me find my way out of the endless cranial labyrinths I got lost in throughout the process. I must also exclaim my appreciation for our Papillon, Hero, whose late-night deskside presence calmed my anxiety about those labyrinths while Samira was busy sleeping. Finally, I would like to thank Carlos Buby, my Bablorixá, and Beremi, my Ialorixá, two spiritual teachers who helped make this book possible on another level. Motumbá!

Samira Kiani

About the Author

Brian Barth is an award-winning independent journalist with bylines in *The New Yorker, National Geographic, The Washington Post, The New Republic,* and *Mother Jones,* among other publications. He lives between the Bay Area and California's remote Lost Coast region, where he is developing a spiritual refuge—open to seekers, broken souls, and all of humankind—amid a foggy, fern-filled forest. *Front Street* is his first book.